# Sitting Pretty
## on a Fixed Income
# 1,001 Personal Finance Secrets
## for SENIORS®

## Publisher's Note

This book is intended for general information only. It does not constitute medical, legal, or financial advice or practice. The editors of FC&A have taken careful measures to ensure the accuracy and usefulness of the information in this book. While every attempt has been made to assure accuracy, errors may occur. Some websites, addresses, and telephone numbers may have changed since printing. We cannot guarantee the safety or effectiveness of any advice or treatments mentioned. Readers are urged to consult with their professional financial advisors, lawyers, and health care professionals before making any changes.

Any health information in this book is for information only and is not intended to be a medical guide for self-treatment. It does not constitute medical advice and should not be construed as such or used in place of your doctor's medical advice. Readers are urged to consult with their health care professionals before undertaking therapies suggested by the information in this book, keeping in mind that errors in the text may occur as in all publications and that new findings may supersede older information.

The publisher and editors disclaim all liability (including any injuries, damages, or losses) resulting from the use of the information in this book.

*For it is by grace you have been saved, through faith — and this is not from yourselves, it is the gift of God — not by works, so that no one can boast.*

*Ephesians 2:8-9 (NIV)*

FC&A Publishing®
103 Clover Green
Peachtree City, GA 30269
www.fca.com

Produced by the staff of FC&A

ISBN 978-1-935574-45-3

# Table of Contents

## Smart money moves that anyone can make

## Healthcare makeover — more value for your money

## Bright ideas to dial down your utility bills

## Come home to savings: better products for less

## Real estate — hot buys and cool savings

## Yard smarts — ideas to save time and money

## Make your home shine on a dime

## Simple ways to stretch your food dollars

## Today's tech at yesterday's prices

## Clever ways to guard against danger

## Awesome ideas to get there on a budget

## Big style — bigger savings

## Celebrate the good times for less

# Smart money moves that anyone can make

# Credit and Debit cards

## Paying with plastic? 5 ways to safeguard your credit score

Would you be more embarrassed to admit your weight or your credit score? A survey from the National Foundation for Credit Counseling reveals more people are ashamed of their credit. Luckily MyFICO, creator of the most widely used credit score, has released the five elements that impact your score. Follow these tips for each category to keep your charging habits from wrecking your finances.

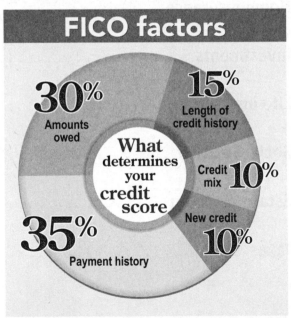

**Never pay late, avoid steep rates.** "Pay your credit card bills on time every month," says Melinda Opperman, Chief Relationship

Officer with Credit.org, a nonprofit credit counseling and debt management service. "This is the single biggest factor in calculating a score, and it's one of the easiest to control."

Most people don't know it, but late payments can stay on your record for as long as some bankruptcies — it could take seven years for the damage to be undone. This is a big deal since your payment history makes up a shocking 35 percent of your FICO credit score. Plus, if you pay late, your card could be hit with a 28 percent penalty interest rate, in addition to huge late fees.

**Don't play chicken with your credit limit.** The second most important FICO factor is how much you owe compared to how much credit you have available. "The best thing you can do is avoid maxing out your credit lines," says Opperman. If your balance is high, a lender may see you as a higher risk.

Experts recommend you use no more than 30 percent of your total credit limit. But you may do well to follow the example of people with higher scores, and use less than 10 percent.

**Build history for a stellar score.** A long, healthy relationship with your credit card boosts your score and establishes reliability with potential lenders. Once you pay off your debt, however, you may be tempted to cancel your accounts altogether. But to keep your credit score glowing, experts suggest you use your card once or twice a month and pay it off immediately.

**Pay in full, earn free loans every month.** To bump up your score, you need to use all your credit lines wisely, says Tracy East, Director of Communication for Consumer Education Services, Inc. One smart move is to pay off the entire balance each month, instead of making just the minimum payment. Not only will you save money by avoiding those lofty interest rates, but it's like getting a short-term loan with zero percent interest.

**Limit new cards to score great credit.** "Be cautious about opening multiple accounts in a short period of time," says East. Whenever you apply for a new card, the credit company sends out an inquiry, which may ding your score. Not to mention, MyFICO says people with six or more inquiries on their credit reports are eight times more likely to declare bankruptcy than people with no inquiries. That's an important detail in the eye of potential lenders.

New credit card offers can be tempting, especially store cards that offer appealing discounts. But before you apply, make sure you're not just trying to get the deal of the day.

## Boost your score, bank $425 a month

True or false: your credit score only affects your ability to open a line of credit. False! Getting the loan is only half of it. Since your credit report reflects how you handled available credit in the past, lenders and insurance companies use it to determine the interest rate they offer.

That means a low credit score could force you to pay top dollar every time you take out a loan, apply for credit, or insure your belongings. But folks who take the five steps mentioned previously can boost their credit and bag huge savings.

|  | Estimated monthly payment | | Monthly savings with good credit |
|---|---|---|---|
|  | With a low credit score | With a high credit score |  |
| $200,000 30-year fixed rate mortgage | $1,056 | $872 | $184 |
| $29,500 5-year new car loan | $701 | $534 | $167 |
| Average homeowners insurance premium | $156 | $82 | $74 |
| Total | $1,913 | $1,488 | $425 |

## Score a lower interest rate in 3 easy steps

One of the first things you notice when shopping for new credit is the dreaded APR (annual percentage rate). That's because a high number here will skyrocket your debt. In fact, a 19 percent APR could force you to shell out more than $3,500 in interest on a $6,000 balance. But if you lowered your APR to 14 percent, you would save over $1,400 in interest. The good news is landing a lower credit card rate may be easier than you think. Just pick up the phone and ask.

According to a recent survey by card comparison service Credit Cards.com, 78 percent of people who asked for a lower APR got their rates reduced. Even better, folks age 50 and above had the most success. It can work for you, too, if you follow this simple strategy.

**Know your history.** Before you make a move, you need to be armored with your credit history. Know how long you've been a customer, if you've paid all your bills on time, how much you charge on the account each month, and your credit score.

**Check out the competition.** Collect those credit card offers that keep showing up in the mail touting rock-bottom rates. Or research the average APR, and compare it to what you currently have.

**Call up your card company.** Share your history with your provider to show you've been a reliable customer. Then, tell them about the lower offers you've been receiving, so they know you have other options. You may need to speak with a supervisor to get results, but be polite. If the creditor agrees to lower your rate, be sure to get it in writing.

## Pay less, demolish debt: 4 proven ways to get out of the hole

Would you ever start a family vacation by piling into the car and driving around aimlessly until you ended up somewhere amazing? Of course you wouldn't, and you shouldn't be that thoughtless with your money either.

According to NerdWallet, a personal finance and information service, most American households are in dire need of a financial GPS. Those that have debt, carry an eye-popping average of $15,762 on their credit cards. Get back on track with these four tips to eliminate bills, slash interest, and finally reach your economic destination.

**Take your minimum to the max.** "The best way to save money is to get out of debt quicker so you are not accumulating high interest rates that keep the debt cycle going," says Tracy East, Director of Communication for Consumer Education Services. You can do this by paying more than the minimum on your credit card every month. Over time, you could save a bundle.

For example, a $5,000 debt with an 18 percent interest rate would cost over $2,660 in interest if you only paid the minimum of $125 each month. But lay out an extra $50 each month, and you could be debt-free two years sooner and save over $1,000 in interest.

By law, your credit card company has to tell you how long it will take to pay off your debt and the total cost if you only pay the minimum amount due. Check out your monthly statement to see for yourself.

**Slash interest with the ladder method.** If you have several credit cards with outstanding balances, consumer experts recommend you pay off the one with the highest interest rate first. In other words, you start at the top of the ladder, and pay more than the minimum, while sticking to the lowest payment on any other cards you have. Once you pay off that top rung, move down the ladder to the card with the next highest interest rate.

This strategy works whether you're just keeping your head above water — or already drowning, because you pay less in finance costs over time, and your debt-reduction dollars go farther.

**Make micropayments, save major moola.** Most card issuers allow multiple monthly payments. Say you pay half your minimum payment every two weeks. You'll get out of debt faster since you're more frequently reducing the amount that's accruing interest. By spreading payments throughout the month, timing them with your paychecks, perhaps, you may also get a better handle on your cash flow. Better yet, you may find you have extra cash for extra payments.

**Press pause and stay out of the red.** Low-cost living doesn't mean living like a pauper. Just follow the 24-hour rule — before you make a purchase, consider if you can pay off the entire amount within a day. If not, maybe you should reconsider. Prioritizing your purchases is the easiest way to save smart, spend smart, and live well.

If your spending habits make you a hazard to yourself, cut up extra cards and stop receiving unsolicited offers of credit, period. Go to *OptOutPrescreen.com* or call 1-888-5-OPT-OUT (1-888-567-8688) to get started. You must provide some personal information, which, according to the Federal Trade Commission (FTC), is handled confidentially and used only to process your request to opt out.

## Scout out surprising perks in the fine print

Have you ever bought a product only to watch the price drop the next day? Some credit companies will spot you the difference — often up to $500 for each item purchased with your card, a max of $2,500 a year.

Hidden in the fine print of credit card policies are details like this that could save you big bucks. Don't pay attention and you're wasting free money from benefits like price drop protection, extended warranties and return policies, refunds, cash advances, or even replacement insurance if something is lost or stolen.

You shouldn't apply for a card solely for these perks, but do review your policy to see if you're missing out on fantastic freebies.

## Swipe big rewards with the right card combos

Airline miles, hotel rewards, merchandise, and more — rewards credit cards offer it all. But to take advantage of these deals, you have to know how to play your cards. Learn the right way to use your rewards, so you can get more without spending more.

**Mix and match cards to maximize payoff.** Credit cards offer rewards when you spend at grocery stores, gas stations, restaurants, and other places you already frequent. Use a regular credit card and you'll get nothing back. But if you have a rewards program, you could play up a particular card based on what you're buying.

For instance, use the 3 percent cash-back gas card when you fill up the tank, and the other card that gives you 6 percent cash back on groceries for trips to the supermarket. Do this every time, and you could earn over $300 a year, just for using your card for things you were going to buy anyway.

**Avoid the rewards trap.** If you don't pay off your charges right away, you could end up wasting money, regardless of how attractive the rewards are. Suppose you have a card that charges 20 percent interest and offers 6 percent cash back on groceries. If you charge $200 at the supermarket, but only send in $25 each month, it would take you almost a year to pay off the balance and cost you $16.50 in interest. How much did you earn in cash-back rewards? A measly $12. Outsmart your bank and stay out of debt by paying off the balance in full.

Experts say the prospect of earning a reward encourages you to spend more. A study by the Federal Reserve Bank of Chicago reveals people who use reward cards that give just 1 percent cash back spend about $68 more a month and increase their debt by $115 each month.

**Hit the jackpot with the best card for you.** If a credit card is your go-to method for most purchases, you might benefit from one with a high limit and solid rewards program. Pay close attention to purchase categories, earning caps, expiration dates, and other terms of agreement.

If you usually carry a balance from month to month, look for one with a low interest rate. You don't want to spend more than you have to. If you pay your card off every month, the interest rate doesn't matter. Get a card with no annual fees.

## 9 ways to make $100 or more a month

Spend money, earn points, redeem for cash. That's the allure of many credit card rewards programs. But when you have to charge $4,000 in three months just to earn $600 in travel rewards, the whole concept quickly turns into a debt threat.

Do you need a few extra Benjamins a month to make ends meet? Instead of chasing rewards, test out these less expensive tactics for netting cash — many you've probably never thought of.

**Rent out your space.** You can earn bundles when you lease an empty bedroom or garage. Also, convenient parking is a big attraction. Consider renting out your driveway when a big event is in town.

**Share your skills.** Can you play an instrument? Give lessons. Are you a math genius? Become a tutor. "In college, I made $200 a month tutoring for just two hours every week," says Kimberly Lewis. Whatever your skill, a job is waiting for you.

**Take to the field.** If you're a sports know-it-all, ref a game or become an umpire. With a little training, youth baseball umpires can make $15 to $30 per game — or more, depending on experience.

**Get crafty.** You love creating things for fun. Why not get paid for it? "Put photos on social media," advises jewelry crafter Ivy Bennett. "When I posted pictures, orders for my $10 to $40 jewelry starting rolling in from all over the country."

**Get paid for your opinion.** Many paid focus groups and surveys out there are duds, so do your research before signing up. Popular websites like *FocusGroup.com*, *eJury.com*, and *UserTesting.com* let you answer questionnaires, explore products, and give feedback for easy money.

**Rake in cash for sitting.** "Recently I made $150 dog-sitting for four days while the owners were on vacation," says Lewis. And don't forget about the classic baby-sitting option.

**Do manual labor.** Some people don't have time for those pesky household chores. Offer your services, and earn money moving furniture, cleaning gutters, or even painting porches.

**Sell your stuff.** Whether you choose the traditional yard sale route or step it up a notch with an online approach, you can earn money by selling your unwanted books, clothes, collectables, and more.

**Save a life.** This one's not for the faint of heart. Sell your blood or plasma, and make up to $200 a month. If you're feeling adventurous, you can even sign up for medical studies through organizations like the National Institutes of Health Clinical Research Volunteer Program. Be sure and talk to your doctor first.

## Master your budget with prepaid debit

Re-loadable cards are convenient for handling finances and dodging debt, especially for the nearly 10 million households that don't have bank accounts. Surprisingly, you don't have to have a checking account to get one of these cards. In fact, you don't even have to get one from a bank. You'll find them in many stores and online. With so many options, it's hard to know which one to choose.

**Prepaid perks are making a comeback.** People of all ages are using these cards to control expenses and secure their money. Check out the benefits of prepaid plastic to learn how it could transform your budget. In general, you can:

- get one without undergoing a credit check.

- use them to make purchases, pay bills, and shop online, just as you would with a bank debit card.

- only spend the amount on your card, which is great for your budget.

- easily load money onto them with cash, checks, and refunds.

- recover your money from a lost card if you registered it first with the issuer — making it safer than cash.

**Watch out for hidden fees.** Prepaid debit cards won't help build credit and may have expiration dates. The biggest disadvantage, though, is their tendency to pile on major fees. The average prepaid debit card could host up to 15 different charges, from purchase and activation fees to transaction and withdrawal fees. Consider how you will use a card, and look at the cost of these fees. For instance, if there will be periods when you won't use your card, make sure you get one that won't slap you with an inactivity fee.

Don't let these add-ons be a deal-breaker. Shop around and you can find cards with no setup or monthly service fees.

**Consider safety.** If you have money in a bank account and the bank goes out of business, the government guarantees you will get back up to $250,000 through FDIC insurance. Prepaid cards issued by a bank may carry some of this same protection. Get a card someplace else, and your funds may not be FDIC-insured. Be sure and read the fine print to know your risk.

Debit cards with rewards programs are no longer as common as credit card rewards. But you can still get the perks you're entitled to by purchasing the right way. Instead of punching in your PIN when you swipe, sign for it. The card processes differently, and you usually reap bigger rewards.

In general, look for a card that is widely accepted and has convenient money loading options, flexible ways to pay bills and make purchases, minimal monthly fees, and unlimited free in-network ATM withdrawals.

## Sign up to save

Remember the old change jar? You just dropped in your pocket change every day, and over time, you saved up enough for a nice vacation or new pair of shoes. Well, some banks have their own change jar programs that will help save you bundles — automatically.

Here's how a program might work. Every time you use your debit card, the bank rounds up the purchase total to the next dollar. The "spare change" is taken out of your checking account and rolled into your savings account. You put away a little bit with each purchase. It's a great tool, as long as you don't use it as an excuse to spend more.

## Think before you swipe: 2 smart ways to save at the register

You may think the only factor that goes into your budget is the price tag on your latest purchase. But did you know that *how* you pay can affect your savings, too? Learn the right times to use cash, credit, and debit, so you can keep more money in the bank.

**Nix cards altogether to sidestep the swipe charge.** "Cash is king" goes the old saying. And it's never been more true. To process credit and debit cards, merchants must pay a "swipe" or interchange fee, which may be anywhere from 2 to 4 percent of your total purchase. That's why many places offer perks if you pay with cash instead.

At the gas station, you may be able to save 5 cents a gallon or more. That might not sound like much, but over a year, it could add up to a couple more tanks of gas. Other places like restaurants, doctor offices, and hospitals sometimes offer cash discounts as well, so don't forget to ask.

**Avoid sneaky debit card drawback.** If you must use a card, it may pay to pay with credit. When you make purchases with a debit card at places where the final amount is unknown — like at a hotel, gas station, car rental, or restaurant — the merchant can put a temporary hold on a chunk of money in your account to make sure you can cover the cost. This puts that money out of action. If your funds are low, you may inadvertently overdraw your account. And that means major headaches and hefty fees.

# Banking and Fees

## Attack of the killer fees: wipe out $600 in ATM and overdraft charges

$6 billion — that's how much the three biggest banks in America made off overdraft and ATM fees in just one year, reports CNNMoney and SNL Financial. The numbers are startling, but you can easily sidestep fees and save bundles by picking up a few tricks bankers don't want you to know.

Would you pay $38 for a latte? Well, that's how much that cuppa joe might cost if you overdraw your account. You can thank your bank's overdraft fee for the pricey beverage.

An overdraft occurs when you don't have enough funds in your account to cover a purchase. The bank loans you the money, then charges a fee — often $34 per transaction. If you overdraw your account once each month and pay back the money immediately, you may be losing more than $400 a year. Luckily, there are a few ways to outsmart overdrafts, and keep that money in your pocket.

**Just say no to overdraft protection.** Banks have to get permission before enrolling you in their overdraft coverage program. So if you want to avoid most ATM and debit card overdraft fees, you can opt out. That means, however, your purchases can be declined, and you have to find another way to pay for your $4 latte.

Depending on your bank, you can still overdraw your account if you've set up automatic payments or write a check without having enough money to cover the transaction. If that happens, you might be charged a non-sufficient funds fee or returned check fee. So watch out.

**Link accounts to allow transfers.** If you don't want to be left high and dry by your checking account, you can link a debit card to your savings, credit card, or credit line. If you overdraw, your bank will take the money from the other account to cover the cost. You will probably still have to pay a fee, but it's usually less than an overdraft fee — about $10 for many banks.

**Sign up for alerts.** The easiest way to avoid overdraft fees is to keep an eye on your account. You can sign up to receive email or text alerts when your balance gets low, so you'll never be surprised.

Banks also cash in on ATM fees. Say you withdraw money from an out-of-network ATM once a week. If you pay the average $4.35 each time, you could rack up $226 in fees in just a year. Skip the ATM fees by following these tips.

**Get cash back at the register after a transaction.** This fee-free option is available at many drug stores, grocery stores, post offices, and more. You can often withdraw up to $100.

**Hunt down an in-network ATM.** Usually you can withdraw money for free by using your bank's ATM. Plan ahead, so you know where to go when you're in a pinch.

**Get your money back.** Some banks will reimburse you for fees charged at out-of-network ATMs. You could get a maximum of $10 to $20 back each statement cycle.

---

### Simple step keeps check fraud in check

Never write checks with a regular pen if you plan to mail them. It could cost you your life savings. Identity thieves steal checks from mailboxes and use common household products to wash off all the handwritten information on the check except your signature. Then they rewrite the check to themselves for any amount they please. To prevent this, use a pen that writes in permanent ink.

---

## How to avoid the bank fee blues: 5 tricks save you $400

Your bank seems to have a surcharge for everything — and it's perfectly legal. From human teller fees to returned mail fees, it's enough to make you start stuffing money under your mattress. But before you do, check out these five ways to beat the most common charges that may be lurking in your statement.

**Meet minimum balance requirements.** According to a recent MoneyRates survey, the average maintenance fee on a checking account runs about $13.29 a month — that's just under $160 a year. You can often waive these fees by upping your balance enough to meet a minimum amount or by signing up for another service, like direct deposit. Check out the options at your bank.

**Take your statement online.** Sue Morrison doesn't like paying money to see how much money she's saved. That's why she gave up paper statements. "My bank sends me an email every month when my statement is ready," says Morrison. "Then I log in to my account and check it out online for free. I save $3 every month."

That's actually a bit low. Some banks charge $5 to print and mail statements each month. You could save $60 a year by viewing yours online instead.

**Cut back on withdrawals.** Think you can withdraw money from your savings account as often as you want? Think again. A common withdrawal limit is six times per statement cycle. After that, you could pay a fee of about $10 each time. Go over the limit just once per month, and you're looking at $120 each year.

If this is normal for you, get in the habit of taking out more money at a time, and cut down on the number of times you withdraw from your account. Also read the fine print. Sometimes you just need to keep your balance above a minimum to get this fee waived.

Is forgetfulness costing you another late fee? Sign up for automatic payments, and never miss another invoice. From insurance premiums to internet bills, all you have to do is set it up with your bank and schedule your payments. Some service providers even offer discounts when you enroll.

**Let your account see some action.** "A while back I tried to save money by limiting how often I swiped my debit card," says Morrison. "Then I noticed a $5 inactivity fee on my statement.

I had no idea the bank could do that. I called them, and they waved the fee since it was the first time."

Inactivity fees can range from $3 to $12 or more a month, and are usually applied after you go 60 days to a year without making a deposit or withdrawal. Suppose your account sits idle for 60 days and you get slapped with an $8 fee. By the end of the year, you could rack up $80 in fees — for doing nothing.

**Beware of sneaky foreign fees.** Buy a wool sweater in Ireland and you expect to see an extra charge on your statement for converting foreign currency to U.S. dollars — often 3 percent of the transaction. But you may be surprised to learn you'll also get pinned with this fee if you use your bank's credit or debit card online to buy something from a company that simply processes the transaction in a foreign country.

Let's say you buy makeup online from a British cosmetic company that has stores in the U.S. If the company processes the purchase using a British bank, you could still pay the international transaction fee. Check out the terms and conditions on any shopping website. They may explain how and where the merchant processes your payment.

## Drowning in fees? Save $160 or more with 3 big-bank alternatives

Mega banks. They provide hundreds of ATMs nationwide, roll out all the latest technology, and make it easier than ever to access your money. Sounds like a win-win. But along with those perks come wallet-busting fees. Consider these big-bank alternatives.

**Hop on over to the bank next door.** If you prefer a personalized experience in a hometown atmosphere, regional and community banks may be right up your alley. MoneyRates.com, a personal finance website that compiles information on bank rates and investing, found that while smaller banks are not always as sophisticated as the big guys, their checking accounts often have:

- lower monthly fees.

- almost half the required minimum balance to waive these fees.

**Move your money online to skip sneaky fees.** Internet-based banks are becoming more and more popular. They have no brick-and-mortar locations and less overhead. As a result, they don't have to charge as much to turn a profit. According to MoneyRates, more than half of online checking accounts surveyed had no monthly maintenance fees. Choose an online bank over a traditional one, and you might save $160 a year in this fee alone.

The downside is that you can't visit a branch to check out the bank before you set up an account. But you can make sure it's insured by the Federal Deposit Insurance Corporation (FDIC), which means the government will cover $250,000 per account if the bank fails.

**Draw more interest when you drop the bank altogether.** Unlike banks, credit unions are not-for-profit organizations owned by members. For that reason, you can usually find lower fees, higher interest rates on savings accounts, and lower interest rates on loans.

For example, the rate for a 4-year new car loan averages 2 percent lower at credit unions compared to banks. It may not sound like much, but over the course of a loan, this lower rate could save you $1,350 in interest.

You may have to meet certain requirements to join a credit union. Many times members live in the same area or work at a particular business, but you can find some credit unions that are open to members nationwide.

The National Credit Union Administration (NCUA) is a federal agency that supervises and regulates credit unions. They also manage the National Credit Union Share Insurance Fund (NCUSIF), which works like FDIC insurance to keep your money safe. Check that this is in place before joining.

## 7 ways to dodge bank fees and fatten your account

Fees can be a real burden on your piggy bank. But put these tips into practice and you'll save bundles every year.

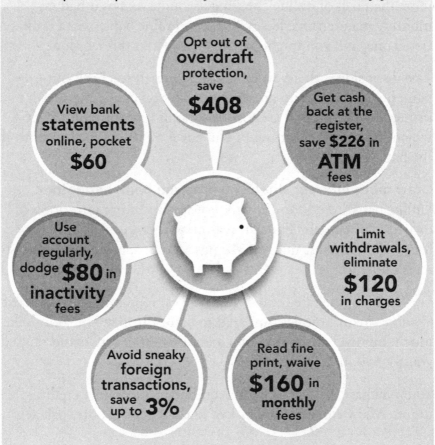

Opt out of **overdraft** protection, save **$408**

View bank **statements** online, pocket **$60**

Get cash back at the register, save **$226** in **ATM** fees

Use account regularly, dodge **$80** in **inactivity** fees

Limit **withdrawals**, eliminate **$120** in charges

Avoid sneaky **foreign transactions**, save up to **3%**

Read fine print, waive **$160** in monthly fees

---

### Secure checks for 74 percent less

A box of checks from your bank could easily drop your balance $25 or more. But here's a little secret your teller won't ever advertise. You can order checks online or at local superstores and save big time.

For instance, if you order duplicate-style checks at Sam's Club instead of Bank of America, you could save 74 percent.

Just make sure the seller is reputable. Look for a small padlock icon on the sample check, to the right of the word "dollars" on the front and next to an explanation of security features on the back. It means extra steps have been taken in designing or producing the checks to defend against counterfeiting.

---

# Mortgages

## 3 ways to kick off retirement mortgage-free

Retirement is just around the corner, and you never thought you'd still be carrying a mortgage when the big day rolled around. But if you still owe on your home, check out these three strategies to help speed up your payment plan. You'll shave months off your loan and save loads in interest.

**Supply a lump sum.** Say you come into some money — an inheritance, bonus, or tax refund. Put it toward your mortgage and you'll not only shrink your balance, but trim your months to payoff, too.

**Add extra annually.** Maybe you don't have a windfall, but can you afford one extra payment a year? You'll still scoop up savings. If you can't do it all at once, try this — divide your monthly bill by 12 and add that amount to your regular mortgage payment every month. It's like making 13 payments a year.

**Chip in each month.** One of the simplest ways to accelerate the process is to pay a little bit extra every month. This doesn't place a huge drain on your finances, yet it's worth the effort, because, as you can see in the example, a small amount over time adds up the most.

Make sure your lender accepts extra payments without charging penalties, and double-check that the additional money will go to the principal, so you're not paying off interest first.

### Accelerated payments knock out your mortgage faster

When Jake was 38, he took out a $150,000, 30-year loan at 4% interest. Currently, his monthly payment is $716 and his balance is $59,000. Jake wants to pay his mortgage off before he retires in 2 years. Here is how different accelerated payment plans can help him do that — plus save money.

| Current payment plan | With extra lump sum payment | With extra yearly payment | With extra monthly payment |
|---|---|---|---|
| $716 a month | +$3,000 one time | +$716 every year | +$250 every month |
| **Jake will pay off his mortgage sooner** | | | |
| 0 months | 5 months | 9 months | 27 months |
| **Total interest saved** | | | |
| $0 | $1,070 | $1,037 | $2,983 |

### Dump your PMI, save cash

Don't get so caught up in slashing your mortgage that you forget a hidden windfall.

Private mortgage insurance (PMI) is usually required when you make a down payment of less than 20 percent of your home's purchase price. But once the principal balance of your mortgage is 80 percent of this original value, you can ask your lender to drop the PMI. For a $150,000 mortgage, that could put up to $1,500 a year back in your pocket.

## Reverse mortgage reform — new changes reduce financial risk

These days, you probably wouldn't touch a reverse mortgage with a 10-foot pole — thanks, in part, to a series of misleading advertisements that only confused viewers. After seniors watched the ads, they were still surprised to learn that reverse mortgages:

- are essentially loans that must be repaid with interest.

- do not let you off the hook from paying property taxes, homeowner's insurance, and property maintenance expenses.

- don't guarantee you will never lose your home.

- can put your retirement security at risk if not managed carefully.

- are not all affiliated with the government.

The concept is pretty straightforward. If you are a homeowner, age 62 or older, you can tap into your home equity for cash. How much you get is based on either how much equity you have or the sale value of your house. You can receive the cash as a monthly payment, a line of credit, or a lump sum. You still get to live in your house, while using this money to cover bills, healthcare expenses, and more. When you die, sell the house, move, or no longer meet the requirements, you or your heirs must pay the loan back with interest.

Sounds pretty great. So what's the problem? Basically, fail to dig into the fine print, and you could wind up in serious financial trouble. Among other complications, you might lose your home if:

- you are a surviving spouse not on the loan.

- you fall behind paying taxes or insurance.

- you can no longer perform basic home maintenance.

While all that is scary stuff, financial experts say it's now time to reconsider this common retirement strategy. It's undergone a makeover in the past few years, and new policies mean less financial risk.

**Moving forward — in reverse.** Only one type of reverse mortgage is federally insured — the home equity conversion mortgage (HECM). And it's only available through a lender approved by the Federal Housing Administration (FHA). Unlike other loans, the HECM comes with more security.

Suppose the housing market runs dry. Even if the loan amount is more than the value of your home, Uncle Sam will cover the cost. Plus, HECM's usually carry a lower interest rate than privately sponsored reverse mortgages.

**Recent changes signal new benefits.** Not only has the FHA cracked down on deceptive advertising, but they've set new rules that mean less risk and more savings.

- Tighter withdrawal limits. As a borrower, you can't take out as much money through a reverse mortgage in the first year. This encourages you to spread out your equity rather than blowing it all at once.

- Stricter financial qualifications. Before your loan is processed, lenders really scrutinize your finances. They want to be sure you'll be able to keep up with home insurance, property taxes, and maintenance expenses in the long run.

- Better protection for spouses. In contrast to previous years, even if your name isn't on the reverse mortgage, you may be able to stay in the home as long as you meet certain requirements.

- New set-aside accounts. You can work with lenders to lay away part of your home equity in advance. This may give you peace of mind about paying your insurance and other future bills.

**Talk to a qualified advisor before you commit.** Still, reverse mortgages aren't right for everyone. Before your application is processed, you have to receive counseling. Take advantage of this opportunity to discuss the financial risks of a HECM as well as other alternatives.

The FHA funds counseling agencies throughout the country that can provide information to you for free or at low cost. Call 800-569-4287 to find a counselor near you.

# Home insurance

## 7 secrets to lowering your insurance rates

Home insurance is one of those things you purchase, but hope you never need. Make paying for it less painful with these tricks that could have you banking hundreds of dollars each year.

**Save bundles when you bundle.** "Consider insuring both your home and auto with the same company," says Teresa Miller, Pennsylvania Insurance Commissioner. "Most companies offer multi-policy discounts."

Todd Jenkins took this to heart and trimmed more than $1,000 off his policy by bundling his home, auto, and umbrella coverage.

**Revamp home security to secure savings.** What do storm shutters, fire sprinklers, and security cameras have in common? They all protect your home from disaster and lower your insurance bill.

"Many companies offer discounts for fire alarms, burglar alarms, smoke detectors, and deadbolts," says Miller.

**Sweep up senior discounts for a bigger bonus.** You can get a senior discount on a hot cup of coffee or brand new shoes, so what about insurance? Yes, that too. Often you have to be over 55 and retired to qualify, but some providers accept bargain hunters as young as 50.

**Quit the habit, fatten your bank account.** Where there's smoke, there's fire. Insurance companies have heard the proverb, too, and they're willing to give lower premiums to residents that don't smoke.

**Claim your reward for a clean record.** Every time your insurance covers a claim, your provider loses money. That's why some insurers offer discounts to homeowners who haven't filed a claim in the past five years.

**Sign up for "easy pay" to easily trim your bill.** Online payments, automatic deductions, and electronic transfers help your provider cut down on costs. Sometimes, they pass on these savings to you, offering discounts when you set up auto pay.

**Find discounts for being faithful.** Without a doubt, you should shop around. But remember, true-blue customers often scoop up sweet deals — frequently for being loyal for at least five years.

Check out these potential savings offered by insurance agencies nationwide. Not all insurers advertise them or allow every discount, so be sure to ask.

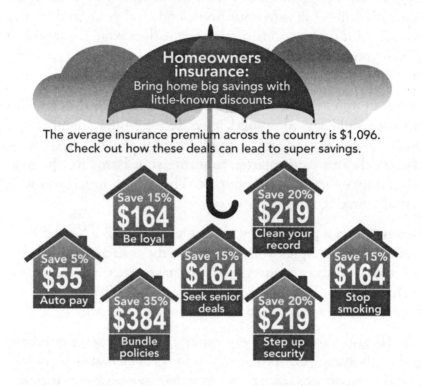

**3 costly insurance mistakes that can leave you in the lurch**

It's not that big a deal if you botch an order at the local cafe. But bungle when buying homeowners insurance, and your bank account will really feel the pain.

**Beware of choosing a low deductible.** When something happens, this is the amount of money you'll have to pay out of pocket, no matter what. So lower is better, right? Think about this. A low deductible can mean through-the-roof premiums every month — whether or not you ever make a claim. On the other hand, raising your deductible from $500 to $1,000 can save up to 25 percent on your premium.

**Don't insure your home for its market value.** How likely is it someone will break into your home and steal your land on the way out? Or that a windstorm or fire will damage the land itself? When you insure your house for its cash value, you're covering your home *and* the land.

"Keep in mind that the market value of a home is different from what it would cost to rebuild," says Teresa Miller, member of the National Association of Insurance Commissioners (NAIC). She says it's cheaper, and smarter, to insure your home for the cost of rebuilding — its replacement cost. This is how much you will actually need if a disaster strikes.

**Never select a provider by price alone.** Price is a huge consideration when you pick your policy, but the Insurance Information Institute (III) also encourages you to make sure the company is licensed in your state and is financially sound. Check out insurance ratings and financial data online at *ambest.com*.

The III also recommends you explore customer service records before choosing your provider. Go to *consumeraffairs.com* for brand comparisons, expert assessments, and customer reviews.

# Investments

## 3 guaranteed ways to grow your money like crazy

You don't have to run out of savings in retirement. These strategies can help you turn small amounts of cash in a retirement account (earning 6 percent interest) into big money over the course of 20 years.

**Maximize your employer match.** Many companies will match your 401(k) contributions. That's free money, and it could double the size of your nest egg. Say you make $40,000 a year, and your company will match your 401(k) contributions, up to 6 percent of your salary. If you pitch in $2,400 annually (6 percent of $40,000), then so does your company. Just look at how it adds up!

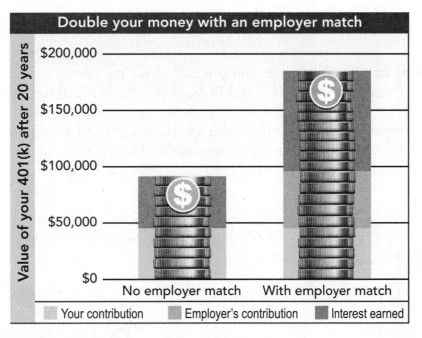

**Double your money with an employer match**

Value of your 401(k) after 20 years

$200,000 · $150,000 · $100,000 · $50,000 · $0

No employer match      With employer match

Your contribution      Employer's contribution      Interest earned

**Weed out expensive investments.** Someone has to run the stock, bond, or Treasury fund you invest in, and that person gets paid by taking a cut of your money. The fee they charge is called an expense ratio, and some funds charge a lot more than others. An inexpensive index fund might charge 0.2 percent a year, while an actively managed fund could charge 1.5 percent. That difference can take a big bite out of your savings. Here's what would happen to $10,000 in an IRA for 20 years, if you invested it in low-fee versus high-fee funds.

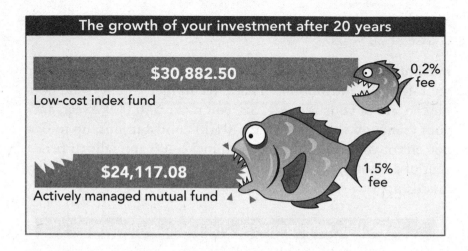

The growth of your investment after 20 years

$30,882.50
Low-cost index fund
0.2% fee

$24,117.08
Actively managed mutual fund
1.5% fee

**Play catch-up.** It's never too late to start saving, thanks to the catch-up rule for 401(k)s and IRAs. While the Internal Revenue Service (IRS) limits how much you can save in these accounts each year, once you turn 50, you can put an extra $1,000 in an IRA and $6,000 in your 401(k) annually. Do it if you can. The more money you save, the more interest you earn.

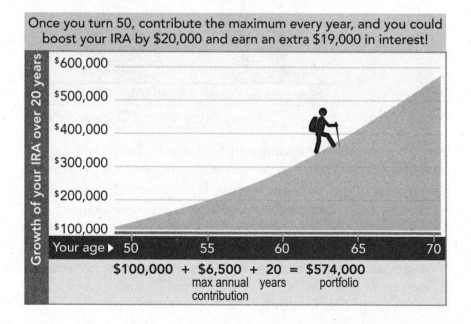

Once you turn 50, contribute the maximum every year, and you could boost your IRA by $20,000 and earn an extra $19,000 in interest!

Growth of your IRA over 20 years

$600,000
$500,000
$400,000
$300,000
$200,000
$100,000

Your age ▶  50          55          60          65          70

$100,000 + $6,500 + 20 = $574,000
max annual   years   portfolio
contribution

## Go treasure hunting: claim your share of lost bonds

The government is holding millions of fully matured, but unclaimed savings bonds worth more than $18 billion.

Most are Series EE and E bonds with 30- and 40-year maturities. That's why you may have forgotten you own one. Fortunately, the U.S. Treasury makes it easy to see if any belong to you. Go online to *treasurydirect.gov*. Click on Treasury Hunt, then Start Search, and enter your Social Security number (SSN). The website will show you any matured Series EE or Series E bonds issued after 1973 that are registered under that SSN.

To find older bonds, or to search by someone's name, call the U.S. Treasury toll-free at 844-284-2676.

## The #1 secret to a richer retirement

Does your retirement strategy involve researching your family tree looking for a long-lost, wealthy relative? "Life doesn't work like that," says one expert with a national brokerage firm. "I've been a financial advisor for 16 years, and I have seen one person get an unexpected inheritance. And yes — they did know the rich aunt."

Besides pinning your future on a financial fluke, he says one of the worst money mistakes you can make in retirement is being too conservative or too aggressive with your investments — especially when you're on a fixed income.

- It's a risky proposition to have all your money in stocks. This investing pro explains if you had retired with 100 percent of your savings in stocks, in 2008, when the market crashed, you would have lost 37 percent of your savings. Not everyone can recover from that financially.

- On the other hand, put all of your savings in Certificates of Deposit (CDs), and these days you'll earn too little interest to survive on.

Both extremes are bad news and could have you running out of money in retirement. Instead, meet with a financial advisor, and together decide on a mixture of investments that's right for you. "You don't want a cookie-cutter formula," he warns. "You want to base your investment plan on your personal health, the longevity in your family, your individual risk tolerance, and your individual needs."

## Tap your retirement early without paying penalties

It's time for a desperate decision. You're facing a financial crisis and the money you need is sitting right there — in your retirement account. But if you're not yet 59 1/2, oh, the penalties. Not only will you pay income tax on whatever you withdraw, but you'll also hand over an automatic 10 percent penalty to Uncle Sam. Take out $5,000 to cover a new roof, for instance, and you'll pay $500 to the IRS, on top of income tax on the withdrawal.

The government isn't completely hard-hearted, though. You can escape the penalty — but not necessarily the income tax — if you're withdrawing the money for one of these reasons.

**You're out of work.** It doesn't matter whether you got laid off, were fired, or quit in a huff. Only two things need to be true:

- You had a 401(k) with this job.

- You were at least 55 years old by December 31 of the year you lost your job.

No matter your age, you can pull money from your IRA penalty-free to pay for health insurance if you lost your job and have collected unemployment checks for at least 12 weeks.

Meet both criteria, and you can start withdrawing money —
but only from that job's 401(k), not an IRA or a different
401(k). Keep in mind this trick doesn't work if you rolled that
401(k) over to an IRA.

**You've racked up huge, health-related bills.** You may be able
to pull money out of your 401(k) or IRA to partially cover unre-
imbursed, deductible medical expenses.

- If you're under age 65, you can withdraw, penalty-free, money
  to pay medical expenses that are more than 10 percent of
  your adjusted gross income (AGI).

- If you or your spouse are 65 or older, figure out 7.5 percent
  of your AGI. Subtract that amount from your medical bills.
  The difference is what you can pull out free of penalty.

You must withdraw money the same year you racked up the
medical bills. Here are some examples:

|  | Under age 65 (10%) | Over age 65 (7.5%) |
| --- | --- | --- |
| Medical expenses | $10,000 | $10,000 |
| Out-of-pocket payment based on an AGI of $40,000 | $4,000 | $3,000 |
| Amount you can withdraw penalty-free from your 401(k) or IRA | $6,000 | $7,000 |

**You need a "take back."** Quick. Pull out this year's contribution
before filing this year's tax return, and, voilà, no penalty. Already
filed? Want to pull from last year's contribution? You can still
withdraw money if you do it within six months of the tax-return
deadline. You'll just need to file an amended return.

**Look for other loopholes.** You also might be able to tap retirement funds early without penalty if:

- you or a loved one need to cover college expenses.

- you are buying, building, or rebuilding your first home.

- you become disabled and can't work any more.

Talk to your financial or tax advisor to see if you qualify. IRS rules are prone to change, and an expert can make sure you're eligible for an exemption and help you fill out any required paperwork.

---

## Don't lose half your nest egg to the IRS

Pull money from your retirement accounts too early and you'll trigger penalties. But take it out too late and the penalties are even bigger — 50 percent of the required withdrawal!

By April 1 of the calendar year after you turn 70 1/2, you must withdraw a certain amount of money from your 401(k) and traditional IRA. It's called your required minimum distribution (RMD). Every year after that, you must take your RMD by December 31. If you forget, you'll owe half of it to the IRS.

An exception kicks in if you continue to work past 70 1/2. You still have to make withdrawals from your IRA, but you can put off taking money from your current employer's plan, such as your 401(k), until April 1 of the year after you retire.

---

## Make your savings last a lifetime

No one wants to run out of money in retirement. So the burning question is how much can you — or should you — withdraw from savings each year?

- Many financial planners suggest following the 4-percent rule. Multiply your initial retirement savings by 0.04, then withdraw that amount every year to live on. You probably won't run out of money this way, but without adjustments, you may take out too little in years when your investments do well and too much in years when they lose value.

- Some retirees try to live on just the income from their investments. That might work for wealthy folks with huge pots of cash earning oodles of interest, but ordinary people would have to live like Old Mother Hubbard and her bare cupboard with this method.

Solid research now shows that two other ways work better, letting you live comfortably without the worry of going broke.

**Plan for your lifetime.** How long will you live, anyway? If only you knew. Should you splurge on that dream vacation or start pinching pennies now? Well, the Internal Revenue Service (IRS) thinks they've nailed down this statistic. They even print it out, in black and white. Call them at 800-829-1040 and request publication 590-B, or download it from the IRS website at *irs.gov/publications*. Then flip to the Life Expectancy tables in the Appendix.

To use this info for financial planning, each year you'll have to do a little math.

1. Figure out how much money you have in your retirement accounts.

2. Look up your current age in the IRS table and note your Life Expectancy. This is the remaining number of years the IRS says you will probably live.

3. Divide your total savings by that number.

4. Withdraw that amount from your retirement account for the year.

Say you have $80,000 in your 401(k), and the IRS table says you will probably live another 14.1 years. Dividing $80,000 by 14.1 equals $5,674 — the amount you can afford to withdraw for the year without threatening your future. Two pieces of this equation will change every year — the balance in your retirement account and the number representing your life expectancy.

One drawback here is that the IRS tables don't take into account your medical history, current health, or gender. And all of these affect how long you'll live. So maybe you'll want a more accurate idea of your life expectancy, to limit your chances of outliving your savings.

Go to the website *myabaris.com/tools* and click on the Longevity Calculator. Answer the questions, and Abaris will tell you how long you can expect to live based on these factors. Subtract your current age from your life expectancy. Then divide your retirement savings by that number to get this year's withdrawal amount.

**Take out the interest, too.** Want to get even closer to the ideal withdrawal rate? Follow the steps above, then figure out how much interest and dividends your savings earned last year and add that to your annual withdrawal. So if your $80,000 earned $2,800 in interest and dividends last year (a return rate of 3.5 percent), this year you can afford to withdraw $5,674 plus $2,800.

---

### Are you missing out on free money?

The pot is a staggering $280 million. You may be owed a measly 12 cents. Or you could get a cool $1 million. That's the range of pension benefits waiting for thousands of people — maybe you — to step up and claim.

Thankfully, the Pension Benefit Guaranty Corporation (PBGC) keeps a list of people who haven't yet collected their benefits. Go online to *pbgc.gov* and click on Find an Unclaimed Pension. You can search by last name, company, or state. Don't have a computer? Write to the PBGC Pension Search Program at P.O. Box 151750, Alexandria, VA 22315-1750.

For help finding lost pensions that aren't insured by the PBGC, plus more information regarding your pension rights, visit *PensionHelp.org* or call 888-420-6550.

## 5 biggest investing mistakes

The riskiest moves you can make with your money aren't what you think. These five mistakes can derail your retirement.

**Playing it too safe.** Generally, the safer an investment, the less interest it earns. Savings accounts and money market funds may be safe, but they may not earn enough interest to keep up with inflation. Higher-yield investments make the most of compounding which helps grow your money like crazy. That's not likely to happen, though, if you keep all your cash in a savings account, because it earns so little interest. Stocks in the form of mutual funds and index funds give you a much better chance of making your money last a lifetime.

**Failing to diversify.** Putting all your eggs in one basket, like stocks, is a recipe for disaster. If that basket falls off a cliff, your nest eggs are scrambled. That's why financial advisors suggest spreading the wealth among different types of stock mutual funds, index funds, bonds, Treasuries, and other investments.

**Borrowing to invest.** Don't give into the temptation of borrowing against your house, credit cards, or future to invest in stocks or bonds. Investments may not earn more interest than you pay for borrowing the money, and stock market cycles are not stable enough to guarantee a good return.

**Betting against the future.** Along the same lines, don't raid your 401k, IRA, or other retirement account to pay for stuff. Not only do you lose out on all that compounding interest, but you may face hefty penalties and taxes.

**Bailing when things get bad.** Everything that goes up must come down, and the stock market is no exception. By pulling all your money out during bad times, you do the opposite of what wise investors preach — you sell when prices are low and miss your chance to buy stocks on the cheap.

# Life insurance

**Insurance policy payoff: 6 secrets to save even more**

Getting and staying healthy can mean big savings on your life insurance. But you've also got lots of other ways to get discounts.

- Bundle with your home and auto insurance.

- Comparison shop, getting quotes from different carriers.

- Ask for a price cut if you're a veteran or a member of certain organizations.

- Pay annually and get a discount of anywhere from 4 to 8 percent.

- Agree to give up some personal health and lifestyle information to your carrier in exchange for reduced premiums.

Want even more cash back? Take the medical exam. Most policies require some type of health screening, however, one exception is guaranteed issue life insurance. Unless you're simply desperate for coverage, it's an option of last resort, because this type of policy has low payouts, restricted coverage, and higher-than-normal premiums. Check out these quotes for a healthy, 51-year-old, nonsmoking man, who shopped around for a $500,000, 20-year term life policy. You'll see that simply by agreeing to a medical exam, he will save $868 a year.

|  | Monthly premium |
|---|---|
| No medical exam | $157.80 |
| With medical exam | $85.42 |
| Savings | $72.38 |

# Win at the Game of LIFE INSURANCE

Improving bad health habits could be worth thousands in savings, whether you're shopping for life insurance or already paying premiums. When twins Ed and Ted turned 51, each decided to get a 20-year term life insurance policy for $500,000. Both had clean driving records, but their different lifestyles led to drastically different rate quotes. See how Ted, through healthy changes and hard work, eventually made his monthly premiums plummet and his savings skyrocket.

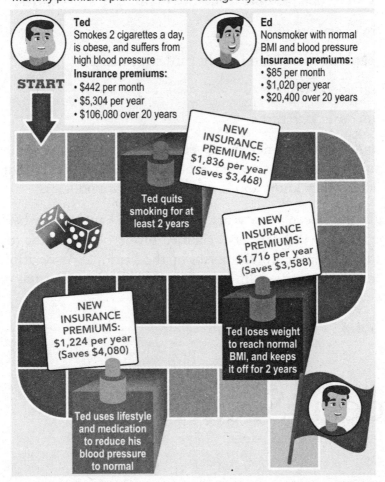

**Ted**
Smokes 2 cigarettes a day, is obese, and suffers from high blood pressure
**Insurance premiums:**
• $442 per month
• $5,304 per year
• $106,080 over 20 years

**START**

**Ed**
Nonsmoker with normal BMI and blood pressure
**Insurance premiums:**
• $85 per month
• $1,020 per year
• $20,400 over 20 years

**NEW INSURANCE PREMIUMS:**
$1,836 per year
(Saves $3,468)

Ted quits smoking for at least 2 years

**NEW INSURANCE PREMIUMS:**
$1,716 per year
(Saves $3,588)

Ted loses weight to reach normal BMI, and keeps it off for 2 years

**NEW INSURANCE PREMIUMS:**
$1,224 per year
(Saves $4,080)

Ted uses lifestyle and medication to reduce his blood pressure to normal

# Big money surprise: claim your share of $1 billion in lost benefits

Rosie is worried about making ends meet after the death of her husband, Sam. But she may be entitled to money she doesn't even know about. According to *Consumer Reports*, nearly $1 billion in lost or forgotten life insurance benefits is waiting to be claimed, with payouts averaging $2,000 per policy.

If you're in a situation like Rosie, it will be easier to track down this money if you can find policy-related documents or evidence that a loved one paid life insurance premiums. Check these:

- mail and email
- banking records and credit card statements
- safe deposit box
- income tax returns

You can also ask former employers, a financial advisor, home insurance agent, attorney, accountant, banker, or other financial provider if they know about any life insurance policies.

Finally, if it's been a few years, benefits may have already been turned over to the state as unclaimed property. Go online to *missingmoney.com*, a website run by the National Association of Unclaimed Property Administrators (NAUPA), and search on the deceased by name.

# Social Security

## Get everything you're owed from Social Security

Single people have a handy rule of thumb that can help you pick the best age to start drawing Social Security. It uses your break-even age — the age at which your choice to claim benefits early or late pays off. Generally, if you're trying to decide between claiming at age:

- 62 versus 66 (full retirement age), your break-even age is around 77 or 78.

- 66 or 70, it's around 82 or 83.

That means if you wait until the older age to claim your benefits, you'll need to live about another 12 years to come out ahead. Consider your family history, and use a longevity calculator like the one at *livingto100.com/calculator* or *myabaris.com/ tools/ life-expectancy-calculator-how-long-will-i-live* to learn how long you might live. If it shows your life expectancy is:

- less than age 77 or 78, you may be better off claiming your benefits early.

- between ages 78 and 82, you might do best claiming at 66 or 67 (full retirement age).

- over age 82, you're better off claiming at age 70.

The time of month you start collecting matters, too. If you plan to file for benefits early, before reaching full retirement age, then retire near the beginning of the month, not the end.

Why? Because if you retire early, the Social Security Administration will send you a check the first month you earn less than about $1,300. You could work part of that month to earn a little extra money, up to $1,300, and still collect a full benefit.

If you plan to file after reaching full retirement age, you should work as much of that final month as you can, until you earn about $3,500. Once you file for Social Security, you'll receive a check the first month you make less than that amount.

# 3 rules you and your spouse should know

Solving the benefits puzzle can be easy, once you know how the Social Security Administration (SSA) treats couples. Take a long-married pair like Arnold and Marie.

- They each can file for benefits on their own work record, or one can claim a spousal benefit on the other's work record.

- Spouses can collect half of what the breadwinner would receive at his full retirement age. If Arnold was the breadwinner and collects $1,000 a month in Social Security, then Marie's spousal benefit will be $500 a month. The exception — if Marie claims her spousal benefit before her full retirement age (66 for most people), it will be less than half of Arnold's.

- Because Arnold and Marie both worked, neither spouse may qualify for a spousal benefit. The SSA will look at both work records and figure how much money Arnold and Marie are each due. They will then get whichever is bigger — benefits based on their own work records, or a spousal benefit.

## Smart ways for couples to supersize their Social Security income

Figuring out when to start collecting Social Security is complicated enough. Being married makes the math even murkier, especially if only one of you works. With a little thoughtful planning and careful timing, you and your spouse can maximize your benefits and ensure a comfortable retirement.

Researchers at Boston College calculated the best retirement scenarios for married couples. They came up with three strategies for claiming Social Security that will give you the biggest bang for your buck.

**You and your spouse are the same age, and only one of you worked.** You should both wait until your full retirement age, generally 66, to claim benefits. The breadwinner will claim the main benefit, and the other person will claim a spousal benefit.

If you're worried about being broke later in life, you should both claim later, at age 68. This guarantees both of you bigger Social Security checks each month for the rest of your lives.

**Your husband is older than you, and he was the breadwinner.** In this case, the best time to claim depends on the age difference between you and your spouse.

- If the wife is one to three years younger, then her husband should file for Social Security at age 68 or 69. She should file at age 66 or 67.

- If the wife is more than four years younger, then the husband should file at age 70, and she should file at age 66.

It boils down to this — the bigger the age difference, the longer the breadwinner should wait to claim Social Security. Why? Because the younger your spouse, the more years she is likely to live after you die.

And if you're the breadwinner, then she is going to rely on her survivor's benefit all those years. Her survivor's benefit will be permanently reduced if you claim Social Security early, which could leave her living in poverty after you're gone.

Want to know if you or your spouse qualify for Social Security benefits? Check out the Benefit Eligibility Screening Tool (BEST) at *ssabest.benefits.gov*. It takes five to 10 minutes to find out if you're eligible for retirement, disability, survivor, Medicare, supplemental security income, or veterans' benefits.

Take Arnold and Marie, for example. If Arnold is the breadwinner, and he files for benefits at age 62, it will permanently shrink his monthly Social Security check. It will also slash the survivor's benefit Marie relies on after Arnold dies.

Say Arnold collects Social Security for 10 years, and Marie gets a spousal benefit. When Arnold dies, Marie lives as a widow for another 10 years.

| | Arnold files at | | |
|---|---|---|---|
| | age 62 | age 66 | age 70 |
| Arnold's benefit + Marie's spousal benefit (per month) | $750 + $500 | $1,000 + $500 | $1,320 + $500 |
| Their 10-year total | $150,000 | $180,000 | $218,400 |
| Marie's survivor benefit (per month) | $750 | $1,000 | $1,320 |
| Her 10-year total | $90,000 | $120,000 | $158,400 |

Marie will collect almost $137,000 more in survivor's benefits if Arnold files at 70 rather than 62. But what if you can't wait that long? If the wife has a work record, she can file for her own benefits as early as age 62, while the husband holds off until at least 68. This strategy brings in a little extra cash each month while allowing the breadwinner's benefit to grow. Delaying the bread-winner's benefit does two things.

- When the husband finally does claim, his wife can switch to her spousal benefit, if it's bigger.

- Because her husband waited until age 68, 69, or 70 to file, the wife will receive a bigger survivor's benefit when he dies.

**You and your spouse both worked.** It's possible neither of you will qualify for spousal benefits if you both worked, unless one of you made a lot more money than the other. Instead, you'll each collect benefits based on your own work record.

That changes your Social Security timing. The closer the size of the wife's benefit is to her husband's, the earlier she should file for Social Security, according to Boston College researchers.

- If the wife's benefit is one-quarter the size of her husband's, she should claim at her full retirement age (generally 66), and he should claim at 69.

Your monthly Social Security check will be 32 percent bigger if you claim at age 70 rather than your full retirement age. If you can't quite wait that long, you can still hold off to bump up your payment. Each year you delay, your benefits increase 8 percent.

- If her benefit is half of her husband's, she should claim at age 65 and he at 70.

Contact the Social Security Administration to find out how much you and your spouse can expect to collect based on your work histories.

## Don't miss out on this $255 gift

The loss of a spouse can mean financial strain for those left behind. A special death benefit from the Social Security Administration (SSA) can help.

The SSA will award you a $255 lump sum if you were living in the same household when your spouse died.

If you were not living together, you can still receive the award if you were already receiving spousal Social Security benefits or you became eligible for benefits upon your spouse's death.

Check with your local Social Security office for details.

## Secret strategy boosts survivor benefits

Losing your spouse, the love of your life, is hard enough. You shouldn't have to worry about losing their income, too. Thankfully, the Social Security Administration has special rules for surviving spouses that can help you stay afloat financially.

Widows and widowers are entitled to receive either their own Social Security benefit or their spouse's. You can claim your survivor benefit starting at age 60, earlier if you are disabled or have young children. Plus, you can do this without touching your own Social Security benefit.

It's a process called restricted application, and it can ensure you earn a bigger payout every month for the rest of your life. Here's how it works.

- You file for Social Security but restrict your application to survivor benefits. These are based on your spouse's work record, not your own.

- When you turn 70, you switch and claim benefits on your record, if yours are more valuable.

Your benefit grows 8 percent every year that you delay claiming it. It stops growing when you hit 70. If your own benefit is worth $900 when you are 66, it will be worth $1,188 at age 70.

Filing for your survivor benefit early, before you reach full retirement age, means you'll get slightly less money each month than your spouse did while he was alive. For instance, if your husband collected $1,000 a month, then you will get $715 by claiming it at age 60.

The "pay cut" might be worthwhile if your personal benefit at age 70 is bigger — maybe much bigger — than your survivor benefit. Talk to a Social Security representative to find out whether this strategy makes financial sense for you.

Married and divorced couples can take advantage of restricted application, too, even if their spouses are still alive. The only difference — the spouse who wants to file a restricted application must have been born on or before Jan. 1, 1954.

If you qualify, you can file for restricted spousal or divorced-spouse benefits when you reach full retirement age (generally age 66), and let your own benefits grow until you reach age 70.

### Web-savvy seniors — get your numbers instantly

You'll be ahead of the game when it comes to figuring out your Social Security income if you can use a computer. The SSA has an online life expectancy calculator that may not be a big hit at birthday parties but is a huge help in estimating benefits. And you can pull up your results instantly.

Use your surfing skills and go to *ssa.gov/planners/ benefitcalculators.html* to check out this calculator as well as 10 more, including these popular options.

- Quick Calculator. Get a rough estimate of your benefits based on current earnings.

- Retirement Estimator. See how age affects your benefits, so you'll know what to expect if you retire early, at full-age retirement, or at age 70.

- Benefits for Spouses Calculator. Use this calculator to check out how your wife's or husband's benefits will change if you file for early retirement.

## The ex files — get all the benefits you deserve

The last few years have been tough for Louise. She and Tom split after 35 years, leaving Louise to worry about her financial future. Since she stayed home raising the kids most of the time, she doesn't have much Social Security and had been counting on Tom's benefits to get through retirement.

Then she learned she could still collect on Tom's Social Security, even after they divorced. Best of all, she didn't need his permission to do it.

If you're in similar shoes, this little-known provision could upgrade your monthly Social Security check to a higher amount. Louise qualified because she and Tom were married more than 10 years and divorced at least two. If you meet these requirements, you may be able to claim spousal benefits, too.

Get everything you deserve from Social Security. You can maximize your payouts with these five easy-to-miss provisions.

- restricted application
- benefits for ex-spouses
- survivor benefits for widows and widowers
- lump-sum payment after the death of your spouse
- delayed claiming

Generally, your benefit is equal to half of your ex-spouse's full retirement amount, and you don't have to wait until your ex claims his benefits to get started. But you do have to meet certain conditions.

- If your ex is still alive, you both must be at least 62 years old for you to claim benefits. Your share will be reduced if you claim early. If your ex is no longer living, you can claim your benefits when you turn 60.

- Thinking about remarrying? You can't collect benefits unless your ex is no longer alive and you wait until you're 60 to tie the knot.

## Sudden windfall? Suspend your benefits to let them grow

It's a strategy called "file and suspend," and it could result in bigger monthly checks down the road. With this tactic, you file and begin collecting Social Security, then you suspend your benefits and stop collecting until much later.

Married couples used to use it as a way to get higher-paying benefits. The government closed that loophole, but you can still use the option in certain circumstances.

Say you get laid off and can't find work. So you file for Social Security at age 63, even though you know that filing early permanently reduces your benefit. A year later your circumstances change for the better. Maybe you land a good job or receive an inheritance. Suddenly, you no longer need Social Security to get by.

If you were 66 — full retirement age — you could suspend your benefits immediately and restart them when you turn 70. But since you started drawing Social Security early, you can't suspend them quite yet. Even though you no longer need the income, you have to collect for two more years.

After that, you can suspend them until you turn 70. Your benefits will grow 8 percent each year you delay them. When you finally file again, your monthly check will be bigger for life.

## Warning — making too much money will slash your benefits

You can keep working while on Social Security, but making too much money can put a dent in your benefits if you start drawing them before your full retirement age (FRA).

**Filing early caps your earnings.** From age 62 until the year you hit your FRA, you're only allowed to earn about $15,700 a year in wages before your benefits get cut. For every $2 you earn above that, you lose $1 of Social Security income. So if you made $23,000 in wages, you would lose $3,650 in benefits.

**Turning 66 raises the limit.** When you turn 66, the government gets more generous. The year you reach full retirement age you're allowed to earn about $42,000 between Jan. 1 and the month you hit your FRA. If you go over, your benefits won't get docked as much — only $1 for every $3.

Say your full retirement age is 66 and 2 months. If you turn 66 in March, then you will reach your FRA in May. You can collect Social Security and earn around $42,000 between January and May without affecting your benefits.

**The limit goes away after FRA.** Once you reach your full Social Security retirement age, you can earn as much money as you want and collect full benefits.

# Estate planning

## Free legal aid —  estate planning without breaking the bank

"It was a complete disaster," recalls Distinguished Professor of Law Amy Morris Hess. She was reviewing wills drafted from forms when she noticed clients had made crucial mistakes, giving away the same assets three times and leaving blanks in places that needed clarification.

"But they didn't know that," she says, "because they didn't understand the language."

This often happens when people choose the do-it-yourself route, but many aren't lucky enough to catch the mistakes in time. Don't trade quality for a lower price tag. Instead, check out these tips to get expert legal help at little to no cost.

**Cutting out the lawyer may not cut down costs.** Bad lawyer jokes are abundant, but it's no laughing matter that legal advice can cost you up to $250 an hour. While low-cost aid is almost as plentiful as legal one-liners, some pros warn that bargain DIY services may end up getting the last laugh.

Although plenty of experts recommend thrifty online services like Nolo and LegalZoom for simple wills, many lawyers say cheap wills give you exactly what you pay for.

"If you really want to save money, let a lawyer draft your will," says Hess, whose specialties include trusts and estates. "It's going to cost your family more to unscramble a will later than it will if you do it correctly the first time."

**Professional aid is a stone's throw away.** "Call legal aid or your local bar association, and tell them you need help with a will and can't afford to pay the going rate," Hess advises. "They should have a list of lawyers who have agreed in advance to take estate planning cases and charge less than their going rate."

Hess is also involved with a university-sponsored clinic that allows people who qualify to get free help from third-year law students, supervised by a licensed attorney. Students help with estate planning documents of all types, including trusts, wills, probate, power of attorney forms, and living wills.

"Those with modest means are welcome to call any law school that has such a clinic and ask if their documents can be done for free by a law student," Hess says.

**Free resources to get the ball rolling.** Don't know where to start? These websites have resources that can help.

- Go to *Eldercare.gov* or call 800-677-1116 to find resources and local assistance for older adults and caregivers.

- Visit *Legalhotlines.org* to search for legal assistance programs by location.

- Access *LawHelp.org* to explore free legal aid programs, information, and forms for your state.

- At *Findlegalhelp.org*, the American Bar Association provides a list of low-cost and pro bono programs in your area.

You can get access to free legal resources online at *AmericanBar.org/aba/html*, *nolo.com* and *SeniorLawyer.com*. You'll find articles on topics like avoiding probate, creating wills, the importance of your power of attorney, and the purpose of living wills — all at no charge.

## 5 simple documents save you up to $5,000

Do you know the best way to wrestle an alligator? If not, you may lose the Worst-Case Scenario board game. But when it comes to real-life emergency situations, like what happens if you can no longer make financial and medical decisions for yourself, the consequences could be much more costly.

In fact, your family could rack up between $2,500 and $5,000 in court fees just to appoint someone to make the calls in your place. Avoid the fees and find peace of mind with five important documents that are absolutely free.

- Financial power of attorney. The last thing you want to worry about is unpaid bills. This legal document allows someone to manage your bank accounts and investments.

- Medical power of attorney. This document allows you to appoint someone to make medical decisions for you if you can't communicate them yourself.

- Do not resuscitate (DNR) order. This form tells health care providers not to perform CPR in a medical emergency.

- Health information release. Doctors are tightlipped when it comes to patient privacy. This form authorizes a chosen person to discuss medical matters with the doctor.

- Living will. This document spells out your desires for medical care treatment. Some states combine the medical power of attorney and living will into one document called an Advance Health Care Directive. Find yours by going to *CaringInfo.org* and clicking the blue box labeled "Download your state specific Advance Directive."

> These documents will do you no good locked away in a safe deposit box. Give copies to your family, your doctors, and the person you named to carry out your wishes.

## 4 beneficiary bloopers you want to avoid

Probate. It's become a dirty word among most Americans, probably because they've heard of the potential headaches involved. Not to mention legal fees that start at $1,500 and up for a small estate to $3,000 and more for a larger estate.

The easiest way to skip a long, drawn-out probate is to name beneficiaries on your accounts. But if you choose this route, watch out for these common mistakes that might have unintended consequences.

**Don't name the estate as your beneficiary.** Be wary of leaving your assets to your estate. It's like not naming a beneficiary at all, leaving authorities to decide where they go. For assets like retirement plans, this means your heirs could lose hundreds of thousands in future growth. Plus creditors could make claims on that account since it's part of your estate.

**Don't forget to update forms.** If you've been married, had kids, or lost your spouse, your beneficiary wishes may have changed. For instance, you may have set up a payable-on-death account with your bank long before last year's divorce to ensure that your checking and savings accounts never go to probate. But if you don't want your money going to your ex, pay your beneficiary form a visit.

**Make sure you name a runner-up.** Your life has probably changed a lot since you bought that life insurance policy 25 years ago. You named a primary beneficiary, but what about a contingent beneficiary in case your first choice predeceases you? If your first-in-line is no longer around, your asset will be on a direct train to probate.

**Never use your will to change your beneficiaries.** Suppose you have a falling out with your sister. You can't dethrone her place as your IRA beneficiary by writing it in your will. A will has no power over assets with a named beneficiary. Don't bother trying to give away these six things in the small print.

- retirement plans

- life insurance policies

- payable-on-death accounts

- investment bonds

- joint ownership property

- living trust assets

## Your digital world — the estate plan you shouldn't forget

Do you know how your heirs will get into your password-protected computer to access important documents? What about your email account or automatic payment subscriptions that will keep draining the bank?

Americans say the digital assets stored on their devices are worth nearly $30,000. Follow these steps so you have a game plan for your most prized virtual possessions.

- Keep track of your online accounts and passwords as well as important computer documents.

- Choose someone to handle your digital estate.

- Leave clear instructions on where to find passwords, accounts, and photos.

You can make these steps easier with popular apps like Sticky Password, which manages all your accounts and data. But you don't have to go high tech. The simplest way is to write your info in a spreadsheet or word doc. Just be sure to keep it in a secure place.

## 5 cost-cutting tips a funeral director won't tell you

Before Tanya's mother passed away, she told the family exactly how to handle her funeral, and for $700, they had a simple cremation. When Tanya's mother-in-law died, however, the family went in without a plan. Their bill added up to a head-throbbing $15,000.

When you don't plan ahead and you're on a time crunch, you may end up going along with whatever the funeral director recommends. And that could cost you big bucks, because what he won't tell you is how to get bargains like these.

**Buy your casket online and pocket over $1,000.** The average price for a casket is more than $2,000, but some on the higher end go for $10,000. You don't have to buy the ones they offer at the funeral home. Caskets at Costco and Walmart start at under $950.

**Burial is free for veterans at a VA National Cemetery.** Thanks to a law first established by Honest Abe, all honorably discharged veterans, their spouses, and dependent children can be buried at a Veterans Affairs National Cemetery at no cost. To reach the regional Veterans Affairs office in your area, call 800-827-1000.

**Going green saves you lots of green.** You could pay $4,000 to have your loved one laid to rest at sea in an environmentally safe Eternal Reef. Then again, going green doesn't have to be that extreme.

If you want to bury your loved one in a cemetery in a way that is kind to the environment — and cost-effective for you — look into having a natural burial.

Green burials cut out the cost of embalming and vaults. Plus you can forgo an expensive casket and choose a biodegradable one or a simple burial shroud. These types of burials are available in 41 states for as little as $2,000.

**Cremation could knock off more than a grand.** The average funeral runs over $7,000, but cremation can knock off more than $1,000 — much more if you choose not to have a service. You don't have to shell out a lot of money for the urn, especially if you're planning to scatter the ashes. You can get a simple one for less than $20.

**To eliminate funeral costs, skip the traditional route.** Most people never consider this benevolent option — donating your body to medical research. Many times, the medical school or private organization you work with will take care of all costs, even transportation and cremation.

To find out more about this option, get in touch with your local medical school. The Anatomical Board of the State of Florida has a fairly comprehensive list of medical schools by state on its website at *Anatbd.acb.med.ufl.edu/usprograms*.

You can also contact private organizations like Science Care, 800-417-3742; BioGift, 866-670-1799; and MedCure, 866-560-2525.

# Taxes

## 3 ways to slash your property taxes

"In this world nothing is certain, except death and taxes." That may have been the case for homeowners in the 1700s when Ben Franklin coined the saying, but now seniors are eligible for breaks that can eliminate property taxes entirely.

**File an appeal to lower your bill.** Not happy with the appraisal your local tax assessor made on your property? That number determines the market value of your home and also affects your final tax bill. If you think it's too high, you can appeal it. And you have a good chance of succeeding, says the National Tax-payers Union Foundation.

The foundation reports that up to 60 percent of property is overassessed, but less than 5 percent of homeowners challenge the market value. Most who do appeal it succeed in lowering the appraisal.

Each local government has a different way of dealing with appeals, so check with your tax assessor's office. To win an appeal you have to prove the market value of your home is lower than assessed. Experts recommend you compare your home value to recent sales in the neighborhood.

Amanda Hersch appealed when her property taxes went up 53 percent all at once. "I pulled housing costs for homes around me to prove the appraisal was overinflated," she says. "They didn't have any facts to back up their assessment, and I was able to get an $11,000 reduction."

**Cut taxes in half with exemptions.** Your local government multiplies the market value of your house by a predetermined rate to get the taxable value. Each tax jurisdiction has its own assessment rate. For instance, Alpharetta, Georgia takes 40 percent of the market value, while Denver multiplies the market value by 7.96 percent.

You can't change your assessment rate, but you can knock down the taxable value of your home. The easiest way to do this is through exemptions. You have to apply for these deals, but it's worth the effort because they could slash your property taxes in half.

Exemptions are often overlooked, so check with your assessor's office to see what they offer. You may be able to pair senior write-offs with special exemptions for homeowners, surviving spouses, or veterans.

**Eliminate property taxes with a small investment of your time.** To calculate your final tax bill, authorities multiply the taxable value of your home by the tax rate set by your district. But you can still knock some numbers off the total. All it takes is rolling up your sleeves and investing a little time and effort in a program offered by your local government.

Tax work-off programs generally allow seniors age 60 and older to complete community service for a tax break. You may put in hours at a senior center, school, library, or even the town hall. Often seniors can knock up to $1,000 off their bills. If you apply for a senior exemption and complete a work-off program, you may wipe out your taxes for the year.

Here's a sample of how these three simple moves can turn your property taxes from yikes to yippee.

## CALCULATING PROPERTY TAXES:
### money-saving strategies that bring down the house

| PROCESS | Original | Reduced | STRATEGY |
|---|---|---|---|
| Market Value | $200,000 | $200,000 $190,000 | Successful APPEALS lower MARKET VALUE. (In this case, it drops by $10,000.) |
| x assessment rate = | | x 100% = | |
| Taxable Value | $200,000 | $190,000 $90,000 | EXEMPTIONS often reduce TAXABLE VALUE. (Homestead and senior deals knock off a whopping $100,000.) |
| x tax rate = | | x 1% = | |
| Property Taxes | $2,000 | $900 $0 | Work program wages may be deducted from total. (You might earn up to $1,000.) |

All calculations serve as examples only

## Tax hacks: 5 overlooked credits can save you thousands

Some tax write-offs are shouted from the rooftops. Shop for a qualified plug-in electric car, for instance, and someone is likely to point out the potential $7,500 tax break. Other credits are not so obvious. These little-known freebies can help you net bigger refunds, even if you don't earn a lot of income.

**Catch a break when you plan for the future.** The Saver's Credit is so hush-hush, 70 percent of folks who qualify don't even know it exists. Formally known as the Retirement Savings Contributions Credit, this break encourages people to save part of their paycheck in Individual Retirement Accounts (IRAs), 401(k) plans, and other retirement investments.

To reward you for padding your nest egg, this credit will cut your tax bill by up to $2,000. The exact amount depends on your income, filing status, and how much you save toward retirement.

**Score tax relief in your golden years — up to $7,500.** The IRS offers a tax break for older folks with lower incomes called the Credit for the Elderly or the Disabled. You usually have to be 65 or older, but you may qualify earlier if you retired on disability and receive taxable disability payments.

The credit ranges from $3,750 to $7,500, but figuring out your amount can be complicated. Check the appropriate box on Schedule R, and the IRS will calculate it for you.

**Snag a max of $6,269 for working hard.** Do you ever wish you were rewarded more for working? You can be. People who work for low wages can benefit from the Earned Income Tax Credit (EITC).

Like most credits, you have to meet certain criteria to qualify. The size of your tax break depends on your income and the number of children you have who meet the requirements. For example, you could receive a $506 credit without children, or up to $6,269 if you have three or more kids.

**Locate loopholes to save up to $1,000.** If your kids are grown, you probably think the Child Tax Credit doesn't apply to you. However, if you take care of a grandchild, niece, or even half-brother, you may be eligible for this break.

Don't take it lightly. The credit could lower your tax bill by as much as $1,000 for each child who meets the requirements. Being the world's best babysitter doesn't count, though. You must be able to claim the child as a dependent.

**Get support for supporting loved ones.** Child and Dependent Care Credits aren't just for children. If you are paying someone to take care of a disabled spouse or parent while you work, you might qualify. The credit makes up for some of the money you spend on care providers.

To figure out the size of your credit, add up the amount you paid for your loved one's care, up to $3,000. You'll get back a percentage of that based on how much you earn annually after deductions (your adjusted gross income, or AGI). If your AGI is less than $15,000, you could get back 35 percent of those care expenses, a maximum of $1,050 for one person's care. The size of the credit shrinks as your income grows.

To minimize taxes with credits, you often have to fill out additional forms. Visit the website *IRS.gov* and click the Help & Resources tab for forms and tips. To order forms and instructions by mail, call the IRS toll-free at 800-TAX-FORM.

## Secret tax breaks for the newly retired

You can't write off your pet parrot as a service animal. You can't deduct a family vacation as a business expense. But you can swipe hidden savings if you're over a certain age. Some deductions are geared toward older folks, but many slip under the radar because people don't realize that write-offs get better with age.

Wouldn't it be great if you didn't have to file taxes at all? Well, if your income drops when you retire, you may not have to. It all depends on your filing status and age. For instance, a single person, age 64, with a gross income of $11,000 a year must file a tax return. When that person turns 65, the income cutoff rises above $11,000, so they no longer need to file.

That doesn't mean you can't. In fact, you may still want to file a return if you expect a refund. If you do file, here are some deductions you don't want to miss.

> Tax credits trump deductions. While deductions lower your taxable income, credits minimize your tax bill dollar for dollar. For example, a $1,000 deduction would cut your taxes by $250, if you're in the 25-percent bracket. A $1,000 credit would slash your bill by the full $1,000.

**Standard deductions.** If you don't itemize, you can claim a standard deduction. When you hit age 65, the write-off becomes a little more exciting — you get to deduct more. For example, a 64-year-old filing single gets a $6,300 standard deduction. Turn another year older, and the deduction goes up by $1,550.

**Hefty health savings.** When you were a youngster, you could only deduct medical expenses that exceeded 10 percent of your adjusted gross income. But when you or your spouse turn 65, that percentage drops, allowing you to deduct medical costs that exceed 7.5 percent of your earnings.

You may be able to write off doctor visits, hearing aids, wheelchairs, reading glasses, prescriptions, and even inpatient hospital or nursing home care in some cases.

**Work write-offs.** You may be retired, but that doesn't mean you don't want to work. Self-employed? You can deduct business expenses for freelance work and consulting gigs. The IRS lets you write off many expenses, from travel costs to home office space.

Just make sure you report everything accurately. The IRS will closely scrutinize your Schedule C, the form for reporting business profits and losses.

## Never pay property taxes again

Senior status does more than earn you discounts at the grocery store. Seniors throughout half the nation are eligible for property tax deferral programs, and you might be, too.

The total amount of tax you can put off varies, but if you meet the program's age and income requirements, you may owe no more property taxes at all for as long as you own and live in the home. Your spouse can also get a deferral upon your death, if they meet certain requirements.

Keep in mind, this program resembles a loan, because interest accrues on the deferred taxes. The good news is, the taxes and interest generally come out of the proceeds from selling your home or settling your estate.

Contact your local assessor's office to see if your city, county, or state offers property tax deferrals for seniors.

## Does new tax law spell bigger savings for you?

If you're a human being living in the United States of America, you probably know you can deduct your state and local income taxes on your federal tax return. It's a no-brainer for many people who itemize their deductions. But now everyone — not just people who live in states without an income tax — have another option.

You can deduct the state and local sales taxes you paid, no matter which state you live in, thanks to the PATH Act of 2015. It's a move that could save you loads of moola and change the way you prepare your return.

**Slash your tax bill with an alternate deduction.** Not everyone will benefit from this write-off, but you might if you either:

- don't pay any state or local income tax OR

- shelled out more in sales taxes than state and local income taxes this past year.

The first situation is obvious, but here's how the second situation might apply to you. Suppose you made a big purchase in the last 12 months — a diamond anniversary ring, your granddaughter's wedding reception, or that new boat you'd been eyeing. Add up the sales tax you paid on those purchases. It might amount to more than what you paid in state and local income taxes for the year. If so, you can take the sales tax deduction on your federal return.

**Simplify your write-off with tools from the IRS.** There's no cap on the amount of sales tax you can deduct, assuming you saved your receipts. If you didn't, you can use the IRS's prefigured sales tax deduction. Most people do. It's based on your total income, the state and local tax rate where you live, and the number of exemptions you qualify for.

Using the IRS sales tax tables, someone making between $30,000 and $40,000 with two dependents might earn a $595

> You have three years to claim your refund. After that, the money belongs to the U.S. Treasury. That means time is running out for about $950 million in unclaimed refunds. The IRS estimates that half of them are worth more than $718 apiece, so don't delay.

deduction in Florida, or a $971 one in Tennessee. This person could also add in the sales tax on special, one-time purchases like a car, boat, home, or even materials for a major home renovation.

You will find more information in the instructions for Schedule A, the form used to itemize your deductions. Figuring out the deduction can be tricky. Luckily, the IRS provides an online calculator at *irs.gov/credits-deductions/individuals/sales-tax-deduction-calculator*.

## 5 red flags the IRS doesn't want you to know about

Your chances of being audited are slim, but that doesn't stop you from feeling a ping of panic every time you hear those three little letters, "I-R-S." Look out for the most common audit triggers on your return, so you can breathe easy the next time you file your taxes.

**Jumbo deductions on a teeny budget.** The IRS compares your write-offs to those of people with similar filing status and income. If your numbers are too big, your tax return will stick out like a sore thumb.

Tax expert Janice Pidgeon from JP Enterprises Tax Service stresses the importance of collecting proper documentation for all deductions. She advises her clients to keep good records and store them in a safe place. The IRS won't settle for your guesses about charitable donations or business travel expenses if you get audited.

**Bogus business claims.** The IRS has a field day with Schedule C, the form where self-employed people write off their business losses and exemptions. Pay special attention to these common audit triggers.

- Hobby losses. You may love refurbishing antique furniture, but you can't write off losses unless you're actually trying to earn a profit from your pastime.

- Home office deductions. You must be able to prove that you regularly use the space for business, and only for business. A room that doubles as a home office and a rehearsal studio for your bluegrass band won't make the cut.

- Travel expenses. Pidgeon says mileage deductions are common audit triggers. Keep a mileage log, so you don't overestimate the distance you travel, and note the reason for each trip.

**Early payouts from retirement accounts.** It's the most common error people make when withdrawing from their retirement accounts early, before age 59 1/2 — claiming an exception to the 10-percent penalty when you don't qualify. Pay close attention to the exceptions listed by the IRS. (Some are explained on page 32.) If you need to make an early withdrawal, expect the IRS to take a close look at your return.

**Wrong wages and other typos.** Even small mistakes can be a big deal. The IRS has all of your forms. That spells trouble if the numbers on your tax return don't add up. It's easy to make mistakes when you file your returns with pen and paper. Anywhere from 10 to 21 percent of paper returns have errors, compared to about 0.5 percent of electronic returns. Avoid costly mistakes by filing electronically. Most online and computer tax programs will automatically check your math for you.

**Rounded numbers on write-offs.** Using too many zeros may make the IRS think you're guessing or pulling deductions out of thin air. Expenses are usually more varied. So if you're writing off a donation, go ahead and put it down as the actual $287, not $300. Always keep your receipts, just in case you do get audited.

## Don't give Uncle Sam an interest-free loan

Looking forward to that big, juicy tax refund? A fat check sounds good, but unless your refund is coming from tax credits, you may actually be losing money.

Most of that refund came right out of your paycheck and went straight to Uncle Sam. If you let the government withhold too much in taxes, it earns interest on that money instead of you. The average tax refund adds up to $3,120. Imagine what you could do with all that money — earn interest in a savings account, pay off debt earlier, even invest in your retirement.

Stop giving the government an interest-free loan. Request a new W-4 form from your employer and claim more allowances on it. Your tax refund will come out closer to zero, but your paycheck will get bigger in return. If you need help, use the IRS withholding calculator at *irs.gov/individuals/irs-withholding-calculator*.

## Federal freebies: ready tax returns for less than a penny

What would you do to get out of paying taxes? A recent poll says 27 percent of people would be willing to get an IRS tattoo. But paying taxes doesn't have to be painful. The government gives you plenty of ways to skip the average $273 fee for hiring a tax professional — without forfeiting the help you need.

**Find personalized advice for zero bucks.** Free one-on-one tax help from an IRS-certified volunteer is right around the corner when you take advantage of Volunteer Income Tax Assistance (VITA) and Tax Counseling for the Elderly (TCE) services.

These programs are conveniently housed in local community centers, libraries, schools, and shopping malls. Trained volunteers will help you prepare and submit your basic tax return at no cost, so you can leave your checkbook at home.

Call 800-906-9887 toll-free to find a location near you. Or go to the website *irs.gov*, click on the Filing tab, and select Get Free Tax Prep Help. There, you'll find the VITA and TCE locator tools, and learn if your age or income qualify you for free help.

**Snap up brand-name software at no charge.** The IRS has another trick up its sleeve for people who want to file for free. It has partnered with major companies such as TurboTax and H&R Block to offer free tax software for people who meet certain requirements. In general, you must make less than $62,000 a year. Some age limits also apply.

Software may sound confusing, but these programs were designed to walk you through the tax process step by step. D. M. Enlow has used tax software for 20 years, and he says it's about as user-friendly as you can get. "I have always been able to figure the ins and outs of how to complete taxes using these services," he says. "And they offer free help and fast filing electronically." That means faster refunds, too.

> It's called surge pricing, and if you're a procrastinating taxpayer, you may already be a victim. As the tax deadline looms closer, the price of tax prep help often climbs higher. Even the cost of tax software can jump 30 percent from February to March. Pay less by becoming an early bird.

**File for free no matter who you are.** If you don't qualify for free tax guidance, you can still file at no cost with Free File Fillable Forms offered by the IRS. The online forms do the math for you to cut down on mistakes, and allow you to submit them electronically. Go to *irs.gov*, click on the Filing tab, then select Free File under Your Filing Options.

# Healthcare makeover — more value for your money

# Prescriptions and Supplements

## Free prescriptions for a whole year — and more

Why pay outrageous prices for prescriptions you can get absolutely free? Stores like Harris Teeter, Publix, Walmart, Costco, and others offer special deals on prescriptions that will save you hundreds of dollars a year.

**Supermarkets: your best source for free medicine.** Do you take amlodopine, metformin, or lisinopril to treat your high blood pressure or diabetes? Need a 14-day dose of amoxicillin or ampicillin? Just drop off your prescription at a Publix pharmacy, and they won't cost you a penny.

Publix offers seven common antibiotics for free, as well as diabetes and blood pressure medications. You'll find similar savings on antibiotics and diabetes drugs at stores like Harris Teeter and Price Chopper.

Harris Teeter requires you to enroll in its Generic Prescription Savings Club, which carries a $4.95 enrollment fee. To receive free diabetes medications at Price Chopper, you'll have to join the Diabetes AdvantEdge program. No worries, though. You can join that one for free.

And don't worry about running out of your meds. You can refill these prescriptions throughout the year at no cost.

**Big boxers join in on the discounts.** Pay less for your prescriptions at Walmart or Costco when you use their prescription discount cards. Both offer up to 75 percent savings on almost all of your medications. And the cards are free.

Head on over to *freedrugcard.us/wal-mart.html* for Walmart's card or *freerx saver.com* for Costco's. Simply print out the card and present it at the store pharmacy.

Walmart also provides generic medications for $4 and up. For a list of other programs in your home state that offer $4 generic meds, go to *NeedyMeds.org*, and search under the "patient savings" tab. You just might find one or two freebies or cheapies that you can pick up right around the corner.

**Support your local small business.** Don't forget to call around to your neighborhood pharmacies and supermarkets to ask about freebies, or near-freebies, before you buy.

"Do a bit of comparative shopping," suggests independent pharmacy owner Jan Smit. "You'll be surprised to find that for the same prescription you can get a variety of prices."

And be sure to ask your local pharmacist for a discount, Smit says, because independent pharmacies have more leeway to negotiate prices. "You can talk to the pharmacist and negotiate a good deal on your prescriptions because he's not bound by corporate rules in determining price."

**Find a bounty of bargains online.** Click away to save time and money on websites like *GoodRx.com* and *Lowestmed.com*. Simply enter your ZIP code, and let the internet do the leg work for you. You'll find free coupons and apps to download, too.

**Get help from the drug companies.** To find patient assistance programs that can help with the cost of your meds, search sites like *NeedyMeds.org, RxAssist.org*, or the Partnership for Prescription Assistance site at *pparx.org*.

These programs offer free or discounted medicines to people who can't afford them. Each program has its own guidelines and application process. You'll find more information about patient assistance programs at *healthfinder.gov*.

## Save on good-for-you probiotics

Keeping your digestive tract in good health will save you money in the long run. And adding probiotics, the "friendly bacteria," to your daily diet is a smart — and cheap — way to do it. These healthy microorganisms can be found in lots of tasty, tangy foods.

**Yo, Gert: here's a cheap source of probiotics.** Yogurt is a popular probiotic food that most consumers know well. In fact, you probably have some in your fridge right now. Popular brands of probiotic yogurt include Chobani, Dannon Activia, Yoplait, and Fage. But which brand offers the best value?

To find out, take a look at the number of CFUs, or colony forming units (the way probiotics' good bacteria is measured) in your favorite brand. Some research says that a daily dose of 1 billion CFUs is the minimum needed for good health, so the higher the number, the better.

Choose brands with the highest levels of CFUs to get the most bang for your buck.

**Check the specs on your favorite yogurt.** Read the label carefully. Be sure to choose brands that have the words "live and active cultures" written on their containers.

Not only do probiotics help your gastro system, researchers are studying them to see if they play a part in boosting your body's immune system, preventing osteoporosis, and even fighting cancer. So check the expiration dates to make sure you're buying fresh, high-quality products.

**Taste a different culture.** Not a fan of yogurt? How about sauerkraut instead? Maybe some cheddar or blue cheese? Perhaps your taste runs to the more exotic, like kimchi (a Korean cabbage dish), kefir (from fermented cow's milk), or tempeh (made from soybeans).

Sound interesting, don't they? Each one would make a healthy addition to your diet, so don't be afraid to try something different.

**Help yourself to a probiotic pill.** If you can't stomach the tastes, textures, and aromas of fermented foods, supplements make it easy to get the probiotics you need.

Check out these six brands of probiotic supplements containing *lactobacillus acidophilus*. You'll see they differ in cost, the amount of CFUs, and the number of bacterial strains in the product.

For the biggest savings, choose one with a low cost per day. If you have questions, your doctor can help you decide which probiotic supplement is right for you.

| Product name | Cost per day | Total CFUs in billions | Number of additional |
|---|---|---|---|
| 21st Century High Potency Acidophilus Probiotic Blend | $0.05 | 2.6 | 3 |
| CVS Probiotic Acidophilus | $0.10 | 1 | 0 |
| Well at Walgreens Super Probiotics | $0.35 | 20 | 1 |
| Nature's Bounty Ultra Strength Probiotics 10 | $0.63 | 20 | 9 |
| Dr. David Williams | $0.75 | 2 | 5 |
| GNC Ultra 50 Probiotic Complex | $1.57 | 50 | 3 |

## Get your money's worth when you buy supplements

Like buying a pig in a poke. Have you ever felt that way after spending your hard-earned cash on vitamin and herb supplements that may — or may not — contain the ingredients advertised on the label?

The U.S. Food and Drug Administration has no control over the quality or safety of dietary supplements until after they're on the shelf. So it's up to you to make sure you're getting what you pay for. Here's how to do it.

**Ginseng, garlic, and houseplant, oh my.** DNA testing of major store-brand herbal supplements found unexpected ingredients hiding inside, like rice, beans, asparagus, wheat, and — believe it or not — houseplant.

That's not all. Researchers found that 79 percent of the products didn't contain any of the primary ingredient listed on the label. So how do you know which supplements are good and which are not?

**Let the government help out.** You can look up a product and check out its label online before you buy in the Dietary Supplement Label Database (DSLD) provided by the National Institutes of Health. Go to *dsld.nlm.nih.gov* to find the serving size, an ingredients list, and the recommended uses.

**Look for seals of approval.** Organizations like these work hard to keep consumers safe from bogus supplements.

- USP. Check for the U.S. Pharmacopeia endorsement on a product's label. A USP mark lets you know the product contains the ingredients listed on the label and was manufactured according to the strictest guidelines. Visit *usp.org* for more information.

- ConsumerLab.com. This independent testing organization puts its seal of approval only on high-quality dietary supplements that it has tested and approved. Look for the logo on the package before you pull out your wallet.

- NSF. Started in 1944 as the National Sanitation Foundation, this public safety organization certifies millions of products, including supplements. When you see the NSF logo, you know the supplement contains only the ingredients listed on the label and nothing else. Look for the logo when you're ready to buy, or search for the supplement online at *nsf.org*.

## Use tax-free money to save at the pharmacy

How would you like to save money before you even spend a penny on prescriptions? It's easy. All you have to do is put money into a tax-exempt account like an FSA (Flexible Spending Account) or HSA (Health Savings Account).

These employer-sponsored accounts let you save pretax dollars to use toward medical expenses, including prescription medications.

An FSA has a yearly use-it-or-lose-it clause, but money in your HSA will roll over. Both accounts limit the amounts you can contribute and have other restrictions. But if you can participate in these plans, your tax savings could be a big help in offsetting your prescription expenses.

Want to see how much you'll save? Check out the FSA calculator at *wageworks.com/employees/support-center/fsa-savings-calculator.aspx*.

## Buy cheap and safe medications online

Ordering prescription medicines online is so convenient, and those tempting prices are hard to resist. But is it a safe way to buy?

**Be aware of the risks of online pharmacies.** Many internet drugstores do not follow well-established pharmacy practices. That's what the National Association of Boards of Pharmacies (NABP) discovered after reviewing more than 11,000 internet pharmacies.

A whopping 96 percent of the websites they reviewed — over 10,000 sites — failed to meet normal pharmacy standards. The NABP says that means you could receive substandard pills with filler like rat poison and drywall. It could also open up your computer to email spam and viruses, and put you at risk for stolen financial and personal information.

And you could see serious health consequences, too. Pharmacist Jan Smit says he's concerned about the safety of drugs bought online.

"They offer very good prices on medications in many cases. But it can be very dangerous," he warns. "Some of those companies were found to recycle expired medication. They repackaged them and sold them again."

Doesn't make you feel too confident about that cheap cholesterol medication, does it?

**Learn how to tell a legitimate site from a shady one.** It is possible to find safe, high-quality medicines at cost-saving prices online. Just make sure you check for these standards.

- Look for the VIPPS seal. It stands for Verified Internet Pharmacy Practice Sites and certifies that the site has been approved by the NABP.

- Do you see the tag .pharmacy at the end of the web address? It's a certification added by NABP to let you know the site meets its standards. You can find a list of these approved sites at *safe.pharmacy*.

- Make sure your medication is subject to FDA standards. "Sometimes those medications are manufactured in countries where there is no quality control," Smit says. To be sure your medications are the real deal, look to see if the site has a company address located in the United States.

- The website should list a phone number for an on-call pharmacist in case you have any questions.

- Make sure the site requires an actual doctor's prescription before you can buy medications.

- Is the website licensed by the state board of pharmacy? Search for your online drugstore at *nabp.pharmacy*. It's one more layer of protection for consumers.

**Double-check the website's security.** To make sure your personal information will be kept safe on any website, look carefully at the site's URL. Does it begin with "https" instead of just "http"? The "s" at the end stands for "secure." A good sign. It means your info is being encrypted.

Next, look for the lock icon somewhere in your web browser's window. But don't assume the lock means the site is secure. Click on it and read the website's security and authenticity. That will help give you some peace of mind when doing business online.

## 6 ways to take the 'bite' out of prescription drugs

Are medication prices gobbling up your budget? You can put a stop to that. Lower your drug costs with these six thrifty tips.

**Pick a card.** A drug discount card, that is. It could save you 20 to 80 percent off your next prescription. Choose from two types.

- The first is distributed by drug companies, and it offers a discount for one particular medicine. For example, if you take the cholesterol-lowering drug Lipitor, go to *lipitor.com* and search for its Choice Card.

- The second type, sponsored by AARP, Costco, NeedyMeds, and others, can be used to buy many different drugs. But some of these cards require an upfront fee, and others have eligibility guidelines you must meet to qualify for their discounts.

**Don't use your health insurance.** Didn't expect that one, did you? Many big-box stores and discount chains offer their uninsured customers generic drugs for less than $4, cheaper than what you'd pay with your insurance.

**Ask for a free sample.** It makes sense to try it before you buy it, right? The next time you start a new prescription, ask your doctor for a trial dose. Enough to last 10 to 14 days should do the trick.

**Look for good-as-gold generics.** Buying generic drugs saves consumers $8 to $10 billion a year, says the Congressional Budget Office. So you can be sure you'll save money when you ask your pharmacist to fill your prescription with generic drugs.

Want more help paying for your prescriptions? Go to *benefitscheckup.org*. Answer a few quick questions, and a list of programs tailor-made for you will pop up on the screen. Click on a program's name to get a fact sheet, contact information, a list of paperwork you need, and an application form.

Before you go to the drug store, search *Drugs@FDA* to find out if your brand-name drug has a generic equivalent.

**Schedule a Medicare update.** Medicare Part D premiums, copays, and deductibles change each year. Ask your pharmacist for a part D annual report. Give him your list of meds, and he can review your information to help figure out the best plan for you.

**Climb out of the "donut hole."** Stuck in the Medicare D coverage gap — that infamous donut hole? Some drug companies offer programs to help you pay for their medications.

Many states, as well as the Virgin Islands, will help pay drug plan premiums and other prescription costs for seniors. Search for the assistance you need at *medicare.gov*.

# Medical costs

## Just say 'no' to 7 medical tests and treatments

Stop the rising cost of health care. Before you schedule that expensive procedure, ask your doctor the one question that could save you money — do I really need to have this done?

There are times when you should certainly say yes to these seven tests to protect your health. But sometimes you can just say no. Talk it over with your doctor before you decide.

**Colonoscopy.** *Approximate cost — $1,780.* This painless exam takes about 30 minutes. It allows a doctor to look at the inside of your colon and rectum for polyps, those small growths that could become cancer.

The U.S. Preventive Services Task Force says you may not need this test if you're under the age of 50 or over the age of 85, and you don't have other risk factors for colon cancer. These include obesity, smoking, a diet high in red meats and processed foods, or a family history of the disease. For more information, go to *cancer.org*.

**PET-CT total-body scan.** *Approximate cost — $1,550.* A positron emission tomography (PET) scan uses radiation or nuclear medicine imaging to show abnormal activity inside your body. A computerized tomography (CT) scan uses a computer and X-ray images to show detailed pictures of your tissues and organs. When combined, these scans help your doctor find cancer, determine its stage, and work with you to plan treatment.

According to the National Cancer Institute, you don't need this test if you have no signs or symptoms of cancer.

**Imaging stress test.** *Approximate cost — $1,400.* This test measures blood flow to your heart while you're at rest and while you exercise.

You shouldn't need this test unless you've been diagnosed with coronary heart disease (CHD), or have symptoms like chest pain, shortness of breath, or nausea, says the U.S. Preventive Services Task Force. If you experience any symptoms of CHD, see your doctor immediately.

**EKG or Electrocardiogram.** *Approximate cost — $775.* This test measures the electrical activity of your heartbeat. An EKG allows your doctor to see if your heartbeat is regular and if parts of your heart are enlarged or working too hard.

According to the American Academy of Family Physicians, you shouldn't need this test if you are at low risk for coronary heart disease, or you don't have any symptoms. But remember, symptoms for men and women may be different. To find out more about your risk for heart disease, visit *heart.org*.

**MRI for lower back pain.** *Approximate cost — $1,200.* MRI stands for magnetic resonance imaging. To have an MRI, you'll lie inside a large, tube-like magnet where radio waves and a magnetic field will make pictures of the organs and tissues in your body.

During the first six weeks of back pain, think twice about this test if you have no other severe conditions like fever, sudden back pain with trauma, or kidney infection, says the American Academy of Physicians. Check with your doctor if you have questions about your condition.

**Pelvic ultrasound for ovarian cancer.** *Approximate cost — $350.* Ultrasound imaging, or scanning, uses sound waves to produce pictures of the inside of your body. It's a safe and painless way to evaluate the uterus, cervix, ovaries, and fallopian tubes.

The U.S. Preventive Services Task Force does not recommend this test unless you have symptoms of ovarian cancer, including bloating, pelvic or abdominal pain, trouble eating, or feeling full quickly. You may also be tested if you have a BRCA1 or BRCA2 genetic mutation, the Lynch syndrome (associated with colon cancer), or a family history of ovarian cancer.

**Bone density scan.** *Approximate cost — $125.* A bone density scan, also called DXA or DEXA, uses a special kind of X-ray to measure bone loss and diagnose osteoporosis.

According to the American Academy of Family Physicians, you may not need this test if you are a woman under 65 (or a man under 70) and have no risk factors for fractures from osteoporosis, such as family history, poor nutrition, or smoking.

## Get all your questions answered — with one phone call

Making a decision about health care plans can be confusing and stressful. Looking for a little relief? Let the government help. Just make one toll free call to 844-USA-Gov1 (844-872-4681) or click on *usa.gov* to get all your questions answered.

Need to know more about the Affordable Care Act and how to choose a health plan? They've got it. Want some help locating doctors and medical facilities near you? They've got that, too.

But this agency isn't just about health services. It's ready to answer your questions about everything from affordable housing to veterans benefits and all the programs in between.

You'll get the help you need in no time. As long as you call at the right time — from 8 a.m. to 8 p.m. Eastern time, Monday through Friday.

## 10 smart (and easy) ways to slash your medical bills

Medical bills can pile up quickly, leaving you trapped under a mountain of debt. These 10 tips can whittle that mountain down to a molehill. You'll kick yourself if you don't try.

**Shop around to save.** Before you have any surgeries, tests, or procedures, get a list of all possible fees in writing. Make sure you include everything and everyone, from the anesthesiologist to the doctor. Then comparison shop. Use websites like Health-care Bluebook (*healthcarebluebook.com*) and New Choice Health (*newchoicehealth.com*) to find prices in your area for the medical care you need.

Here's a real eye-opener. Suppose you need knee repair surgery, and you live in a small, midwestern city. If you have the procedure at an outpatient center, you could pay as little as $2,100. Choose a hospital instead, and your total bill could skyrocket to a whopping $14,400.

**Keep your eyes peeled for errors.** Scrutinize those bills. According to the Medical Billing Advocates of America, more than 80 percent of medical bills contain mistakes. Be sure to ask for an itemized bill so you can verify all your charges. Keep an up-to-date file of the paperwork you receive. That way if you end up disputing a charge, you'll have all the records you need right at your fingertips.

**Be a CPT code cracker.** Find out the current procedural terminology (CPT) code for your tests or surgery. Knowing the code will make it easier to compare prices, and you'll be better prepared to make sense of your bills once they start rolling in. Ask your doctor's staff for help, or conduct your own search at *icd10data.com*.

**Ask for the Medicare rate (even if you're not a senior).** Medicare pays doctors, hospitals, and other health care providers the lowest fees. You can request the same rate for yourself. Even if they say no, you can still use those numbers to negotiate your way to a lower medical bill.

According to a survey by the Consumer Reports National Research Center, only 31 percent of Americans have ever tried to lower their medical bills. The great thing is, most of them were successful, with more than a third saving over $100 on their bill.

**Make sure your insurance pays its part.** Sometimes it doesn't. If the insurance company denies your claim, you are entitled to receive an explanation in writing. If you disagree with their decision, you have six months to appeal.

To get help with your insurance claim, contact the Consumer Assistance Program in your state at *cms.gov* or call the Health Insurance Assistance Team of the U.S. Center for Consumer Information and Insurance Oversight at 888-393-2789.

**Settle up with cold, hard cash.** If you can afford it, offer to pay your doctor one lump sum — at a significant discount. The doctor will be pleased to get his money right away, and his office staff will be saved the time and trouble of filing insurance claims — or possibly hiring attorneys and collection agencies.

**Negotiate a payment plan.** Talk with the billing department about your financial situation, and ask to set up a payment plan. Many doctors' offices and hospitals will allow you to make payments at zero percent or very low interest. That will lower the "amount due" on your bill to a more manageable amount.

Decide on a time frame and payment you're comfortable with, then make sure you pay your bill on time each month.

**Keep your credit card in your pocket.** That little piece of plastic may be convenient, but it's one of the most expensive forms of financing because interest rates are so high. Plus, your health care provider could hit you with a processing surcharge of up to 4 percent to boot.

**Consider other ways to pay.** Take advantage of your company's health savings account (HSA) or flexible spending account (FSA) to cover the cost of care. Ask your provider for a "prompt pay" discount while you're at it.

If you don't have this option, check on discount programs available through your health care provider or hospital. But you have to be pro-active — in other words, you have to ask for help.

**Call in professional help.** Experts report that medical billing advocates can help you save up to nearly 50 percent on your medical bills. A professional advocate will do a line-by-line analysis of your bill, looking for clerical, coding, and other types of errors.

But beware. You may be charged as much as $100 to $200 per hour for their services. Or the advocate could charge you 25 to 35 percent of whatever he saves you. You'll have to decide if the extra help is worth the price.

Is help available for uninsured patients? Yes, says Dana W., a medical billing specialist. "The usual cost for a doctor visit here is $216. If the uninsured patient pays cash on the day of the visit, the charge drops to $140. That's a 35 percent discount." The bottom line — always ask.

For more information, go to websites like the Medical Billing Advocates of America at *billadvocates.com* or Medical Cost Advocate at *medicalcostadvocate.com*.

## Get health care for free

You don't have to go without health care because there's no room in your budget. You can get treatment for free or at little cost.

Health centers managed by the Health Resources and Services Administration (HRSA) will provide you with quality health care, even if you have no insurance. You simply pay what you can afford based on your income.

The centers provide services that include well-patient checkups as well as treatments when you're sick. Some even provide mental health, dental, and eye care.

To find an HRSA health center near you, go to *findahealthcenter.hrsa.gov*. Contact your local center directly to make an appointment.

## This admission scam could cost you thousands

You've tossed and turned in that uncomfortable hospital bed for three long nights. You've choked down enough green Jell-O to last a lifetime. Finally, you're ready to be discharged, and you find out your status has been listed as "outpatient under observation" for your entire stay.

Inpatient. Outpatient. What's the big deal? Big money, that's what.

Being "out" could end up costing you an arm and a leg. As an outpatient, your hospital stay isn't covered under Medicare Part A, which pays the charges above your $1,288 deductible. Instead, outpatient services are billed under Medicare Part B, which means you pay 20 percent of the hospital costs. Plus, there's no cap on the bill you might be saddled with.

Want another example? After your hospital stay, you need to move to a skilled nursing facility for rehab. The median cost per day for a semi-private room is $220.

You assume Medicare is handling the bill because you were in the hospital for three days, which covers the Medicare requirement. And Medicare pays for 20 days in a skilled nursing facility so you're all set, right?

Only if your status in the hospital was listed as inpatient. Uh oh. Your outpatient status means you have to pay the $4,400 rehab tab yourself.

Hospitals are caught in the crossfire. The average cost per day for a hospital stay is $2,212, and the average stay is about four and a half days. That's almost $10,000. And of course, Medicare doesn't want to pay the high price of inpatient treatment.

To keep Medicare expenses down, the government is pressuring hospitals to serve more patients on a cheaper outpatient basis.

Those who don't comply risk legal action, fines, and penalties. So even respectable facilities are doing it. Then they have to deal with patients who complain about the out-of-pocket medical bills they're stuck with because Medicare Part A refused to pay. All because they were listed as outpatient.

How can you protect yourself? Know your hospital status. Are you "in" or "out"? If you're listed as an outpatient, especially if you need rehab, ask your doctor to help reverse your status before you're discharged.

## Guard your health with these 'rights'

Protect yourself from medication mistakes with these five must-ask questions.

**Right patient?** Be certain your nurse checks the name on your wristband before you take any medication.

**Right medicine?** Make sure you're being given the right drug. Don't be afraid to ask questions about a new medication.

**Right dose?** Ask your doctor or nurse about any changes in the amount or strength of your medicine.

**Right time?** Check the clock. It's important to take your meds at the correct time.

**Right method?** The medicine must be administered correctly. Find out if you need to take it orally, intravenously, or by some other method.

## Protect yourself from this costly — even deadly — hospital blunder

Seven thousand. The estimated number of deaths each year caused by medication mistakes that happen in hospitals across the nation.

The cost of these nearly four million medical errors? About $16.4 billion. And guess who typically foots the bill for the extra treatments and procedures needed to fix these mistakes. The patients and their insurance companies, that's who.

Here's how you can protect yourself and your wallet the next time you're scheduled for a hospital stay.

**Be on the lookout for drug mistakes.** It's tough to be at your best when you're lying in a hospital bed. But try to be alert when it comes to your medicines. Watch out for these common mistakes.

- They give you the wrong dose.

- They give you the wrong drug.

- The medicine is not given the right way, for example orally versus intravenously.

**Bring your medicine bottles with you.** If you take certain drugs regularly, bring them with you. If that's not an option, take a picture of the label with your cellphone. It's not enough to just copy information off the labels. You could make a mistake, too.

Be sure to include your over-the-counter meds, herbs, and supplements so your health care team can review them. Have the medicines or pictures ready for your doctors and nursing staff to see.

**Ask questions about new medications.** Check with your doctor or nurse about any new meds you're prescribed while in the hospital. Find out what they're for, and ask about side effects you might experience.

**Don't try to go it alone.** An extra pair of eyes and ears can help keep you safe, especially when you're under sedation. Bring along someone you trust to watch out for you. Give them an up-to-date medication list, too.

**Go to a tech-savvy hospital.** Hospitals that use the computerized provider order entry (CPOE) system require doctors to enter their prescriptions into a computer that sends them directly to the pharmacy. One study estimated that using CPOE could reduce hospital medical errors by as much as 48 percent.

Pairing CPOE with the clinical decision support system (CDSS) is even better. That gives the doctor immediate access to information like default doses of the drug, possible medication interactions, and even patient allergies.

To find out what hospitals in your area use CPOE, check *leapfroggroup.org*, and click on the tab marked "Compare Hospitals Now."

## The digital doctor will see you now (right now!)

"Ground control to Major Tom." Those well-known lyrics from a song about space fit right in with the new age of telemedicine. The idea for telemedicine was hatched back in the 1960s when NASA wanted to monitor the health of its far-flung astronauts. Now it's available to earthlings everywhere, 24 hours a day at low-cost, out-of-this-world prices.

When you're running a temp at 3 a.m., reach out to a telemedicine doctor. Through two-way video, email, smartphone, and computer, telemed doctors can help you with allergies, flu symptoms, fevers, coughs, and many other common complaints. They can also monitor your heart rate, blood pressure, and body temperature — right over the internet.

> A 10-minute consult with a telehealth company costs between $30 and $50, but you may owe nothing more than a $15 copay. Compare that to the average $1,400 middle-of-the-night emergency room tab, and you'll see why telemedicine's star is on the rise.

Some telemed doctors can even prescribe medications for you. "My daughter has that option with her health insurance," Ann H. says. "She was able to get medicine for the flu right away."

But coughs and colds are just the beginning. Dermatologists and even psychologists are considering the many ways telemedicine can meet their patients' needs.

Interested in scheduling your own virtual visit? First, check your health plan to see if telemedicine is covered by your insurance plan. If not, go online and schedule appointments on your own with companies like MDLive at *mdlive.com* or American Well at *amwell.com*.

Look for these features when choosing your online provider to keep your interactions safe and secure.

- Check for this seal from the American Telemedicine Association. It certifies the website has met the established guidelines for patient security, provider qualifications, and pricing information.

- Make sure you can easily access your doctor's qualifications and credentials.

- Check the site's security information to verify that your private information is protected.

- You should be able to access your medical records through a secure patient portal on the site.

- Scroll through the site to answer these questions. Is it easy to change doctors? Can you make appointments online? How do you give feedback?

- Avoid sites that recommend a particular brand of medication. Sometimes a drug manufacturer may sponsor a website just to promote its own products.

---

### Save time and money when the doctor comes to you

Remember the good old days when doctors made house calls? Mobile medical teams like GoMed and Mobile Medical Specialists are bringing those days back by taking modern medicine right to your door.

"Medical care can be affordable and accessible and doesn't have to take up a large part of your day," says Barret McDowell, co-founder and chief operating officer of GoMed. "Care is more well-received and more effective when the patient is most comfortable, and that's usually in their own home."

Like an urgent care center on wheels, GoMED can treat everything from cuts and wounds to strep, flu, and pneumonia. They'll even do lab tests. And a home visit costs no more than a normal office visit, McDowell says. But just think of the money you'll save on transportation and expensive trips to the emergency room.

Want to know more? Visit the American Academy of Home Care Medicine at *aahcm.org.* Click on "Find a Provider" to find a service near you.

---

## Googling your symptoms — money saver or mistake?

You have a scratchy throat and a fever. Feeling a little achy, too. You could follow the age-old, tried-and-true advice — take two aspirin and call the doctor in the morning. Instead, you decide to check out your symptoms online.

You're not alone. About one-third of U.S. adults search the internet for health information. Cheaper than a midnight trip to the emergency room, right? Maybe not.

Symptom checker websites are designed to figure out what's wrong with you and what you should do to fix it. But taking medical advice from the internet can have unforeseen results.

**The internet can turn you into a "cyberchondriac."** Do you find yourself feeling nervous and fearful as you read through all the strange diseases that may be causing your symptoms? There's a name for that health anxiety — cyberchondria. And it can cost you big bucks if you decide your symptoms call for expensive tests like MRIs or CT scans — despite what your doctor says.

That fear can also make you more likely to buy online treatments and "miracle" remedies that are more con than cure.

**It can push you into medical care you don't need.** A recent study by Harvard Medical School found that symptom checker websites often give advice that encourages patients to seek unnecessary care — think expensive trips to the ER or urgent care centers — when self care would have worked just fine.

**You can end up with bad advice.** Correct medical advice was given in only about half the cases monitored in the Harvard study. The websites did better with emergency cases, getting those right about 80 percent of the time.

Online medical advice can never replace a talk with your health care provider. Don't let the internet be your only source of information. When you have a concern, call your doctor.

**Improve your odds by choosing the right websites.** If you decide to search your symptoms online, choose reputable websites to get a more accurate diagnosis.

- Visit sites that have .gov, .edu, and .org addresses. Those three little letters mean you can trust the websites are run by the government, a college or university, or a professional organization.

- Find out who wrote the site's content. Make sure it's been reviewed by qualified health care professionals before it found its way online.

- Check references. The website should provide information sourced from medical journals and scientific studies.

- Look for content that is recent, not more than two to three years old.

- Don't rely on just one website. Search other sites to verify the information you find.

## Calling all veterans — this benefit puts thousands in your pocket

Don't miss out on a pension that could boost your income by up to $2,500 every month. "Aid and Attendance" is a little-known veterans assistance program that provides monthly payments to vets and their spouses who need personal care assistance.

Approximately 10 million older adults — about a quarter of all Americans over 65 — could qualify to receive this extra income, but only about 5 percent have applied. Find out if you, or your loved one, is eligible.

- You must have an honorable or general discharge from military service, or you are the unmarried surviving spouse of a veteran.

- You must be at least 65 years old, or officially disabled if younger.

- You need help with daily activities like bathing, feeding, and dressing.

- You or your spouse must have served in the armed forces for at least 90 days, with one or more days of service during World War II, the Korean War, the Vietnam War, or the Gulf War.

Your income has to be less than the pension amount you could receive. For example, if you're a veteran with no dependents, you're eligible for $1,788 every month. If your monthly income is $1,000, then you can get an additional $788.

However, you may rake in more than you think. "Countable" income is the key. The Veterans Administration allows you to deduct lots of expenses like Medicare and other insurance premiums. You can take off all your medical-related costs for yourself and your spouse, too. You don't even have to count your Supplemental Security Income (SSI).

Are you a resident of an assisted living facility? That's a pricey $3,500 every month, according to national averages. Good news — you can deduct that, too.

For more information, go to *benefits.va.gov* and type "Aid and Attendance" in the search box. Or call 800-827-1000 to speak to someone at the Department of Veterans Affairs.

## Peace-of-mind insurance: what's best for you?

Long-term care (LTC) insurance covers extended health care if you're over age 65. If you can afford it. If you qualify. And that's always been the kicker. Now seniors who worry about facing a medical hardship have another option, short-term care (STC) insurance. It's a cheaper alternative, certainly. And only about 8 percent of 61- to 70-year-olds who applied were denied coverage. But is it right for you? There are some serious differences you need to understand.

# Long-term care vs short-term care costs

## What are you willing to pay?

Short-term care (STC) insurance generally has lower premiums compared to long-term care (LTC) insurance. Here are sample premiums for a 65-year-old.

| STC Annual Premium: $420 | LTC Annual Premium: $2,760 |

## What kind of care do you need?

| | Average cost of care | Insurance type | Coverage | Your out-of-pocket cost per day |
|---|---|---|---|---|
| **Home Care** | The median cost is about **$184 per day**. | STC | $50 per day | $134 per day |
| | | LTC | $200 per day | $0 |
| **Assisted Living** | The average stay is 21 months at about $3,450 per month. **Total cost: $72,450** | STC | $1,500 per month for up to 12 months | $54,450 |
| | | LTC | $6,000 per month for up to 60 months | $0 |
| **Nursing Home** | The average stay is 15 months at about $7,590 per month. **Total cost: $113,850** | STC | $1,500 per month for up to 12 months | $95,850 |
| | | LTC | $6,000 per month for up to 60 months | $0 |

Your coverage and out-of-pocket costs may differ according to the terms of the plan you choose.

## How long will you wait for benefits?

The elimination period, or waiting period, is the number of days from the time you begin receiving care until you actually get benefits. Generally speaking, the longer the elimination period, the smaller the premium you pay.

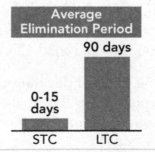

Average Elimination Period

90 days

0-15 days

STC       LTC

# Medicare

## 5 Medicare pitfalls that cost you money

Navigating the long and winding road through Medicare can be confusing, and the pressure is on to make the right decision from the get-go. This list of common stumbling blocks can help keep you on track.

**Hesitating to apply for financial help.** You may qualify for programs that lower your Medicare premiums, deductibles, and copays. For example, with a Medicare Savings Program, or MSP, your state pays the Part B premiums and possibly some other expenses.

Or check out the federal Extra Help program. You'll get cheaper Part D prescription drug coverage if you qualify.

**Choosing a drug plan simply because your spouse picked it.** The plan that's right for your husband or wife may leave you high and dry. Use the Medicare Plan Finder to estimate your individual out-of-pocket prescription costs. Go to *medicare.gov* and type the words "plan finder" in the search box.

**Forgetting to review your coverage every year.** Research studies show this simple step could save you more than $300. Look over your plan annually to make sure it still pays for all the medicines you take, and check that the premiums haven't gone up.

You can find this information in your Annual Notice of Change report that will be mailed to you every September. Use the notice to compare other plans in your area. You'll be armed and ready to make a switch when the open enrollment period rolls around — Oct. 15 through Dec. 7.

**Ignoring the Medicare income cutoff.** If you're single and have an income of more than $85,000 — more than $170,000 for a couple — your Part B premiums will be much higher than this year's average of $121.80. In fact, you can expect to pay between $170 and $389 per month for Part B if you go over the income limit.

Your Part D drug premiums will be pricier also, adding as much as $72.90 to the basic monthly payment. How do you get around this pitfall? Avoid financial moves that might hike your adjusted gross income for the year, like rolling a traditional IRA over to a Roth. And don't make any big withdrawals from a tax-deferred retirement account.

**Making these decisions all by yourself.** Need some help? State Health Insurance Assistance Programs (SHIPs) help people like you with questions about benefits, coverage, premiums, deductibles, and coinsurance.

They'll walk you through the Medicare complaints and appeals process, and even guide you through changing your Medicare Advantage, Medigap, and Part D prescription plans. Visit *shiptacenter.org* or call 800-633-4277 for information about programs in your state.

## Save these dates — and save a bundle

Medicare is very particular about its enrollment periods. If you want to avoid penalties, there's no room for error. Check this list to make sure you sign up on time, every time.

**Initial Enrollment Period (IEP).** This includes the month of your 65th birthday, plus the three months before and after your birthday month. Sign up during this time for Part A, Part B, Medicare Supplement (Medigap), Medicare Advantage plan, and a Part D Prescription plan.

**Enrollment Period**

**Medicare Supplement (Medigap) Open Enrollment Period.** This begins the month you turn 65 and are enrolled in Medicare Part B. During this six-month period, you can sign up for any supplement plan, regardless of your health. You can apply at a later date, but you may be denied coverage or charged more because of your health conditions.

**Enrollment Period**

**Medicare Open Enrollment Period.** From Oct. 15 through Dec. 7, Medicare beneficiaries can enroll in, or change, their Medicare plans, including Medicare Advantage. New coverage will go into effect on Jan. 1 of the new year.

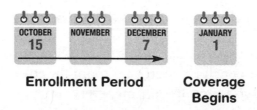

**Enrollment Period          Coverage
                             Begins**

**General Enrollment Period (GEP).** If you didn't enroll in Medicare during your IEP, you have another chance to sign up between Jan. 1 and March 31. Your new coverage will begin on July 1. Some penalties may apply.

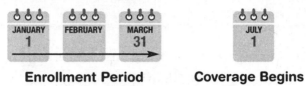

**Enrollment Period**          **Coverage Begins**

**Medicare Advantage Enrollment Period.** Sign up between April 1 and June 30 for a Medicare Advantage plan if you already have Medicare Part A coverage, and you got Part B for the first time during the GEP. Your coverage begins on the first day of the month after you sign up.

**Enrollment Period**

**Medicare Advantage Disenrollment Period.** Between Jan. 1 and Feb. 14, you can switch from a Medicare Advantage plan to original Medicare and a Part D prescription plan. However, you won't be able to switch from one Medicare Advantage Plan to another or switch from one Part D plan to another during this period. Your coverage will begin the first day of the month after the new plan gets your enrollment form.

**Disenrollment Period**

**Special Enrollment Period (SEP).** If you're a new beneficiary who didn't enroll during your IEP, you may be able to enroll during an SEP. You must meet certain requirements to qualify. For example, you might be granted an SEP if you move out of your plan's service area, you lose your current coverage, or your current plan changes its contract with Medicare.

---

## Good news — you can switch plans with no penalty

You want to change Medicare Advantage plans, but the open enrollment period doesn't kick in until October. And you definitely don't want to pay a penalty.

You're in luck. Medicare allows you to make one penalty-free change to certain Medicare plans each year during a special enrollment period that lasts from Dec. 8 through Nov. 30.

What's the catch? You have to switch to a five-star program. Every year, Medicare awards Medicare Advantage plans one to five stars based on quality of care and customer satisfaction. Five stars is tops.

But only 17 plans in the country secured a five-star ranking in 2016. To find out if one is located near you, go to *medicare.gov*, and search the plan finder.

---

## Don't get slapped with a pricey penalty

Medicare is not always free, especially when you get slapped with lifelong penalties for signing up late. Stay out of the Medicare penalty box with these pointers.

**Know when your enrollment period starts and ends.** You're automatically enrolled in Medicare Part A hospital insurance and Part B medical insurance when you turn 65 if you're already receiving Social Security benefits. But you'll need to sign yourself up if you've postponed filing for Social Security or if you're not eligible for premium-free Part A.

Medicare gives you a seven-month window to get this done. Your Initial Enrollment Period (IEP) starts three months before your 65th birthday month and lasts three full months afterward. You have no reason to wait because, for most people, Part A is free thanks to the Medicare taxes taken out of their paychecks.

Get ready to be socked with a hefty penalty if you wait to enroll until after your IEP has expired. If you do have to buy Part A, you'll be charged an extra 10 percent of your premium every month for twice the number of years you waited to enroll.

Here's an example. Suppose your Part A premium would have been $450 if you'd signed up during your IEP. If you wait three years before enrolling, you'll pay an extra 10 percent ($45) every month for six years, raising your monthly premium to $495. That means you would pay an additional $3,200 in Part A premiums.

So don't put it off. To apply for Medicare Part A, visit your local Social Security office, call 800-772-1213, or contact the Social Security Administration at *ssa.gov.*

**Don't wait to enroll in Part B.** You'll steer clear of costly Part B penalties if you make a decision about your plan when you enroll in Medicare during your IEP. You can delay enrolling in Part B without paying a penalty if you're over 65 and get health insurance from an employer who has 20 or more workers.

The Part B penalty works like this. You'll be charged 10 percent of your monthly premium for each full 12-month period that you could have had Medicare Part B but didn't take it.

An example? Suppose your Part B premium is $121.80 each month. Let's say your IEP ended Sept. 30, 2016. You decide to wait to sign up for Part B until the general enrollment period in March 2019. Your delay makes your Part B premium penalty 20 percent because it included two full 12-month periods.

By waiting to enroll, you've upped your monthly premium from $121.80 to $146.16. And you'll be paying that penalty for life.

**Sign up for the drug plan even if you don't need it.** Don't skip your Part D sign-up just because you don't take any prescription drugs right now. You will pay a late enrollment penalty if you don't have a Medicare Prescription Drug Plan (Part D), Medicare Advantage Plan (Part C), or other Medicare health plan that offers prescription drug coverage. A penalty kicks in 63 days after your IEP ends.

If you enroll late, you will pay an extra 1 percent of the average monthly prescription drug premium. In 2016, it was 1 percent of $34.10, or 34 cents. Multiply 34 cents by the number of months you were late, rounded to the nearest 10 cents to get your penalty.

Here's the math. If you were 12 months late in enrolling, you'd multiply 34 cents by 12 months, which equals $4.08. Round that to $4.10 per month. That's the penalty you'd pay on top of your original $34.10 premium, for a total of $38.20.

And here's the worst part. Every year your penalty will be recalculated based on that year's average so it can rise — along with the premium — for as long as you have Part D coverage.

## Pocket over $3,000 with free Medicare services

You've made your decisions and signed up for your Medicare plans. Now it's time to cash in on the benefits you've been waiting for.

**Preventive services keep you fit as a fiddle.** Here's a list of just a few screenings, treatments, and tests you can get for free with Part B — as long as your provider accepts "assignment." That means your doctor agrees to accept the Medicare-approved amount as full payment for his services.

- breast cancer screening (mammogram)

- heart disease screening (once every five years)

- diabetes screening (up to two each year if you're at risk)

- flu and pneumonia shots

- lung cancer screening

- prostate cancer screening

- colonoscopy (once every 10 years, or every two years if you're high risk)

If you add up the cost of the first six screenings, your savings would total about $1,045 depending on where you live. Figure in the cost of a colonoscopy, and that grand total soars to a colossal $2,544. Treat yourself to a free preventive doctor visit and save another $321. The savings keep piling up.

**Medicare welcomes you with a free checkup.** During your first year with Medicare Part B, you're entitled to a free "Welcome to Medicare" exam. The doctor will counsel you about preventive services, including certain screenings or tests you should have.

When you call the doctor's office to make an appointment, be sure to mention you are scheduling your "Welcome to Medicare" checkup. This visit will be free as long as your doctor accepts assignment.

**Make sure all is well with a once-a-year, no-cost visit.** At this free wellness visit, your doctor will update your personalized health plan. You and your doctor will discuss your current health and risk factors and the steps you can take to stay healthy. Let your doctor's office know you are scheduling your annual wellness visit when you call to make your appointment.

The one-time preventive visit and annual wellness visit come with a price tag of $321 each, according to Dana W., a medical billing specialist. Add that amount to the $2,544 for the screenings, and you've hit pay dirt with a savings of $3,186.

---

### Fight for your prescription rights — and win

You went to pick up your medication at the pharmacy and, to your surprise, your Medicare plan doesn't cover that drug anymore. What can you do?

You can appeal. You have the right to ask your health plan to pay for a medicine you and your doctor think should be covered. Here's how you do it.

Ask your Medicare drug plan to send you a written explanation, called a coverage determination, of why the medication was denied. Your pharmacist can tell you how to do that. Next your doctor must submit a request for an exception, explaining the medical reasons why your prescription should be approved. If you're still denied coverage, you can request a review.

For help with this process, go to *medicare.gov*, and search for claims and appeals. Just don't give up. In one recent year, nearly eight out of 10 prescription denials were eventually approved.

---

## Wipe out your medical bills in one easy step

Forget about Medicare limitations. This little-known government program could pay all your hospital and nursing home bills.

Back in 1946, Congress gave money to hospitals, nursing homes, and clinics to help them upgrade their buildings and equipment. This was known as the Hill-Burton Act. As payback for these grants, the facilities are required by law to treat a certain number of patients each year for free or reduced costs. About 150 hospitals, clinics, and nursing homes across the country participate in this money-saving program.

**Find out if you qualify.** You are eligible for Hill-Burton assistance if your income falls within the U.S. Health and Human Services (HHS) poverty guidelines. And even if your income is twice or, for nursing homes, even three times that level, you may still receive reduced-cost treatment. Visit *aspe.hhs.gov* and click on Poverty Guidelines to check your eligibility.

**How and where you can apply.** First, look for a participating hospital or medical center near you. Go online to *hrsa.gov* and search for Hill-Burton obligated facilities, or call the Hill-Burton hotline at 800-638-0742. You may apply for Hill-Burton assistance before or after you get medical care — even if your bill is past due.

Your next step is to visit the hospital's business office and ask for a copy of its Hill-Burton Individual Notice. It will tell you if your income qualifies you for free or reduced-cost care and where you should go to apply for help. This notice will also list the treatments they offer.

You may have to look elsewhere for assistance if the hospital has already met its quota of discounted procedures for the year.

Next, fill out the application forms and gather the necessary paperwork, including pay stubs to prove your income level. Then go to the hospital, file your application, and request a Determination of Eligibility. Check your Individual Notice to find out how long the hospital can take to approve or deny your application.

**Will the program cover Medicare and Medicaid payments?**
You can't use Hill-Burton funds to cover your Medicare deductible or coinsurance. But Medicaid copayments and spend-down amounts are eligible.

## The secret to uncovering hidden benefits

Ever heard of SPAP or SNAP? How about MSP? SSI? Sounds like a toddler learning the alphabet song. But these unfamiliar acronyms stand for programs that can save you M-O-N-E-Y. And they all spell out benefits your tax dollars entitle you to.

Many adults over age 55 need help paying for the basics, like prescriptions, housing, utilities, even food. The National Council on Aging (NCOA) took note and started the free screening service *benefitscheckup.org*.

Tucked away in its database are almost 2,500 public and private programs from all 50 states and the District of Columbia. Since 2001, the website has helped more than 5 million people uncover over $16 billion in benefits.

NCOA has found that more than half the people they screen are eligible for help to buy food, and over a third are entitled to receive Supplemental Security Income (SSI). A quarter qualify for Medicare Extra Help, and about one in five are eligible for Medicaid.

Ready to claim some hidden benefits of your own? Just click your way through a few questions on the website to receive a personalized list of programs tailored to fit your needs. Here's a sample of the programs available through *benefitscheckup.org*.

- Medicare Extra Help works with your Medicare Part D plan to cover the costs of prescription drugs.

- Medicare Savings Programs (MSPs) help you pay Medicare premiums, deductibles, and copays.

- State Pharmaceutical Assistance Program (SPAP) assists Medicare patients with drug plan premiums.

- Supplemental Nutrition Assistance Program (SNAP) helps low-income individuals and families buy food.

## Save over $500 a year with a little 'extra help'

Is it getting hard to divvy up your dollars for prescription meds, copayments, and deductibles? Maybe it's time to check out the Extra Help program. More than 2 million seniors qualify for this Medicare money-saver, but up to 40 percent don't take advantage of it.

A recent study found that seniors receiving Extra Help saved an average of $529 on out-of-pocket spending for medicine and premiums each year. Some participants saved even more — up to a whopping $4,000.

Extra Help goes the extra mile to get you a sizable drug discount. You'll pay no more than $3 for generic prescription medicines and less than $8 for brand-name drugs once you're enrolled in the program.

To qualify, you must be signed up for Medicare Part A and/or Part B. You can't earn more than $17,820 per year if you're single or $24,030 if you're married.

They also count other assets like bank accounts, stocks, and bonds — but not your house, car, or life insurance policies. Those must be under $13,640 for singles and $27,250 for couples.

It's easy to apply for Extra Help. You or a family member can get started by going online to *ssa.gov* or by calling the Social Security Administration at 800-772-1213.

## Claim denied? Don't take no for an answer

Don't let Medicare take away money that's rightfully yours. Even if your claim has been denied, you can still take steps to get the decision reversed. Stick to your guns — like thousands of others — and you can change Medicare's mind.

The Medicare appeals process has several levels. Scaling the steps is not easy, but perseverance can put cash in your pocket. In a recent year, almost 25 percent of the people denied hospital benefits got the decision reversed at the first level. For medical claims, that figure jumped to 40 percent. About one in five achieved a favorable outcome at the second level for both Part A and Part B claims.

Claim denied by Medicare Advantage? Apply for reconsideration within 60 days. Your next step is an Independent Review Entity (IRE). If IRE turns you down, appeal to an administrative law judge. No luck? Try the Appeals Council. The U.S. District Court is your last chance for reversal. Call 800-MEDICARE for help.

Call your doctor's office and ask for help as soon as you find out your claim has been denied. Medicare's denial could have been caused by something as simple as entering an incorrect CPT code.

If that doesn't fix the problem, you'll find the information you need to begin the appeals process on the back of the Medicare Summary Notice (MSN) you get in the mail every three months. At *medicare.gov*, you can find links to all the forms you'll need for the appeals process. Or you can call 800-633-4227 for information about your claim.

Worried this might be too much to handle alone? Help is available. Claims Assistance Professionals (CAPs) have extensive experience in the medical claims and health insurance industry. They'll put their expertise to work for you for a fee ranging from $60 to $150 per hour. Search *claims.org* to find the locations of CAPs in your state.

# Manage your Medicare appeal

**Level: 1**

## Ask for a redetermination

**Act within 120 days**

If you disagree with Medicare's denial of coverage or payment, you can request a redetermination by the company that handles claims for Medicare. Your Medicare Summary Notice (MSN) contains information about getting your appeal started.

**Decision within 60 days**

**Level: 2**

## Move on to reconsideration

**Act within 180 days**

If you are unsuccessful at Level 1, a member of a separate review organization, known as a Qualified Independent Contractor or QIC, will consider your appeal. Send your request to the QIC listed on your redetermination letter.

**Decision within 60 days**

**Level: 3**

## Schedule a hearing with an Administrative Law Judge (ALJ)

**Act within 60 days**

To file an appeal at this level, the amount of money in dispute must be more than $150. An ALJ will review the facts of your case before issuing a new and impartial decision. This hearing can be held in person, by phone, or by videoconference.

**Decision within 90 days**

**Level: 4**

## Take your case to the Medicare Appeals Council (MAC)

**Act within 60 days**

An appeal to the MAC is also known as "a request for review." The MAC may adopt, change, or reverse the ALJ's decision, send the case back to the ALJ for further action, or dismiss the appeal.

**Decision within 90 days**

**Level: 5**

## Request a judicial review by the U.S. District Court

**Act within 60 days**

You can only make this appeal if the amount of money being disputed is more than $1500, but you may combine claims to meet this limit. There's no timeframe for a judicial decision.

**No limit for a decision**

# Eye care, Dental services, and Hearing aids

## You'll love these 'specs'-tacular savings

Pay $500 for new eyeglasses? No way. How about $8? Now that's more like it. You can save hundreds on everything from specialty lenses to designer frames — if you know where to look.

**Eye spy low prices online.** You can get great glasses no matter where you live. Just shop online for deals. Click on over to *goggles4u.com* or *zennioptical.com*, for example, and feast your eyes on prescription glasses for eight bucks a pair or less. But make sure that deal includes both the frames and the lenses. You can search for online coupons, too, that will help you snag a rock-bottom price.

In the market for eye-catching designer frames? Let's say you saw a fabulous pair of Tiffany and Co. frames at a brick-and-mortar LensCrafters for around $240. Nice, but a similar pair at *myglasses.com* might be yours for more like $130. That's a discount of almost 50 percent.

**Check out all the details.** A few tips to help you compare before you buy:

- Several sites, like *glasses.com*, let you download a photo of yourself so you can 'try on' your new glasses. Check it out at *glasses.com/virtual-try-on*.

- Know the shipping costs. For example, *zennioptical.com* charges $4.95 to ship your first pair anywhere in the United States. The rest of the glasses in your order ship for free.

Online competitor *goggles4u.com* has a slightly pricier shipping policy — $5.95 ships your glasses to any location in the U.S.

- Online retailers will make your bifocals and other specialty lenses, too, but plan to pay a little more for those. And buyer beware — it's harder to get a good fit when you purchase eye wear online. So if you have extreme nearsightedness, farsightedness, or astigmatism, or wear bifocals, you could end up with glasses that just aren't quite right.

- Don't forget to read each company's return policy. You don't want to be stuck paying for glasses that make you look like Mr. Magoo.

- For reviews of online companies and their products, take a gander at *toptenreviews.com*, and search on eyeglasses.

**Have your numbers ready before ordering.** You'll need to gather some stats before you place your online order. First, get your vision checked by your eye doctor to get an updated prescription.

Next you'll need your PD, or pupillary distance. You can ask your eye doctor for it, or you can measure it yourself. Just remember that if the PD is not accurate, your new glasses won't fit properly.

Want a DIY to find your PD? *39dollarglasses.com* and *goggles4u.com* are two of the many sites that will show you how to get the correct measurement.

**Online shopping not your style?** Keep your eyes peeled for great deals at warehouse stores like Costco or discount stores like Walmart and Target.

And if you feel comfortable choosing your frames online, you can have the prescription filled locally. Walmart charges $10, plus the cost of the lenses, if you bring in your own frames. Costco has a similar deal, but you'll pay $18 to start.

## Free vision exams — a sight for sore eyes

Haven't had those twinkling baby-blues checked in a while? Take a look-see at this list of organizations ready to help you get your eyes examined for free.

**Medicare: take advantage of all your benefits.** If you have diabetes, eye disease is a real concern. Medicare will pay for you to have a dilated eye exam to make sure your eyes stay healthy. Your doctor will determine how often you need it.

And, if you're at risk for glaucoma, Medicare will pay for an eye exam once a year to test for it.

**EyeCare America: easy on the eyes and the wallet.** EyeCare America is sponsored by the American Academy of Ophthalmology. It offers free yearly eye exams for qualifying seniors. It will also provide a year's worth of care for any eye disease diagnosed during your first exam.

Just meet these guidelines, and you're on your way to a free exam.

- You must be a U.S. citizen or legal resident age 65 or older.

- It's been three years or more since your last eye checkup.

- You don't belong to an HMO or have eye care coverage through the Veterans Administration.

- You don't have an eye doctor.

Concerned about glaucoma? You may be eligible for a free glaucoma exam if you're at risk because of factors like your age, race, or family history, and you haven't had a vision checkup in a year. If you need treatment, the doctor will start it right away.

Find out more about EyeCare America's benefits at *aao.org/ eyecare-america*.

**Lions Clubs International: setting their sights on serving your community.** This all-volunteer service organization can help you buy glasses or get eye exams at discounted prices. Scout around for a club near you at *lionsclubs.org*.

**Mission Cataract USA: put that gleam back in your eyes.**
Mission Cataract USA provides free cataract surgery for people of all ages who have no Medicare, Medicaid, or any other way to pay. Surgeries are scheduled for one day each year. To find a participating doctor near you, go to *missioncataractusa.org*.

## Money-saving dental deals put a smile on your face

Finding low-cost dental care is a hassle. Like pulling teeth, right? The cleanings, the crowns, the root canals and other out-of-pocket expenses could break anybody's bank. So how can you afford to keep those pearly-whites shiny and bright? Mind your molars — and your wallet — with these sure-to-make-you-smile tips.

**Is your cash as scarce as hen's teeth?** But your toothache just won't quit? You don't have to pay for dental care. Here's how to get it for free.

Find relief through the U.S. Health Resources and Services Administration (HRSA). Nearly 1,300 HRSA health centers in more than 9,000 locations will provide free or discounted dental care, all based on your financial need. To find a center near you, visit *FindAHealthCenter.HRSA.gov*, or call toll-free 877-464-4772.

Another source for free or reduced-price dental care is *freedentalcare.us*. Just select your state and search the listings.

**Ask for a discount.** Plain and simple. Your dentist might offer a 10-percent discount to uninsured patients. Some will even give you a discount for paying your bill in cash at checkout. If you're a little long in the tooth, say over 55, ask for a senior discount.

Also, it helps to know the prices of dental procedures before you go. The consumer website *fairhealthconsumer.org* is a great tool for planning your dental and medical expenses.

**Head back to school for a budget-friendly smile.** Dental students need the experience, and you need the discount. Make an appointment at a university's dental school, and you could save up to half of what you'd pay a traditional dentist.

In other words, a $90 exam will cost your around $45. And your treatment will be supervised by experienced, well-qualified instructors. For a list of dental schools near you, go to *ADA.org/dentalschools*.

For teeth cleanings, call on the students at a local dental hygiene college. You'll nab a 50- to 75-percent discount, cutting your cost from about $95 to $50 or less.

Want to have your teeth whitened? Depending on the procedure and the city you live in, your dentist could charge a whopping $1,500. But a dental hygiene student could do the job for around $135. Now that price is sure to have you grinning from ear to ear.

**A deal U.S. veterans can sink their teeth into.** If you're a veteran or former prisoner of war, and you have a service-connected dental condition or disability, you may be eligible for free dental care. Even if you don't qualify for the free plan, the Veterans Administration offers vets the option to buy dental insurance through Delta Dental and MetLife at a reduced cost. Find out more at *VA.gov/dental*.

**Join a dental club and save.** Like the big-box stores, you pay an annual membership fee of $80 to $200 per year. In return you'll get 10- to 60-percent off cleanings, root canals, crowns, and other costly procedures.

To locate a plan that fits the bill for you, go online to *dentalplans.com*, or call toll-free 855-204-1325.

## Now hear this: save hundreds on hearing aids

A pair of hearing aids may cost you up to $6,000. And to make matters worse, Medicare and most private insurance companies are no help at all. What are you supposed to do? Listen up. Find the help you need at prices you can afford.

## Boost your hearing for thousands less

Do you have a hard time keeping up with conversations in a noisy restaurant? Is your TV a little too loud? A personal sound amplification product (PSAP) may be just what you need to boost your hearing.

The devices don't require any testing or fitting and are ready to use right out of the box. Several styles even work with Bluetooth technology, letting you listen to audio books or stream music.

The FDA advises that PSAPs should be used by people who want to amplify certain sounds, but not for those with hearing loss.

Prices range from around $25 to upwards of $500. A savings of thousands of dollars over regular hearing aids, and a great first step towards better hearing.

**Used hearing aids can work as well as new.** Has your dad upgraded his hearing aids? Don't toss out his old ones. They might be the perfect solution for you.

First, have a doctor decide if the used hearing aids will work for your type of hearing loss. Next, have the aids inspected to be sure they're not damaged. Finally, make sure they can be reprogrammed for your hearing needs. If you get the all-clear, you'll only have to pay for testing and fitting fees.

If it turns out the used aids won't work for you, find an organization that accepts donations. They might just fit the bill — and the ear — for someone else.

**Turn to generous providers for hearing help.** Private organizations may be the answer for you as well. Contact your local Lions Club and ask about used hearing aids. The national website, *lionsclubs.org*, can point you to the nearest one.

The Sertoma organization offers used hearing aids, along with financial help if you qualify. Find out more about Sertoma's program at *sertoma.org*, or give them a call at 816-333-8300.

You may find just the hearing aids you're looking for at *starkeyhearingfoundation.org*. Under the heading "Initiatives," click on the link to "Hear Now," a program that provides hearing aids to those in need.

> Hard of hearing? These free smartphone apps can help.
>
> **SoundFocus:** adjusts frequencies on your phone so music sounds clear.
>
> **BeWarned:** vibrations, flashes, and changing colors warn you about danger.
>
> **ClearCaptions:** adds captions to phone conversations.
>
> **Dragon Dictation:** turns your spoken word into written texts and e-mails.

And if you're internet savvy, you can find used hearing aids on Ebay or Craigslist. Just be careful. Do your research so you know what you're getting before you buy.

**Check prices at warehouse and discount stores.** Depending on the style of hearing aid you need, Costco may have just what you're looking for. The website touts prices as low as $499, heading upwards to around $1,800. Big boxer Sam's Club's prices are comparable to Costco, starting at around $350 and topping out close to $1,800.

Many of these stores offer free hearing tests, but call for an appointment. They get booked up months in advance.

**Lend them your ear: sign up for a clinical trial.** Check online at sites like *centerwatch.com* for hearing aid manufacturers that might be holding trials of their new products. You can also contact the companies yourself and volunteer to participate in a study.

Generally, once the study is complete, participants get to keep the hearing aids for free. And that's music to your ears, right?

# Healthy living

## Best drink for your health — for less than a penny

Henry David Thoreau may have said it best when he wrote, "I believe that water is the only drink for a wise man." Maybe he knew something you don't. Read on to find out a few of the many ways a simple drink of water can improve your life.

**Water keeps you wealthy.** Straight from your faucet, it's healthy and cheap. Perfect for the frugal household.

A gallon of drinking water from your kitchen faucet costs less than a penny, according to the American Water Works Association. That's right. Less than 1 cent.

You can buy a case of 16-ounce bottles of water for around 8 cents per bottle at a warehouse store. You'll need to drink four bottles if you're trying to get in eight, 8-ounce glasses of water daily. So you'll spend at least 32 cents every day. In a year, that'll cost you $117. And that's if you buy the big-box brand, not the pricey stuff.

If you drink the same amount of water from your tap instead, you'll spend only 73 cents in one year. Quite a savings, isn't it?

But wait, you can save even more. By ordering water instead of soft drinks, coffee, or tea at your favorite restaurant, you'll cut your bill as much as 20 percent. So that $10 meal will cost $2 less because you wash it down with a glass of water with lemon. Dessert, anyone?

For more savings, try the great soda swap. The average American family spends an estimated $850 every year on soft drinks. Remember how little it costs to drink tap water for one year? Do the swap for 12 months and enjoy your savings. You may even have enough for a weekend getaway the whole family can enjoy.

**Water keeps you healthy.** It's a no-muss, no-fuss way to better health. Check out some of the extraordinary ways water benefits your body.

- Washes away the blues. Dehydration can contribute to fatigue and short-term memory problems. It can also play a part in that bad mood. So drink up and smile.

- Soothes those achy joints. Take in a little more H2O to help cushion and lubricate your hips, shoulders, knees, and toes.

- Protects your heart. Staying hydrated helps your heart pump blood more efficiently, the American Heart Association says. (It helps your other muscles work better, too.)

- Helps shed those extra pounds. Drinking water before meals may help you drop that stubborn weight. Obese people who drank about two cups of water 30 minutes before eating a main meal lost more weight over a three-month period than those who didn't, researchers found. This "preloading" makes you feel fuller, so you don't eat as much. Cut calories and save money. It's a win-win.

## The dollar store deal that steals your health

What dangerous substance is hard to spell, tough to pronounce, and nearly impossible to avoid? The correct answer is P-H-T-H-A-L-A-T-E-S, and it's pronounced "thah-lates."

Phthalates are chemicals that are used to make plastics stronger and more flexible. Sounds like a modern marvel, right? But research suggests exposure to phthalates may lead to liver and kidney damage as well as other health issues.

So how can saving a little money cost you your health? Let's say you go shopping for the grandkids at the dollar store. You pick a pretty pink headband for your granddaughter. Grandson gets a pack of plastic silly straws. And while you're there, you remember to grab a new vinyl floor runner for that messy mud room. A steal for $1 each, but the poisonous chemicals lurking in your dollar-store deals spoil the savings.

**Don't bargain with your health.** Each item you just purchased contains phthalates in quantities much higher than the 0.1 percent allowed by the U.S. Consumer Product Safety Commission for children's products.

That headband showed a phthalate content of almost 19 percent when tested by the pros at *ecocenter.org*, a consumer education and protection organization. Those silly straws scored lower, at around 2 percent. But the phthalate content of your vinyl floor runner came in at a frightening 24 percent.

Phthalates enter your body through your food, your water, and even the air you breathe when you:

- eat food packaged in phthalate-laced plastics.

- drink from plastic bottles that leach the chemicals into your beverage.

- absorb phthalates through your skin by using certain cosmetics and lotions.

- breathe in dust or fumes from products that contain vinyl. That "new car" smell you love? You guessed it — phthalates.

The good thing is, your body breaks down phthalates into waste products that quickly pass through your system. But scientists are concerned about the effects of long-term exposure.

**Find the phthalates hiding in your home.** The table shows where 10 common phthalates are lurking. The first six are the most dangerous, and the United States and Europe have restricted the amounts used in children's toys. But they're still found in products manufactured in countries like China and India, so check labels carefully.

| Phthalate | Found in these products |
|-----------|-------------------------|
| DEHP | dolls, shoes, raincoats, floor tiles |
| DINP | clothes, paints, drinking straws, food |
| DBP | cosmetics, car care items, coatings on medicines, home furnishings |
| DiDP | electrical cords, leather for car interiors, flooring |
| DnOP | garden hoses, pool liners, conveyor belts |
| BBP | food wrap, adhesives, artificial leather, sealants |
| DEP | toothbrushes, tools, aspirin, cosmetics |
| BBzP | food packaging, upholstery, carpet tiles |
| DMP | personal care products and cosmetics, adhesives |
| DnHP | vinyl gloves, flea collars, tool handles, dishwasher baskets |

**Steer clear of plastic peril.** You can't make your home phthalate-free, but you can follow these steps to limit your exposure.

- Read the label. Stay away from products marked "fragrance" or "parfum." Both words indicate phthalates are present. Look for products that are labeled "no synthetic fragrance" or "phthalate-free."

- Sweep wood floors often, especially under and around beds to get rid of airborne phthalates. Vacuum carpets frequently.

- Eat organic food, and purchase a water filter to avoid insecticides made with phthalates.

- Never buy this item at the dollar store or anywhere else for that matter — plastic food containers made from PVC and marked with a #3 recycling label. The plastic may leach phthalates into your food when the containers are heated or cooled. Store and cook food in glass, ceramic, or stainless steel — never plastic.

## Invest in your health with filtered water

If the taste or smell of your tap water bothers you, a water filter may be worth the investment.

A pitcher-style Clear2O CWS100A water filter, rated highly by *Consumer Reports*, will cost about $30. You need to replace the filter after 50 gallons, about every three months or so, at about $15 each, bringing your total first-year expense to $90. After that, you'll only pay for the filters.

A faucet-mount filter is similarly priced. The Culligan FM-25 is rated "excellent" by *Consumer Reports*, and it also costs close to $30. Replacement filters run $12 to $15 and need to be installed every two months or 200 gallons. So, after the first year, your annual cost will range from $72 to $90.

It's still cheaper than bottled water. And much better for your health — and the environment.

## Save $3,000 a year when you break this 1 bad habit

Don't watch thousands of dollars go up in smoke. Snuff out that cigarette and pack away your cash instead.

**Break the habit, not the bank.** In 2016, the average price of a pack of cigarettes in the U.S. was $6.28. So let's say you're an average smoker, lighting up a pack and a half every day. That's 30 cigarettes. Not so bad, right? Now multiply that 30 by $0.31, the average cost of one cigarette. That equals a daily expense of $9.30.

See where this is heading? $9.30 x 365 days in a year = $3,394.50. That's over $3,000 you're spending each year on cigarettes.

But that's just an average. Your numbers may be lower or higher. Would you like to know exactly how much you can save by breaking the habit? Plug your numbers in at *smokefree.gov*.

**Smoking's not-so-little hidden costs.** Don't forget about these extra expenses that come along with lighting up.

- You'll pay higher life insurance premiums. A 50-year-old male smoker can expect to pay around $320 per month for a $500,000 life insurance policy. A same-age nonsmoker will pay just a quarter of that price.

- You'll pay more for health insurance. Smokers pay 15 to 20 percent higher premiums. So if a nonsmoker pays $500 for his monthly premium, a smoker can expect to shell out upwards of $600. That's a difference of $1,200 a year.

- Even home insurance is affected. Prepare to pay 20 percent more in your premiums.

- It impacts auto insurance, too. A typical nonsmoker's discount is around 5 percent.

**Get fired up and quit for good.** Start right now. Make a list of all the things you'd like to do with that extra $3,000 every year. Some ideas to get you going: Take a cruise. Pack away some cash in your grandkids' college fund. Remodel your kitchen. Make a down payment on a little cabin in the woods, and breathe in that fresh mountain air.

## Get healthy — and stay 'fiscally' fit — with fitness trackers

You've made the decision to take better care of yourself. You're eating right, taking the stairs, trying to get more rest. All things that are good for you — but how can you tell if they're actually doing you any good?

A fitness tracker might be just what the doctor ordered. It can give you a boost by showing you what you've accomplished. Here's the skinny — including prices and apps — on the gizmos and gadgets that promise a healthier you.

**A $5 pedometer can get you started.** Walmart's Sportline Step and Distance model may not do more than count your steps, but at five bucks it's an inexpensive way to begin.

For a few more dollars, take a look at a clip-on pedometer like the one by Timex. It sports a low $14 price tag and is rated by *Consumer Reports* as accurate and easy to use.

**Step up to a $50 fitness tracker.** Researchers found that beginners enjoyed using simple devices with uncomplicated apps and comfortable wrist bands. A basic model, like the Jawbone Up Move, may be just what you're looking for.

At this price, you can get a tracker that will count your steps and calories as well as monitor your sleeping habits. But you won't get a heart rate sensor, watch, or stair counter. It may not have a display, so you'll need to sync it with your computer or smartphone to access your fitness data.

**Get all the bells and whistles your tech-savvy heart desires.** If you're a fitness fanatic, a tracker or smart watch in the $200 price range will treat you to all kinds of high-tech gadgetry. Along with the basics found in the cheaper models, pricey trackers usually offer a real-time heart rate monitor and a GPS.

Some will calculate your blood oxygen level and monitor your skin temperature, body weight, and body mass. A few can even receive phone calls, e-mails, and text notifications from your smartphone.

Expect to get plenty of accurate workout data and tons of custom options, too. Devices at this price point usually sport large, easy-to-read displays that help you keep up with your workout stats.

**Stay motivated by choosing the right device.** If you compare one tracker to another, you may end up with different stats, but that doesn't really matter, experts say. These devices succeed because they are "in-your-face" reminders that you need to get up and move to make those 10,000 steps.

Still, studies report about one third of users stop wearing their devices after six months, and only a half are still using them after one year. Common complaints? Some users said the tracker was uncomfortable or the data didn't seem to be accurate.

So how do you decide what's right for you? Ask these questions before you buy.

- How much are you willing to spend?

- Is the device easy to use?

- What fitness stats (like heart rate, sleep patterns, calories burned) does it track?

- How will you get your data? Through the device's display or on your computer or phone?

- What is the device's battery life?

- Is the tracker comfortable to wear?

- What do the user reviews say?

If you still can't make up your mind, give them a try before you buy. Visit a website like *lumoid.com*. For $30, you can work out with five different trackers for two weeks. If you decide they're not for you, simply send them all back.

# Bright ideas to dial down your utility bills

# Electricity and Gas

## Smart way to 'strip' your energy bill

Seems like the world gets smarter by the nanosecond, what with all the smart gadgets out there. Now you can add special power strips (surge protectors) to the list of ultra-intelligent technologies. And they can save you hundreds of dollars on your energy bill.

Electronics account for up to 10 percent of your monthly energy bill, states the U.S. Department of Energy. So if your power bill averages $170 a month, that's $17 or over $200 in a year. But plug in a smart strip or advanced power strip, and you can cut the amount of energy your electronics drain, plus pocket a good bit of cash.

Used primarily in a home office or entertainment center, smart strips detect when you've turned off a device such as your television, and respond by cutting off power to it. Once that primary electronic is turned off, smart strips shut down peripheral items like a DVD player, game console, and receiver.

And smart strips start as low as $25, so you get your money back after using one over a couple of months.

Here are a few other features they come with, depending on the one you get.

- "Always-on" outlets for things you don't want to shut down, like a modem or DVR

- Built-in timers, so you can set up on/off times

- Motion sensors, which power on or off depending on your physical presence in a room

- Wireless remote control you can use from up to 60 feet away to turn on or off your home office equipment or entertainment center

You don't have to be a rocket scientist to see how smart these are and how helpful they can be.

---

### Free government program could save you $350 a year

How would you like to get $6,500 worth of energy-saving improvements made to your house for free — and save more than $350 a year on your energy bill? It doesn't matter whether you rent or own your apartment, house, or mobile home.

If you qualify, energy experts will come in and install insulation, seal ducts, repair heating and cooling systems, and run health and safety tests on heating systems and appliances. And these measures will save you money for 10 to 15 years, even twice that if the home's walls and roofs are insulated.

It's all thanks to the government's Weatherization Assistance Program for low-income families. More than 40 million households are eligible for the program, but not everyone knows about it. Check *waptac.org/Grantee-Contacts.aspx*, and click on your state to see if you qualify.

---

## 4 ways to pay less for utilities

Not everyone gets to pick and choose their utility providers, especially if you live in an area with a monopoly on gas, water, electric, and so forth. But if you're one of the lucky Americans who do get to choose, learn to pay the price you want with these tactics.

**Get the "new customer" deal.** Remember getting that great deal when you first signed up with your power company? But then a year slipped by and your rates went up — way up. Don't hesitate to ask for that great deal again. Your current company may honor your request if you commit to another year.

**Ask for a price match.** Find out what deals your company's competition is offering. Just make sure you do your homework first. Read the fine print and understand the terms and conditions.

If it's still a great offer, call your current provider and ask them to match it. Ask to speak to someone who has the authority to negotiate with you, and be prepared to read the competitor's terms. Doing this one thing, can save you more than you imagine.

**Compare rates with the government's help.** Hop on to the internet and check your state's public service commission or public utility commission. They have online tools that help you compare rates for the utility providers in your area.

**Use an aggregator to shop online.** You can get a better deal online if you use a site that shows all the deals available in your area. Most people don't even know you can do this.

Visit *allconnect.com* to compare prices for everything from gas and electric to cable and internet in your locale. You can even sign up or switch online for free.

Just check first to see if other providers in your area are available as well. Not all utility companies list their prices on Allconnect.

## Program slashes 10 to 15 percent off your energy bill

Timing is everything, even with your energy usage. That's why power companies raise your rates if you use electricity during high-demand times. But if you turn on your oven or run your dishwasher during off-peak (or low-demand) times, you could save a bundle.

Companies charge way less, 90 percent less in some states, if you use electricity when energy is not in high demand. Many companies have created special programs so you can take advantage of the lower prices. Look for "time-of-use" programs like the Energy Planner run by Tampa Electric.

"Customers are in full control of when they use that electricity," says Cherie Jacobs, spokesperson for Tampa Electric, "and most people who participate in the program save up to 10 percent on their electricity cost."

A look at programs around the country suggests the following:

- You will need to sign up with your power company and make a one-year commitment.

- The "standard" rate — the rate you pay if you're not on the program — is higher than off-peak, but lower than at high-demand times. To save money on the program, you'd need to use electricity during off-peak times as much as possible.

- If your bill goes up on the program instead of down, companies will give you a refund for the difference.

- More than likely you will see a 10- to 15-percent drop in your annual electric bill.

- Most companies install a special device to your electric meter for free while others require a monthly meter charge.

- Some programs, like Tampa Electric, require you to have broadband internet service so a special device can transmit energy usage back to headquarters.

- High-demand rates do not apply on weekends and holidays.

The best way to take advantage of a time-of-use program is to shift your habits, especially if you're home during high-demand hours. For instance:

- resist the temptation to do laundry or run your dishwasher just because you're home.

- plan your meals in advance and bake goodies on the weekend so you use your oven during off-peak hours.

- set timers on appliances (like your pool pump) to operate during off-peak hours.

- install a timer on your water heater so it kicks in during down times.

- set your air conditioner higher and your furnace lower during high-demand hours and when you're not at home.

Contact your power provider or check online to see if there's a time-of-use program in your area. Take a look at the phenomenal savings.

|  |  | Peak | Off-peak | Savings |
|---|---|---|---|---|
| Con Edison New York | June-Sept | 18.99 cents/kWh | 1.34 cents/kWh | 93% |
| Tampa Electric Florida | year-round | 16.47 cents/kWh | 7.13 cents/kWh | 57% |
| NV Energy Nevada | July-Sept | 40.6 cents/kWh | 6.2 cents/kWh | 85% |

## No-fuss, surefire way to shrink your power bill

Want the power company to pay you for a change? All you have to do is sign up for a little-known program that saves power and puts cash in your pocket. You can be like Josefina, a Florida

Power & Light (FPL) customer, who is happily pocketing an extra $137 a year.

The program is known as a "load management program," but it goes by different names across utility companies nationwide. And it works by easing the demand on power plants during peak usage times. Here's an example of how they do it.

A utility company places energy-management devices on certain appliances. In Florida, FPL will install the device on the central air conditioning unit (AC), electric water heater, central heating system, and in-ground pool pump through its On Call program. The device then shuts down the appliance during peak hours for a predetermined amount of time.

- Josefina can choose if she wants her central AC and heating system shut off for up to 17.5 minutes each half hour for a total of six hours during peak months. That's April through October for her AC, and November through March for her furnace.

- She can also register her water heater and pool pump for the extended program. FPL will then turn them off for up to four hours during a 24-hour period all year long.

- Her AC and heat can be on the extended program, too. They get switched off for up to three hours at a time.

- She will get credit on her monthly bill and can save up to $137 a year even if FPL never switches off her equipment.

- But what if Josefina doesn't want her AC shut down during her Fourth of July cookout? No worries. The program doesn't operate on holidays or in the evenings and weekends. Typically, it only works early to late afternoons over the summer.

- And the best perks of all — enrollment is free and she can cancel any time.

That's just one way a load management program works. Otter Tail Power, which services communities in Minnesota, North Dakota, and South Dakota, offers a Cool Savings program. Participants get a $7 credit on their power bill from June to September for allowing Otter Tail to cycle their AC on and off every 15 minutes during peak hours.

Ask your power company if it has a similar program in your area.

## Rebate programs keep money in your pocket

Get paid for your energy-efficient purchase with the help of *DSIREUSA.org*. A quick search could mean money in your wallet.

DSIRE stands for the Database of State Incentives for Renewables & Efficiency. Simply put, it's a website where you can find all sorts of rebates and incentives from state and federal programs. Here's what you do.

Say you live in Colorado Springs, and you want to install a new gas furnace.

1. Go to *www.DSIREUSA.org*.

2. Fill in your ZIP code and click Search.

3. Click Apply Filters.

4. Click Technology, then Energy Efficiency, then HVAC.

5. Check the box in the Furnaces tab.

6. Scroll to the bottom and click Apply Filters.

7. Your search results will display state and federal programs available in your area.

Click on a link, for instance Colorado Springs Utilities — Residential Energy Efficiency Rebate Program. There you'll find a gas furnace incentive for $250. Click on the link provided for Colorado Springs Utilities to learn more, and you could be well on your way to getting a check.

## Save up to 15 percent on your energy bill with one simple tool

Do you play with your thermostat like a yo-yo, up and down, up and down? Play no more, suggests a heating, ventilating, and air conditioning (HVAC) pro. Do this instead, and pocket hundreds in savings.

Get a programmable thermostat. This amazing tool lets you set your home's temperature based on when you're home, away, or asleep. But you're still in charge, because you can override settings without affecting the schedule you've set.

"Using a programmable thermostat can save you anywhere from 8 percent to 15 percent off your heating bill," says Steve Reyes, an HVAC technician in New York.

Changed your HVAC air filter lately? If it's been over a month or two, you're wasting money. Dirty filters hinder air flow and make your unit work harder. Slash your energy bill up to 15 percent — that's $130 a year for the average household — with this simple task.

In winter months, for instance, "keep the day/night setting within 10 degrees," Reyes suggests. He recommends 70 degrees during the day, and 60 to 65 degrees at night or when you're not home.

Programmable thermostats cost as little as $22 at home improvement stores, so they pay for themselves in a flash. Plus, this inexpensive gadget will keep you from making a huge energy error — shutting off the heat completely.

"Some home owners shut the heat off when they are not home and when they return, the house is very cold," says Reyes. "It takes a long time to reheat the house." This means constantly running the furnace to warm up your house, and that equals a big waste of bucks. Take his advice: "Don't shut off the heat."

---

### Slash your heating bill by $149

Here's a little savings secret — for every degree you lower your thermostat, you save up to 5 percent on heating costs. The average U.S. household pays $597 for electric heat over winter months. So if you set your thermostat to 67 degrees instead of 72 degrees, you could lower your annual heating bill by 25 percent. That's a $149-a-year utility savings!

---

## Feel warm all winter without turning up the heat

It's chilly outside and you're tempted to turn up the heat. But you don't want your utility bill to go through the roof. So turn up the humidity instead. It's the one thing you can do to feel warmer without raising your thermostat — and your utility bill. Here's why.

In the winter when the air in your home is dryer, your furnace has to work harder. That's because air low in humidity doesn't hold as much warmth. By cranking up the humidity, you can turn down your thermostat. And the lower your thermostat, the lower your utility bill.

Single-room and whole-house humidifiers range from $30 to $240. But you can humidify your home for free with these tips.

- Fill a stockpot halfway with water, and place it on the back burner of your stove to simmer.

- Pour water and spices (for a sweet scent) into a crockpot, and turn it on low.

- Keep your bathroom door open while you take a shower, and leave the exhaust fan off.

- Fill pans with water, and place near windows and heating vents.

- Hang damp clothes and towels around the house to air dry.

- Mist indoor plants regularly.

- Skip the drying cycle on your dishwasher. Open the door and allow dishes to air dry.

## Unplug your way to $125 in savings

You've got the power to save money on your monthly utility bill — and it's all in your fingertips. Just reach for your outlets and start unplugging things you don't use.

That's what Erica does to save close to $100 a year on electricity.

It's the one household item you should never unplug, because it'll cost you more than the energy you save. It's your inkjet printer, and each time you plug it back in, it goes through a cleaning cycle, wasting both energy and pricey ink. Better keep this one plugged in.

"I unplug lamps and clock radios in rooms I don't use much," she says. "In the kitchen, I only plug in the toaster, coffee maker, and blender as needed. But when I have overnight guests, I plug everything back in."

You may not think unplugging a few things around the house will add up to much, but it does.

Most U.S. homes have about 40 items plugged in and on standby. That means you're wasting 5 to 10 percent of your energy — and money.

Check out the graphic to see some of the things that drain your wallet simply by being plugged in. The numbers reflect connections 24 hours a day, 365 days a year, using the U.S. average of 12 cents per kilowatt-hour (kWh).

While it may not be practical to unplug your appliances and electronics all the time, pulling the plug for just 12 hours a day would save you about $125 a year — and that's not chump change.

## COST OF STAYING PLUGGED IN 24/7

**Desktop computer, on idle**
1584 kWh
**$190.08**

**Mini audio system, power off**
215 kWh
**$25.80**

**Cordless power tool, ready & charged**
123 kWh
**$14.76**

**Microwave, ready**
43 kWh
**$5.16**

**Surge protector, power on**
61 kWh
**$7.32**

**Coffee maker, power off**
24 kWh
**$2.88**

**Cable modem, on standby**
36 kWh
**$4.32**

Unplug these items just 12 hours a day and save as much as **$125 a year**

Some information used from Berkeley Lab, a U.S. Department of Energy National Laboratory Managed by the University of California

## Flick a switch for 'fan'-tastic savings

Once upon a time women snapped open beautiful, accordion fans and waved them furiously in front of their faces to stay cool. Fast forward to today, and keeping your cool with fans takes on a whole new meaning.

With the flick of a switch, you can keep your house cooler or warmer, depending on the season. Just make sure you understand how your fans operate, or you could be blowing away money.

**Ceiling fans — pay attention to the blades.** Should they spin clockwise or counterclockwise? Let the seasons guide you. Those sturdy blades can help keep you warmer in the winter and cooler in the summer, depending on which way they're whirling.

To feel a comfortable breeze on a sizzling, summer day, set your fan to spin counterclockwise, otherwise known as the "normal" setting. And use a higher speed so you feel the airflow. This will let you turn up your thermostat a degree or two and still feel comfy.

To feel warmer on a frosty, winter day, set your fan to rotate clockwise. Your fan will grab the warm air rising to the ceiling and force it down. Use a slower speed — you just want warm air to circulate.

And if you're in the market for a new fan, look for Energy Star certified. They are 60 percent more efficient than conventional fan/light units, saving you more than $15 a year on utility bills.

**Exhaust fans — keep the vent short and sweet.** Oh, the joys of venting. Well, not that kind of venting. The kind where you flip a switch to suck up all those unpleasant bathroom or cooking odors or the steam from your hot, morning shower.

But ventilating fans can do more harm than good if you forget to switch them off. Leave your kitchen or bathroom exhaust fan on for a couple of hours, and you could blast away your home's warm air. And that's like tossing money in the wind.

Turn them off as soon as they've done their job, and save your heat.

**Attic fans — give them the support they need.** Here's the ideal scenario. You install an attic fan, and it works by drawing in cool, outside air while blowing out hot, indoor air. But there's a catch. You've got to make sure your attic is sealed off from the rest of the house. Otherwise, you'll end up cooling your attic with your air conditioner, making the unit work harder and driving up your summer utility bill.

To get the best bang for your buck, seal the air ducts throughout your house, insulate the attic, and install attic vents that allow for natural air flow.

## Your small space heater could cost you big bucks

Cranking up a space heater will make you feel warm all over, especially if you find one for less than $50. But if you think it's saving you money on your energy bill, think again.

Space heaters run on electricity, an expensive fuel source. If you get cozy with one while running your furnace, you could drive your power bill sky high.

Energy experts say the only way a space heater saves you money is to shut off your furnace. Not practical, of course. So instead, use a portable heater only to take the chill out of a drafty space.

"They can help reduce energy costs when you're using one to heat a small area like a family room," says Cherie Jacobs, spokesperson for Tampa Electric in Florida. "Only use one in areas that are occupied, and don't use them overnight because of safety concerns."

## Swap bulbs to slash energy bill by $1,400

Do you know how many light-bulb sockets you have in your house? The Department of Energy says around 40 for the average

U.S. household. And all those light bulbs add up to 20 percent of your annual electric bill, or about $200.

But switch to Energy Star light bulbs and you'll save more than you can imagine. Check out the table to see how they compare.

| Type of light bulb | Initial cost per bulb | Replacement cost over 7 years | Operating cost for 3 hours/day | Total invest-ment |
|---|---|---|---|---|
| Traditional 60 watt incandescent | 25¢ | $1.75 | $48 | $50 |
| Energy Star 12 watt equivalent | $5 | 0 | $10.40 | $15.40 |

That's a difference of about $35 over seven years. Doesn't sound like much until you multiply that by 40 light sockets. Now your savings is a whopping $1,400!

# Insulation

## Discover the $200-a-year utility savings secret

Want to see your high energy bills vanish into thin air? Then insulate — it's one of the cheapest and easiest things you can do to save money on heating and cooling your home.

Ninety percent of single-family homes in the U.S. are under insulated, according to the Environmental Protection Agency (EPA). That means your house is probably full of holes. Not like potholes, but tiny gaps and cracks that let in drafts while allowing warm or cool air to escape to the great outdoors. Sealing these leaks can save you up to $200 on energy bills annually, says the EPA.

Slash your heating bill (gas or electric) by up to 30 percent! How? By maintaining your furnace, sealing air leaks, adding insulation, and getting a programmable thermostat, a nifty device that helps keep you snug for less. For more about saving money with an energy-saving thermostat, see page 133.

To check for leaks, try hanging toilet paper in front of openings you think might be a problem, suggests David Coakley, a builder with Carlino Construction in Atlanta. "The toilet paper is light and will detect the slightest amount of air coming through," he says. "Keep in mind if air is coming in, air is leaving as well."

You only need three products to make most leaks airtight — caulk, foam spray, and weatherstripping. Here's a breakdown of what to use where.

**Close cracks with caulk.** Every morning you spread a line of toothpaste on your toothbrush. That's what it's like to apply caulk. You can get it in a squeeze tube or a rigid tube that requires a caulk gun. These run anywhere from a few dollars to 50 bucks, while caulk tubes range in price from $2 to $11.

Since you have lots of different types to choose from, Coakley recommends buying "a good siliconized caulk — something that will stay pliable for years."

- Use around the exterior of doors and windows, suggests Coakley.

- Seal gaps around plumbing, ducts, and electrical wiring through walls, floors, and ceilings.

- Fill air leaks around your furnace and water heater vent flues.

- Plug cracks and open spaces along baseboards.

- Apply around ceiling lights and fans, medicine cabinets, and bathtubs.

**Fill gaps with foam spray.** Where caulk is good for small cracks up to a few millimeters, foam spray fills and expands in larger holes to seal them off. Use sparingly at first until you get the hang of it. After you apply it, wait a few days before trimming the excess with a utility knife.

Choose between high-expansion spray for really large gaps and low-expansion for doors and windows. Individual cans cost between $4 and $18.

- Spray around the interior of doors and windows, recommends Coakley.

- Use around ceiling fixtures, bathtubs, utility pipes, ducts, and vents.

**Seal doors and windows with weatherstripping.** Check out the weatherstripping aisle at your hardware store, and you'll find dozens of choices.

"First, identify what you are trying to seal, then choose the weatherstripping for that task," Coakley says.

Choices include the V strip (or tension seal)

Adding insulation to your home is so energy efficient, the federal government wants to reward you with a tax credit. In years past, the credit was for 10 percent of the price you paid for materials up to $500. Check *energystar.gov* to see what types of credits are available today.

used along the sides of double-hung and sliding windows, thick foam tape for inside door frames, and door sweeps that you install along a door's interior bottom. Read packages carefully before choosing.

And no need to fret over cost. These handy tools comes in rolls for just a few dollars or in strips for not much more.

Once you've made your home as airtight as possible, don't forget to check your work once in a while. Coakley says one of the costliest mistakes people make is not making sure the weatherstripping still works and not maintaining caulking around windows.

So don't wait — insulate.

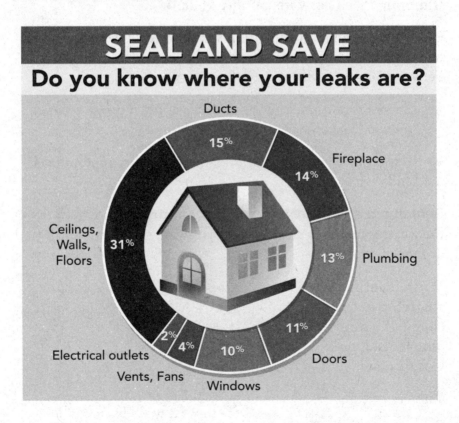

**SEAL AND SAVE**
**Do you know where your leaks are?**

Ducts 15%
Fireplace 14%
Plumbing 13%
Doors 11%
Windows 10%
Vents, Fans 4%
Electrical outlets 2%
Ceilings, Walls, Floors 31%

## Turn a 10-cent investment into $50 in savings

Here's a little way to save a whole lot of money — insulate the switches and outlets on your exterior walls with foam inserts. These cheap insulators block drafts from sneaking into your house, saving you up to $50 a year.

Buy a pack at your local home improvement center, or order them from *energyfederation.org* for 10 cents each.

To install, shut off the power supply to the area you're working in. Unscrew the switch plate or outlet cover, push the gasket in so it fits securely, and screw back on. Then think about what you want to do with that extra 50 bucks!

## Easy ways to seal and save with your fireplace

Some of the best things in life are free, like a roaring fire in your fireplace with logs you cut down yourself. But when you're not using your fireplace and air is freely wafting in and out of your home, that's like money going up in smoke.

Fireplace and chimney gaps account for 14 percent of air leaks in your home. Seal them up and save yourself some cold, hard cash. Here's how.

**Fill the flue with a DIY fix.** It's easy for drafts to come in and out of the flue, even with the damper closed. You could buy a fireplace plug you inflate like a balloon, but they're pricey at $56 and up. Energy experts have a cheaper solution — make your own.

- Stuff fiberglass batt scraps in a trash bag and shove it in the flue. Attach a durable cord so you can easily see it and pull it out when you want to light a fire. Play it safe and leave yourself an additional reminder next to your matches or gas switch. If you ask a contractor or builder friend to save you his fiberglass scraps, you're only out the cost of a trash bag.

- You could also take a piece of rigid foam board, cut it to size, and wedge it up into the flue. A 1/2-inch board costs under $15. Remember to attach a cord so you can pull it out easily.

**Frame the front with a decorative screen.** Another spot you can seal is your fireplace's opening. You could install tight-fitting glass doors but they're expensive — $250 and up.

Rigid board          Pipe
insulation        insulation

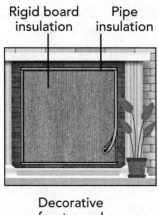

Decorative
front panel

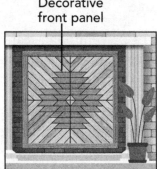

Use rigid board insulation attached with pipe insulation around the edge. Pipe insulation costs a little over a buck for a 1-inch by 6-foot piece. When finished, you can decorate the front to match your room's decor with things like peel-and-stick vinyl tiles, bead board, cloth, pallet wood, or magnetic chalkboard.

If the insulation has a smooth surface, you can place your decor directly on the rigid board. Otherwise, you'll need to attach a thin piece of plywood to the board before decorating.

**Seal the gaps in your attic and roof.** You may find other gaps you can seal when you inspect the rest of your flue and chimney.

- If your flue goes through the attic, seal around it with aluminum flashing, stapled or nailed into place. You can find sheets of flashing under $10. Finish sealing with high-temperature caulk.

- Head to the roof and use 26-gauge sheet metal to close the gap between your home's framing and the chimney. Sheets start at $5. Seal with high-temperature caulk.

Don't forget the attic access, say energy experts. It's another source for air leaks that is cheap and easy to fix. Cut a piece of fiberglass or rigid foam board insulation the same size as the hatch, and tape or glue it to the back. Place weatherstripping around the edges of the opening.

# Water and Plumbing

## Easy ways to whittle down your water bill

You use a whopping 36,000 gallons of water every year. Yes, 36,000! But spend $5 at the hardware store, and you can cut your water usage by thousands of gallons a year.

It's easy with a little device called a faucet aerator. You can even install it yourself. Just unscrew the mouth of your kitchen faucet by hand or with a wrench, and screw on your new aerator. Ta-da! It's that simple. Here are seven other straightforward, easy steps to shrink your water bill.

- Test your shower flow rate. All it takes is a 1-gallon bucket and a minute of your time. Aim the showerhead into the bucket and turn it on full blast. If the bucket fills in less than 20 seconds, you need to replace your showerhead with a low-flow model. Look for those labeled WaterSense.

- Turn off running water while you brush or lather up. You'll save up to 4 gallons a minute while brushing your teeth and 150 gallons a month while lathering your hair in the shower. And only turn on your hose while rinsing your car if you wash it at home.

- Catch the cold water with containers while waiting for it to get hot. Use that to water your plants and pets.

- Don't use oversized pots and pans to cook or boil small meals. Reach for the right-size cookware for the job.

- Pull out your favorite pitcher, fill it with water, and keep it in the fridge. That's better than running the tap every time you want a glass of water.

- Keep the leftover water you get from cooking or steaming food. Use it as a starter for a savory, nutrient-rich soup or stew.

- Test your toilet for leaks by putting a few drops of food coloring in the tank. You'll know you have a leak if the water in your bowl changes color within 15 minutes. Remember to flush so you don't stain your toilet.

Before you lather up again, read this. Showering for 12 minutes uses about 15 gallons of hot water. Do that every day, and that's $100 worth of hot water over the course of a year. But if you trim that long, leisurely shower down to eight minutes — the average for most Americans — you'll cut your hot water cost by one-third!

## Every drop counts — plug money-guzzling leaks in 3 smart steps

Remember "Stop, drop, and roll," the famous fire-safety saying? Well, there's a new motto in town, and putting it into practice could save you thousands of gallons of water.

"We have a real simple mantra we like to tell people," says Kathleen Brady, Vice President of Eastern Research Group, a consulting firm that works closely with the Environmental Protection Agency's WaterSense program. "It's called Check, Twist, Replace." According to Brady, the EPA promotes it every year during Fix a Leak Week, generally the third week in March.

But why wait until March to get started? Follow Brady's advice now and start racking up the savings.

**Check.** "First, check your home for leaks," says Brady. It's easier than you think.

- Examine your winter water bill. "Winter is typically the lowest time of year for water use," she explains. If your bill shows that your household used more than 100 gallons of water per person per day — the national average — you probably have a leak. For a two-person household, anything over 6,000 gallons per month in winter suggests a leak.

- "Walk around your home with eyes and ears open to find leaks," suggests Brady. "And don't forget to check pipes and outdoor spigots."

- Look for silent leaks under your bathroom vanity and kitchen sink. Check for water pooling under the pipes.

- Take a close look at your showerhead when showering. According to Brady, sometimes water is just spraying off in the wrong direction because of calcium buildup. "Or sometimes," she says, "water comes out where the shower-head connects to the wall." Both are big wastes.

**Twist.** If you find leaks, pull out your toolbox and do the twist. "Give leaking faucets and showerheads a firm twist with a wrench," says Brady. "Then apply pipe tape to be sure plumbing fixture connections are sealed tight."

Leave bigger problems to the pros, though. "For anything more complicated, we recommend you see a licensed plumber before a little plumbing project turns into a big one."

**Replace.** "If you just can't nip that drip, it may be time to replace the fixture," says Brady. "Look for WaterSense-labeled products. They use at least 20 percent less water and are independently certified to perform as well as or better than standard plumbing fixtures." By saving all that water, your new fixtures should pay for themselves in no time.

---

### Free home repair — and more

You've sprung a leak and it's pricey to fix. No worries. If you're age 60 or older you may qualify for free home repair services for seniors, no matter your income.

Area Agencies on Aging (AAA) funds all types of services that seniors might need, from housekeeping chores to legal assistance. People with the most economic or social needs are first in line for services, but, if enough funds are available, anyone over age 60 can get help.

Contact your local AAA for more information. Call 800-677-1116, and a specialist will connect you to the AAA nearest you. You can also locate specific services in your area at *www.eldercare.gov.*

---

## Stop wasting money: slow the flow with WaterSense products

Here's a win-win scenario: You purchase a WaterSense product for your home. Not only can you save thousands of dollars on your water bill, you can also help save billions of gallons of water. That's right, billions!

That's because products sporting a WaterSense label meet the Environmental Protection Agency's (EPA) criteria for efficiency and performance. So when you purchase one of these products, you save both money and the environment.

**Showerheads.** "WaterSense-labeled showerheads use 20 percent less water than standard showerheads and provide the same spray force and coverage you expect in a typical shower," says Kathleen Brady, Vice President of Eastern Research Group (ERG), a consulting firm that works closely with the EPA's WaterSense program. Best of all, they cost about the same as regular showerheads — just $12 and up at your local hardware store.

"By replacing one showerhead with a WaterSense model, the average family can save enough water to run more than 70 loads of laundry, enough electricity to power their home for 13 days, and more than $70 per year on utility bills," says Brady.

What's more, if every U.S. home installed WaterSense showerheads, Americans would save more than $2.2 billion on their annual water bills and more than 260 billion gallons of water each year.

**Toilets.** It's all about the flush. Older toilets use up to 6 gallons of water to swish things away. WaterSense toilets use a little more than 1 gallon per flush. That's a savings of up to 60 percent, or about $110 a year and $2,200 over the toilet's lifetime. WaterSense toilets cost the same or even less than regular toilets, starting at just $99.

**Faucets.** "WaterSense faucets and accessories, such as aerators, use 30 percent less water than standard faucets, without a noticeable difference in flow," Brady says. "Replacing old, inefficient faucets with WaterSense-labeled models can save the average family 700 gallons of water per year." And since using less hot water means using less energy, you'll cut your electric or gas bill, too. Once again, WaterSense faucets cost the same as regular ones, starting around $25.

Convinced yet? Maybe this will help. Check out the EPA's WaterSense rebate program. You could get a check from your local government for $100 if you buy a WaterSense toilet, or $200 for a high-efficiency clothes washer. Visit *epa.gov* and type "WaterSense rebate finder" in the search box. Click on Product Search in the results, then search by state for rebates where you live. Or contact your local water provider to learn about available rebates.

No more second-guessing. Ask your water provider if you can track your usage online. Better yet, sign up for alerts. If you get close to the monthly water limit you set for yourself, you'll get an email notice — a surefire way to flush out more savings.

## 2 things you must know to stay out of hot water

"Where are they now?" You've seen the headline a dozen times, usually in relation to child movie stars and big-haired rock bands. You may not know where they are, or care. But if someone asks, "Do you know where your water meter and shutoff valve are?" you need to answer, "Yes." Here's why.

Every year the average household wastes about 10,000 gallons of water in leaks, say experts. That's enough water to wash 270 loads of laundry. In fact, household leaks waste more than 1 trillion gallons of water across the country each year. That's millions of dollars sucked down the drain.

Before you waste another minute, and another drop of water, you need to locate the following two items.

**Uncover your shutoff valve.** Don't save this for a rainy day. Put it on your to-do list this week. Find your shutoff valve and figure out which tools you need to turn it off — before disaster strikes, or simply before you go out of town. "It doesn't hurt to turn all the water off when you leave for any extended amount of time," says Denny Hicks, owner of Hicks Plumbing. "It could save you thousands of dollars in damage from a house flood."

- In warm climates, look for the valve on an exterior wall of your home or underground near the curb.

- In colder parts of the country, you'll find the valve inside your house in a closet, a basement, or behind a panel.

Some valves require a special key while others need only a crescent wrench. If your valve is indoors, a firm turn with your hand should do it. Always turn the valve to the right to shut it off.

**Become a leak detective.** Water meters aren't just for meter readers. They're for people like you who want to know if there's a mysterious leak in your home. Look for your meter near the main shutoff valve or where the main water line enters your home.

Now, turn off all the appliances in your home that use water, including the ice maker and clothes washer. Don't flush the toilet, take a shower, or run the faucets for two hours. Check the reading on your meter at the beginning and at the end of that two-hour period. If the dial moves, you probably have a leak.

## Save thousands of dollars of damage with simple gadget

Fire and water: two of the most destructive forces in your home. Just like you need an alarm to sound if your house is going up in smoke, you also need an alarm to alert you if you've sprung a disastrous leak. A $10 sensor could spare you $1,000 to $5,000 in water damage.

You can pick up water alarms at your local home improvement store. Installation is easy. Some you simply peel and stick to a surface, while others you mount to a wall or door. You can even lay them on the floor. Put one anywhere there's a risk of flooding — beside the water heater, in your basement or crawl space, next to toilets, by the dishwasher and clothes washer, and under sinks.

A sensor hangs from the alarm on to the floor, delivering a piercing screech if it detects as little as 1/32-inch of water. Like smoke detectors, water alarms run on batteries, so you'll need to check and change them regularly.

---

### Toilet tricks prevent $85 house call

"I love it when my toilet clogs up," said no one, ever. Here's what you can do to bypass irritating clogs and slow drains.

- Invest in a toilet auger or snake. It's the number one thing plumbers say you should own. Best of all, they cost under $10, and they're easy to use.

- Try single-ply toilet paper. That's what Annie did when she moved into her new home. She couldn't under-stand why both of her toilets kept clogging, so she asked a plumber. After ruling out a couple of things, the plumber suggested she switch from two-ply to single-ply. The results — no more clogs!

Can't give up your cushy two-ply? Try toilet paper made from recycled paper or brands labeled "septic safe," even if you're not on a septic system. These break down easier during flushing.

---

## 3 water heater tips earn back a tankful of money

Shower on. Shower off. It's easy to get in a rut. But here's some-thing that will wake you up even more than your morning routine. Your water heater may be working harder than necessary, sending money down the drain every time you bathe. Try these tricks to make your appliance more efficient.

**Wrap it warmly.** An insulation blanket costs around $20, but you'll earn that back in a single year by reducing heat loss. In fact, you'll save more than $30 a year simply by wrapping an old water heater. Just make sure you take a few precautions.

- Before you do anything, check your appliance. Some water heaters come with a "do not cover" warning, so don't wrap these.

- Leave room to access your water heater's safety valve.

- Do not cover the tank's thermostat.

- Keep insulation away from the burner and top vent, if it's a gas appliance.

While you're at it, insulate the first 6 feet of cold and hot water pipes coming out of the water heater.

**Turn down the heat.** Thermostats aren't just for houses. Water heaters have them, too, and they're easy to adjust. Chances are, yours is set too high. Here's how to tell. Turn the hot water all the way up in the shower. If the water gets too hot to bathe in, then you can definitely turn down the heat.

How low can you go? Probably down to 120 degrees without sacrificing comfort. Energy experts say you can save up to $30 a year for every 10 degrees you lower the temperature. If you go from 140 degrees (the setting used by most manufacturers) to 120 degrees, you could pocket an extra $60 a year. Play with the thermostat until you get it just right, then enjoy the savings.

**Shop ahead.** Stay in your home long enough, and it's bound to happen. Probably while showering. In winter. Eventually, your water heater will break and need to be replaced.

Do your homework in advance, so you can make an energy-wise purchase when the inevitable occurs. Water heaters are rated with an Energy Factor (EF). The higher the EF, the more efficient the unit — and the more money you'll save on your monthly bill.

## Discover the $2,046-a-year household savings secret!

Make one or two of these changes each month and watch your bank account swell as your utility bills shrink. Read the stories throughout this section to learn more about these tips.

| | Potential Annual Utility Savings |
|---|---|
| **TIME-OF-USE PROGRAM** Sign up through your electric company and shave up to 15% off your bill. | $309* |
| **PROGRAMMABLE THERMOSTAT** Install this inexpensive gadget and learn to use it correctly. | $130* |
| **THERMOSTAT SETTING** Lower your heat by 5° in winter. | $149* |
| **ENERGY WASTERS** Unplug appliances and electronics when you're not using them. | $125 |
| **CEILING FAN** Install an Energy Star ceiling fan. | $15 |
| **AIR FILTERS** Change these regularly in your heating and air conditioning system. | $130* |
| **AIR LEAKS** Seal around doors, windows, fireplaces, and more. | $200 |
| **WINDOWS** Replace old, single-paned windows with Energy Star certified windows. | $465 |
| **WATER HEATER** Turn down your water heater from 140° to 120° ($60 savings) and wrap it with an insulating blanket. ($30 savings) | $90 |
| **REFRIGERATOR** Buy an Energy Star refrigerator. | $150 |
| **TOILET** Switch to a WaterSense toilet. | $110 |
| **SHOWER** Replace 2 shower heads with WaterSense models ($70 savings each) and trim your shower time from 12 minutes to 8 minutes. ($33 savings) | $173 |

*Savings based on U.S. energy bill average of $2,060 a year.

**TOTAL SAVINGS $2,046**

# Come home to savings: better products for less

# Appliances

## Fix-or-ditch timeline saves hundreds on broken appliances

The smell of rotten food greeted Lizzie Branson when she returned home from an out-of-town funeral. And she knew immediately what it was — her refrigerator. "It had stopped cooling and everything in the fridge and freezer had gone bad," says the registered nurse. Should she call a repair guy to see if he could bring it back to life? Or was it time to buy a new one? "The refrigerator was 17 years old, so I figured it was time to say good-bye," she says.

Smart move. She saved herself at least an $85 service call, plus the average cost of an appliance repair — around $275.

Like the best-buy date on packaged foods, appliances can only last so long. And one that's operating on borrowed time may not be worth repairing.

| Appliance | Estimated life in years |
|:---:|:---:|
| Air conditioner, room or window unit | 5-10 |
| Dishwasher | 9 |
| Microwave oven | 9 |
| Washer | 10 |
| Water heater, gas or electric | 10-11 |
| Freezer | 11 |
| Garbage disposal | 12 |

| Appliance | Estimated life in years |
|---|---|
| Range, electric | 13 |
| Refrigerator | 13 |
| Dryer, gas or electric | 13 |
| Air conditioner, central | 15 |
| Range, gas | 15 |
| Furnace, gas, oil, or electric | 15-20 |
| Water heater, tankless | 20+ |

If your crotchety appliance is well below these numbers — and even if it's not — don't automatically kick it to the curb.

- Make sure it's plugged in and the circuit breaker hasn't tripped.

- Clean out vents and filters. If these are clogged, your appliance may not work properly.

- Look over your appliance's paperwork to see if it's still under warranty. If so, schedule a service call.

- Check the appliance's manual or search online for do-it-yourself repair videos, and try to fix it yourself. Take safety precautions first, like unplugging it or turning off the circuit breaker.

- Factor in how much you've used the appliance and how well you've maintained it over the years.

## Never pay top dollar for new appliances

Buying a new appliance has become a wallet-busting experience. But how would you like to save up to 80 percent, just by shopping outside the box?

**Search scratch-and-dent deals.** That's what Minnie Hopper did, and she found just what she was looking for — at half the price!

"I bought a stainless steel fridge with French doors and paid $500 for it," says Minnie. "At a big retail store, it was selling for $1,000." And the only flaw was a tiny dent the size of a dimple on one of the doors. It lasted a little over 10 years.

Visit your local appliance dealer and ask to see its inventory with cosmetic flaws. Or try a charity thrift store like Habitat for Humanity's ReStore. Betsy Horton saved $400 by buying a brand new Hotpoint fridge at Atlanta's ReStore. What was wrong with it? Nothing, except for a couple of dings on the door.

**Sign up for retailer alerts.** It's an easy way to get the scoop on upcoming sales and special promotions via text or email. Some stores even offer coupons just for signing up. You can also load the retailer's app on your smartphone or tablet to search for products and compare prices.

**Know when to shop.** Big appliance sales happen in January, May, September, October, and around major holidays. Labor Day weekend is a prime time to find slashed prices on older models as next year's inventory starts to slide into stores. And there's always Black Friday, if you don't mind the crowds and long lines.

**Buy the floor model.** Retailers will reduce prices dramatically on these otherwise new items. One couple picked up a $2,800 stainless steel fridge for $1,200 with free delivery and installation, all because they asked about the floor model. That's a savings of almost 60 percent off the regular price. Best of all, you should get the same warranty as with a new, in-the-box appliance.

**Trade old for new.** Some stores will give you a discount on a new appliance when you bring in your used one. Ask dealers in your area if they have a trade-in program.

**Purchase refurbished.** Look for "certified factory refurbished" products and save up to 80 percent. These returned or overstocked appliances are inspected, serviced, and repackaged, and most come with warranties same as new. They're usually sold through their manufacturers or authorized dealers.

**Shop online.** Merchants like Abt.com offer discounts and free shipping on thousands of appliances. And if you find a better deal elsewhere, this online retailer will try to meet or beat the price.

**Compare prices with apps and online tools.** Start with *google.com/shopping* and type in the exact item you're looking for. Google will show you a list with price comparisons and where the item is available, including if it's ready for pickup near you.

Or try *pricegrabber.com* to compare prices all over the internet, and *camelcamelcamel.com* to track Amazon's prices.

---

### Repair or replace?
### Simple formula helps you decide

Your clothes washer decides mid-cycle to simply stop working. Do you repair it or replace it? Here's a quick formula to help you decide for this, and most other appliances.

First, get a repair estimate. You'll have to fork over the service call fee, but most companies will waive it if they repair the appliance. Next, figure out the answer to these two questions:

- Is your appliance more than halfway through its average life span?

- Is the cost of the repair over 50 percent the cost of buying new?

If it's a yes to both, you should replace, not repair. So back to your washing machine. Let's say it is 7 years old, with a typical life span of 10 years. It will cost $250 to fix, while you can buy a new one for as low as $300. Guess what? You're going shopping.

---

## 3 ways to snag an extended warranty for free — and save up to $150

"Do you want the extended warranty? It's only $70 and will cover you for three years." The cashier waits. You run scenarios in your head, and start to sweat. The pressure is on.

Like insurance, extended warranties, service plans, or service agreements hedge against disaster, such as a major — and expensive — meltdown. They can range in price from $30 for two years of coverage on a small appliance like a mixer or a toaster oven to $150 for five years on a major appliance like a fancy new fridge loaded with bells and whistles.

Sounds like a smart idea, but is this extra expense worth it? Consumer experts say no. In fact, you should never pay for one, because there are several ways to get an extended warranty for free.

**Cash in with your credit card.** Call your credit card company before you buy an appliance. Many offer an extra year of protection after the manufacturer's warranty expires if you buy the item with your card. And make sure you ask how to register the appliance once you've bought it.

**"Seal" the deal.** If you see the Good Housekeeping Seal on your new purchase, you're in luck. This 100-year-old institution offers an automatic two-year limited warranty on any product that carries its seal. Go to *goodhousekeeping.com* for details or write to Consumer Services & Seal Coordinator, Good Housekeeping Magazine, 300 W. 57th Street, New York, NY 10019.

**Let the law protect you.** Your state's consumer protection agency probably has you covered, thanks to an implied warranty of merchantability required by all states. If your product doesn't do what it's supposed to do, you're protected. Say, for instance, your new freezer doesn't maintain a low enough temperature to freeze. You can return it under the warranty of merchantability. Go online to *usa.gov/state-consumer*, find your state's consumer protection agency, and contact them for details.

## Energy labels help take the sting out of your monthly bill

When you're shopping for a new appliance, it pays to compare. But not just the ticket price. Those bright yellow and black Energy Guide labels help you make smart shopping decisions and save you money in the long run. Think of them as your energy "saviors." Here's what the numbers on the labels mean.

- That big number in the middle of the label estimates how much it will cost to run an electric appliance for a year, based on the nation's average energy cost. Use it to compare annual operating costs between models. The more energy-efficient the appliance, the lower your monthly utility bill. And that's money in your pocket.

- To get a more accurate reading of your operating cost, look for the kWh (kilowatts per hour) number on the label's bottom half. Multiply this by your local electricity rate, which you can find on your bill.

- Some labels may also have an additional box with a dollar figure giving the average cost to run a gas appliance annually.

- And some carry the Energy Star logo in the bottom-right corner. This means the product exceeds the government's minimum standards for energy efficiency, so it's better for the environment.

Just make sure you compare like labels. Over the years, Energy Guide labels have undergone a couple of changes.

Newer ones have a black box in the middle with numbers in yellow. Appliances with these labels have undergone updated energy efficiency tests. Older labels are all yellow with numbers in black.

If you don't see a label, don't go crazy looking for one. Some appliances — like ovens, ranges, clothes driers, and dehumidifiers — don't get them. Those that do include boilers, central and window air conditioners, clothes washers, dishwashers, freezers, furnaces, heat pumps, refrigerators, and water heaters.

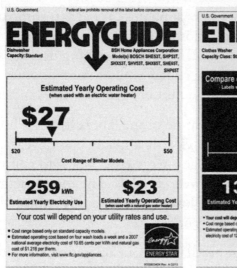
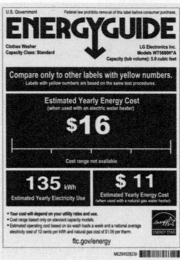

Old label                                    New label

## Cool ways to add years to your refrigerator's life

"The number one thing you must do to make your appliances last longer," says Leo, a technician with Atlanta Appliances Repair, "is keep them clean." That means clearing filters of gunk and lint, wiping splatters in microwaves and on stove tops, and immediately mopping up spills in refrigerators. This cheap and easy secret could keep your home appliances running 10, 20, even 30 years or more.

Refrigerators especially need extra TLC. Otherwise, they have to work hard to keep food cool, driving up your utility bill.

**Don't make your fridge bust a gut.** The more the compressor in your refrigerator struggles, the more likely it is to blow. Try these tips to prevent your appliance from overdoing it.

- Check the magnetic seals or gaskets around the doors once a year, and look for wear and tear. If you see a problem area, try the "dollar bill check." Place a bill half inside the fridge with the other half sticking out, and close your door. If you can't pull the dollar out, the seal is OK. But if it slips out easily, you've got a problem.

- Your refrigerator needs something to cool. So even if you eat out a lot, don't run it empty. Instead, place water bottles inside.

- Clean and vacuum condenser coils once a year. You'll find them underneath or on the backside of your appliance.

**Play it cool — but not too cool.** You can actually run your freezer too cold, says Leo. And if you do, you risk freezing your water lines, which will shut down your water and ice dispensers. "The best temperature is usually around zero degrees," he says.

**Avoid the end of the ice age.** Ice dispensers are notorious for breaking. But these simple steps will keep you in cubes for many years.

- Replace the water filter every six months to keep fresh water running through your supply lines and debris out of them. Besides that, "If you don't replace the filter," Leo says, "you're probably consuming contaminated water."

- Notice a drip from your dispenser or icicles in your ice maker? You may have a water valve problem. "Not every customer can replace a valve," says Leo. "Call your technician to come and see what's going on with your water lines."

## Easy fixes foil costly washday disasters

Wash. Rinse. Dry. Repeat. It's the never-ending cycle of doing laundry week after week. And all of that washing and drying adds up to big bucks, especially if your appliances aren't performing at their best. These cheap and easy maintenance tips will help you soak up the savings — and avoid major headaches to boot.

| Washer | |
|---|---|
| **Smart step** | **To avoid this** |
| Replace cracked rubber supply line hoses | Leaks, flooding |
| Install stainless steel supply line hoses | Leaks, flooding |
| Don't overload top loaders | Water spills, bouncing |
| Don't overload front loaders | Broken door hinges |
| Place rubber pads under machine | Vibration |
| Wipe down front loader gasket with micro-fiber cloth; leave door open between loads | Mold and slime buildup |
| Run a cycle with vinegar, no clothes, and no detergent | Detergent buildup in washer |
| Install an automatic water shutoff system like Floodstop or TimeOut | Leaks, flooding |

| Dryer | |
|---|---|
| **Smart step** | **To avoid this** |
| Clean lint filter after every use | Clothes not drying, fire hazard |
| Clean exhaust vent once a year | Clothes not drying, fire hazard |
| Replace plastic ducts with metal ducts | Fire hazard |
| Clean moisture sensors with rubbing alcohol | Buildup on sensors that prevents "auto-dry" setting from working properly |

## Slash drying time by a third with these DIY gizmos

Does the thought of never buying fabric softener or dryer sheets again sound appealing? How about reducing dryer time by one-third? All this is possible with energy-saving wool dryer balls.

Maybe you've seen them in the store. They look like large, white tennis balls, and at around $15 for a 4-pack, make an economical, all-natural alternative to commercial products and even plastic dryer balls. Here's how they save you money. They:

- bounce around in your dryer like a pinball, separating your clothes and allowing more hot air to circulate.

- soften garments and reduce wrinkles by pummeling clothes.

- pull moisture out of clothes so they dry faster.

- reduce static.

- last for years, so you can save hundreds of dollars on dryer sheets and fabric softener.

- protect the environment from nasty chemicals because they're natural.

Clean your dryer's lint filter. You've heard it hundreds of times. But Leo, an appliance technician with Atlanta Appliances Repair, can't stress it enough. "Every week I remove two full garbage cans of lint," he says.

Don't address this major fire hazard and it can cost you thousands of dollars in damages.

Want to save even more money? Make your own wool dryer balls for less than five bucks. The homemade ones are basically balls of wrapped yarn that look like something you'd roll on the floor for your cat to play with. You need a skein of 100 percent wool yarn and an old pair of pantyhose.

1. Wrap yarn around two or three fingers about 20 times.

2. Slip off and wrap yarn around the middle.

3. Pinch your tiny ball and keep wrapping yarn around it tightly.

4. When it's about the size of a tennis ball, cut the yarn, and tuck the end into your ball.

5. Repeat until you've made two to four balls with your skein.

6. Cut off one leg of a pair of panty-hose. Place the balls in your hose, tying off each one separately with string or acrylic yarn. You'll end up with a lumpy "snake."

7. Now you're ready to start felting, a process which fuses the fibers together. Throw your snake into your washer's hot water cycle followed by a hot dryer cycle.

8. Congratulations. You now have wool dryer balls. Want to make them bigger? Wrap each one with more yarn, and go through the felting process (hot water, hot dryer cycles) again.

Bonus step. Give your clothes a fresh scent by sprinkling a few drops of lavender or citrus essential oil on your wool balls before tossing them in the dryer with a load of laundry.

## Double your dishwasher's life with 3 clever tips

Gunk, funk, and junk. Sound like the name of a heavy metal band? No worries, it's not. But it is what's clogging up your dishwasher. Here's how to get rid of the gunk for good — and save $300 on a new dishwasher.

**Don't load "dirty" dishes.** It sounds like a contradiction. After all, isn't that why you have a dishwasher, to clean your dirty dishes? Yes, but unfortunately, the dirtier the dishes, the more likely you are to clog up your appliance's drain lines, spray arms, and pump assembly. And a repair could cost you a hefty $140. Better to follow one reader's suggestion.

"Do a quick rinse of your dishes before placing them in the rack," says Michelle, who's had her original machine ever since she built her home over 20 years ago. That's amazing, considering most dishwashers only last nine years. "Food won't clog up your washer, and it will last longer."

**Flush out funky filters.** Even if you scrape and rinse your dishes, food particles can get trapped in your dishwasher's filters. Most models come with one or two of these, and according to Leo, a technician with Atlanta Appliances Repair, they need a good scrubbing about once a month. "Clean out all the objects that are bigger than a green pea," he says.

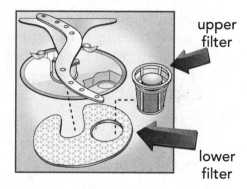

upper filter

lower filter

Look for these filters on the bottom of your dishwasher, below the sprayer arms. Pull them out, place in a sink full of warm, soapy water, and scrub with a toothbrush. You can also check your dishwasher's manual for tips on how to clean your filters. If you don't have a manual, do a Google search with your appliance's make and model.

**Deodorize and freshen.** Dishwashers can sometimes smell yucky. They can't help it, what with all the food deposits and mineral buildup from hard water running through the inner workings. So Leo recommends using commercial dishwasher cleaning products about once every six months. "These will clean all the gunk out of your pipes and dishwasher," he says. "And it will smell better."

## Give your oven some lovin' — and save up to $2,000

A new oven could cost anywhere from $400 to $2,000. But the smallest of chores can keep your old one cooking for years to come.

- Don't let anything spill on the heating element inside your oven. It could burst, and a repair could cost a whopping $100 to $250.

- Keep children from hanging onto the doors. The hinges run a hefty $50 each, plus you'll have to pay a service call of a couple hundred dollars.

- Clean glass surfaces immediately after spills. Otherwise, you can damage your surface trying to scrape up something that's burnt on. And a replacement is very expensive.

- Wipe your oven's window with a mixture of water and vinegar.

- Leo, an appliance technician, recommends you never use the self-cleaning oven setting. While it burns away oils and food particles, it can also damage the oven's electrical parts. "I've never seen any benefit from using self-cleaning," he says. Instead, just use regular oven cleaner.

- Every time you slam the door, you risk breaking the oven's latch or locking mechanism. "Be gentle," says Leo. "It's your appliance."

- Remove any dried-up gunk in the oven with a nonabrasive scrubber. Use a scrub brush to clean oven racks.

- Pour salt over spills that happen while you're baking. You'll have an easier time cleaning up the mess once the oven has cooled.

# Furniture

## Secrets to buying yard sale furniture like a pro

Before you load up that used table or dresser, ask yourself, does it appeal to you, do you have a place for it, and does it fit into your decor?

That's what amateur furniture restorer Karen Gross recommends. She's been scouring yard sales for 10 years looking for pieces to update and resell at Kudzu Antiques in Atlanta.

Next, look at the condition, she suggests. Make sure it has "good bones or good lines." Otherwise, a $10 steal could be a waste of money.

Want to score the best furniture pieces at rock-bottom prices? Check out her other helpful tips.

- Look for hardwood pieces. "I like to get real wood," says Gross. Wood is easy to clean and even easier to update with chalk paint, no sanding required. Gross has purchased wooden chests and dressers for $5 and $10 and resold them for over $100 by painting them and adding new knobs.

- Stay away from cheap wood. "I don't like particle board stuff," she says. "For the most part I stay away from veneers because they often have a lot of problems with chips, and those are very hard to repair."

- Steer clear of chairs, too. "Chairs are particularly hard to fix if they're wobbly or shaky, because there are so many joints in a chair," Gross says.

- Tables, including end, side, and dining, are great finds. "Tables are pretty easy to work with even if they're a little shaky," says Gross. You can fix them easily and cheaply with glue or screws.

- Stay away from mattresses and bedding. But freshen up an old metal headboard in a fun, trendy color. New ones start at $100, but you can pick one up at a yard sale for $10 and make it look good as new with a $4 can of spray paint.

- If it's upholstered, walk away. "You don't know what people have in their houses as far as pets and smoking," says Gross. "And you might not notice an odor if it's outside, not until you've got it in a closed space." Plus, bed bugs, fleas, and other infestations can be tucked away in upholstered furniture. So that $25 dream couch could turn into a $1,000 pest-removal nightmare.

## DIY chalk paint on the cheap

Why pay $35 for a quart of high-end chalk paint when you can make your own for a lot less? Here's a cheap and easy recipe.

Mix 1 1/2 tablespoons water with 2 1/2 tablespoons plaster of Paris. A 64-ounce tub runs around $6 at craft stores. Use a coupon and cut the price by a couple of dollars.

Pour the mixture into one cup of latex paint. If you have some in a color you like, you're good to go. If not, pick up an 8-ounce color sample for just a few dollars at a home improvement store.

Stir and make sure it's smooth like pancake batter. Apply with any paint brush, and turn that bargain into valuable treasure.

# Flooring

## Floor-buying tip that will save you thousands

Nothing in your home takes a beating like the floors. They endure everything from mud tracks and wet boots to spaghetti spills and coffee stains. So when it's time to replace your floors, you need to get the best bang for your buck.

That means considering the long-term cost of flooring, not just the initial cost of materials and installation, suggests a study from the Brook Byers Institute for Sustainable Systems. Experts looked closely at the cost of upkeep over the 61-year life span of a typical home. Here's what they learned.

Carpeting may be cheap on the front end, but it must be replaced every 10 years. That's at least five times over the life span of a home, making carpet a costly option.

Ceramic tile on the other hand (or foot) costs a little more to install, but it only gets replaced once over six decades. And since it's relatively low maintenance, it's a cheaper option overall. So if you're planning on staying in your current home for many years, ceramic tile is a sweet deal.

Take a look at the chart to see five flooring options, the average price for materials and installation for a 250-square-foot room, and how much they cost to replace or refinish over 60 years. Then consider how long you plan on staying in your home. The choice you make could save you thousands of dollars in the long run.

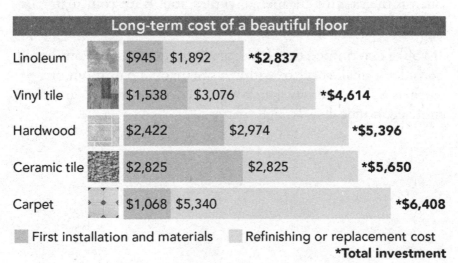

## Long-term cost of a beautiful floor

| | First installation and materials | Refinishing or replacement cost | *Total investment |
|---|---|---|---|
| Linoleum | $945 | $1,892 | *$2,837 |
| Vinyl tile | $1,538 | $3,076 | *$4,614 |
| Hardwood | $2,422 | $2,974 | *$5,396 |
| Ceramic tile | $2,825 | $2,825 | *$5,650 |
| Carpet | $1,068 | $5,340 | *$6,408 |

## Design secret slashes tile costs by $4,000

Yes, ceramic tile can make a floor go from boring to beautiful. But it can break your budget, too. Learn this secret to laying tile, and cut your cost dramatically.

At one time, laying tiles diagonally was all the rage. Designers loved it because it could make a room appear larger. That's because your eye focuses on the wide angles of the tile borders rather than the narrowness of the room.

But a diagonal design comes with a hefty price tag. You have to buy 20 percent more materials if you lay diagonally over straight, say flooring experts. Every tile around the perimeter of the room (against the walls) must be cut. Plus, if you have professionals install it, your labor costs could triple.

The average cost of materials and supplies to tile a 250-square-foot room is about $670. Add 20 percent to that for a diagonal design, and you're looking at an extra $134.

Labor for that same size room runs about $2,087 if you lay straight on. But it jumps a whopping 200 percent if you tile diagonally. That's another $4,179.

Such is the case for cheaper vinyl tiles, too. Both your materials and labor costs will shoot up if you lay them diagonally.

If you're determined to tile diagonally somewhere in your home, consider a small space or within a square on a bathroom or kitchen wall. Otherwise, stick with the equally attractive — but more economical — straight pattern.

# Real estate — hot buys and cool savings

# Home buying and selling

## Safeguard your home with this small investment

Do you have homeowner's insurance? If so, that's good. But there's one other type of insurance you also need on your house that almost nobody buys, or even knows about. And it could save you thousands of dollars.

School kids are taught that Abraham Lincoln was born in a one-room cabin built on a little piece of Kentucky farmland. But did you know that when Abe was just two years old, his family was forced out of their home? That's right. When Tom Lincoln's claim to the property was challenged in court, he didn't have the necessary papers to prove he owned the farm. But somebody else did. So the Lincolns were fresh out of luck — and out on their ears.

What could have saved Tom and his family from this heartache? Title insurance, that's what.

**Be sure you own it fair and square.** Title companies search public records for outstanding liens or "clouds" on a title. They hunt for things like legal judgments, special assessments, or unpaid taxes. Anything that might make the property unmarketable. In most cases, the title company quietly clears up the clouds, so the sale can go through without a hitch. Then the insurance company issues a policy promising to defend the title in court, should it be challenged by anyone, anytime, anywhere.

Remember Abe's dad? Title insurance protects you from the possibility that someone could come along and contest your ownership of a property, as with Tom Lincoln. Perhaps the old owner's ex-spouse pops up, or an unknown heir unexpectedly appears. What if they really do have a legal claim? Title insurance will protect your investment by covering your financial losses.

**Neither a borrower nor a lender be — without title insurance.** Yes, lenders usually force you to buy title insurance before you take out a mortgage. But that insurance doesn't protect you. It protects the lender's investment in the property. You could still lose your down payment or any equity you have in the home.

As the borrower, or owner, you can buy your own title insurance to protect your investment in the property. This type of policy is called owner's title insurance, and it remains in effect as long as you own the home. It will keep your equity safe and give you peace of mind for years to come.

You usually purchase a title policy with a one-time premium paid at closing. You could pay anywhere from $1,000 to less than 1 percent of your loan. Use a rate calculator like the one at *ratecalculator.fnf.com* to see how much you can expect to pay for title insurance in your state.

**Snag a sweet deal.** That's a lot of money, but you can ensure you get the best price by following some savvy advice.

- Shop around. Call several title insurance companies and compare their coverage and rates. Ask your real estate agent about locally owned companies.

- Buy your lender's and owner's policies at the same time and from the same company.

- Ask about a cheaper "reissue" rate if the house has changed hands in the past few years.

## How to pay less for your next home

Maybe it's time to buy that vacation home you've always dreamed of. Want to move closer to the kids? Or maybe you'd just like to downsize. Whatever the reasons for your change of address, be sure your finances are up to the challenge. The right planning — before you buy — is the key to real savings.

**Get your credit score up to snuff.** Companies use credit scores to predict how likely you are to pay back a loan. This number is based partly on your credit report and will fall somewhere between 300 and 850, with 850 being perfect credit. The higher your number, the lower your monthly payment. It's that simple.

Lenders know your credit score, and you should, too. Some websites, such as *creditkarma.com*, will estimate your score for free. For a more accurate number, check with your credit card companies. Many now let their customers check their score once a month for free. Is your score below 660? Get ready to pay higher interest rates. Scores from 700 to 720 will earn you pretty good terms on your loan. But over 750? You're golden. Expect to snag a great deal.

Ready to go house hunting? It's best to have a price in mind before you head out. Conventional wisdom says that your house payment should not exceed 28 percent of your gross income. Don't want to mess with the math? Plug in the numbers at an online payment calculator like *usmortgagecalculator.org*.

Consider this. On a $200,000 30-year, fixed-rate mortgage, a borrower with a credit score of 620 may pay around $1,061 per month. A borrower with a score of 760 may pay about $877. That's a savings of $184 each and every month — for 30 years.

In one year alone, your good credit could save you $2,208. That adds up to $66,240 in savings over the course of 30 years!

It takes time to raise your credit score from the cellar to, well, stellar. So don't delay. Here are some tips to get you started.

- Pay your bills on time, every time. Set up electronic payment reminders if those due dates tend to slip by you. Or use your bank's online bill pay system to schedule your payments ahead of time.

- Don't max out your credit cards and don't apply for any new credit. That may look bad to a prospective lender.

- Pay off debt rather than shifting it to other credit cards, especially if that brings you too close to your card's limit.

- Don't close unused accounts. Dust off the unused card from time to time to pay small bills, so the credit card company doesn't close your account. Then immediately pay the balance in full. Having the same account for many years helps build your credit history. Lenders like that.

If you're in serious financial trouble, don't hide from it. Talk to your creditors directly to work out an affordable repayment plan, or find a reputable credit counselor to get you back on track.

**Say no to PMI.** Another mortgage cost-cutter? Make a down payment of more than 20 percent of your loan, and you'll avoid paying private mortgage insurance (PMI). That could save you close to $100 each month on a $200,000 mortgage.

**Squirrel away extra cash.** Tuck away three to five months of mortgage payments in a savings account. This shows the mortgage company you mean business, and it may land you a better deal on your loan.

## Not your grandpa's mortgage: new ways to buy your home and save money

The big bank boys aren't the only game in town anymore. So before you sign, consider these alternatives.

**Credit unions.** Known for their lower fees, they offer flexible options — some with no closing costs or PMI.

**Costco.** Yes, the big-box giant now markets mortgages through First Choice Loan Services. Lender fees are limited to $650 for Gold Star members and $350 for Executive members.

**Nontraditional financing.** Consider owner financing. Or talk to your seller about renting to own.

**Online lenders.** Quicken Loans and Nationwide are just two of the many companies that offer mortgages with a click of the mouse.

**Mortgage brokers.** They help you find the best deal, but they charge a fee for their services — either paid by you, the borrower, or the lender. It's generally a very small percentage of the loan amount.

## Sell it yourself to pocket thousands

Hire a real estate agent to sell your home, and you'll pay him a commission of around 6 percent. On a $200,000 home, that's a colossal $12,000. Rather cut the commission and keep that cash in your pocket? Don't mind working for it? Then For Sale by Owner (FSBO) might be right up your alley. Here are six tried-and-true tips to get you going.

**Price it right from the start, and save.** Setting too high a price for your old home can keep you from moving into your new one. And if you've already purchased that new house, you could end up with two mortgages. Also, lowering your home's price over and over sends the wrong message to buyers.

Go online for some easy-to-use pricing help. Enter your address at websites like *trulia.com* or *zillow.com* to find the prices of comparable homes in your neighborhood. *ForSaleByOwner.com* and similar sites can help you figure out a price range with their online appraisal service. Or, pay a real estate agent to do a market analysis for you.

**Go where the buyers are — advertise online.** Experts say 42 percent of home buyers begin their search by browsing the internet. Help those buyers find you by advertising on sites like *owners.com*. They'll even get you started for free.

More extensive advertising takes more cash. For example, pay a fee of $695, and *owners.com* will post your home on their site and several others, including the ever-important Multiple Listing Service (MLS), for 12 months. Other real estate sites offer similar packages, so compare carefully before you commit.

**Let your friends on social media get the word out — for free.** Facebook, Twitter, and Instagram are great platforms for marketing your house. Post lots of clear pictures and videos to entice buyers to come take a look. And a well-composed, 250-word description of your home can help boost your selling price. Include words like luxurious, impeccable, remodeled, and landscaped for the best results.

**A low-cost yard sign still gets their attention.** Make it bright and eye-catching. Don't forget to add your phone number and possibly a new email address you set up just for this purpose.

**Invite them in with an open house.** Be sure your house is buyer-ready: neat, clean and ready to be seen. Have a professional-looking brochure or flyer to hand out to visitors. Follow up with an email or phone call.

**Consider a real estate attorney to help you close the deal.**
You'll want every i dotted and t crossed when that buyer is ready
to sign. Expect to pay a flat fee or anywhere from $150 to $350
per hour for this kind of legal help.

FSBO isn't for everyone. One exasperated seller shared these
important points:

- Showing the house yourself can be a hassle. You may get
  calls at inconvenient times.

- Be aware of security risks. Don't show your house alone.
  Safety in numbers, remember?

- Prospective buyers may not share your decorating tastes. Be
  prepared for unflattering comments.

- You're stuck negotiating with prospective buyers yourself,
  which can sometimes be uncomfortable, especially with
  lowball offers.

---

### Save $5,000 with fee-for-service realtors

Sometimes you want the appetizer, salad, entrée, and
dessert — a set menu. Other times you'd rather pick and
choose. Go à la carte, as they say. That's the idea behind
fee-for-service realtors. You pick and choose the services
you want. For instance, for a flat fee of about $500, you
could purchase a package that includes a listing in the local
MLS, photos, signs, and a few other basic services. But if
you want them to host an open house for you, that'll cost
an additional $400. Want an ad in the paper? That could be
another $25. How about a virtual tour online? You'll pay out
a couple hundred dollars. Sure it can add up, but if you
chose just these options on a $100,000 home, you'd still
save almost $5,000 on the traditional agent's commission.

## Negotiate like a pro to snag a great deal

In 1783, while negotiating an end to the American Revolution, John Adams made one of the best bargains in real estate history. Aware of Great Britain's financial floundering, the patriot swooped in and secured all lands east of the Mississippi, north of Florida, and south of Canada. Want to negotiate your own historic deal? Time to get schooled.

**Know your opponent.** John Adams had this down pat. The one who knows the most about his opponent is sure to win the battle. So make it your job to study the other side. Are they under pressure to get the deal done? Check out their social media pages. You might find some helpful info there. Use it to your advantage at the bargaining table.

**Know your market.** In a seller's market, homes are scarce and demand is high. A house might attract multiple bidders. In that case, a fair bid will be the asking price, or even 1 to 3 percent higher. And offering more earnest money can show the seller how much you're interested.

In a buyer's market, home sales are sluggish. An acceptable offer might be 8 to 10 percent below the list price. The deal depends on how long a house has been on the market and if there have been price reductions.

**Seal the deal.** Try these strategies when you're ready to get down to business.

- Be collaborative, not confrontational. Find ways both parties can win.

- Stop talking. Try the 70/30 rule. Listen 70 percent of the time, talk the other 30. When they throw out a number, stay quiet. They might think you're dissatisfied and revise the deal — without a word from you.

- Play nice. Sincere flattery can knock down the other side's defenses and open the door to a better deal for you.

- Be ready to walk. Have a specific price in mind that you won't go above, or below, and be prepared to walk away.

---

## 1 smart way to build family wealth

Mike's parents made the tough decision to move out of their life-long home. They wanted a place with minimal upkeep and zero financial stress. A condo, they concluded, would be a perfect fit for them. But they didn't want to spend their nest egg, and they struggled to find a rental they could afford. Besides, who knew what kind of landlord they'd end up with if they rented?

The solution — Mike bought the condo and rented it to his parents. With the help of a lawyer, the family designed a deal that benefited everyone. His parents paid an affordable monthly rent, which Mike applied toward the mortgage. The condo made a great investment for him, and the extra deductions helped with his tax bill. Meanwhile, Mom and Dad enjoyed a forever home with a landlord they loved. A win all around.

---

## Set the stage for a quick sale and top-dollar offers

Post that "sold" sign in no time. Whether you hire a professional stager or opt to do it yourself, showing off your home in its very best light will get you the very best deal. Fast.

**Surveys say staging works.** The National Realtors Association reports that buyers offer up to 5 percent more when a home is professionally staged. So for a home priced at $200,000, that's an increase of $10,000. Cha-ching.

And a study by the International Association of Home Staging Professionals found 95 percent of professionally staged homes sold, on average, in 11 days or less. And they sold for 17 percent more than non-staged homes. On the other hand, non-staged homes sat on the market much longer — almost 3 months longer. This could end up costing the seller (that's you) big bucks in extra mortgage payments.

**Bring in the professionals, take out your wallet.** A stager's job is to make potential buyers fall in love with your house. If you choose to hire one, however, keep your wallet handy. Prices for professional stagers can start with $200 for a "walk-and-talk" consultation. If you opt for top-to-bottom staging, the numbers can soar as high as $7,000.

**Show the pros to the door, and keep your cash.** DIY staging starts with the rooms that experts agree absolutely, positively must be staged: the living room, the kitchen, the master bedroom, dining room, and bathroom. Get rid of extra or bulky furniture, and rearrange the pieces you keep so your spaces look inviting but still have good traffic flow. Accentuate the positives in every room with accessories.

# Moving

## The truck stops here: don't get taken for a ride on moving day

Those butter-fingered moving men just dropped your 50-pound, flat-screen TV. The one that cost you a cool $1,000 now lies shattered in pieces on your driveway, and all you can legally recoup from the moving company is a paltry $30. How can you protect yourself from moving-day mayhem like this?

**Get the right price.** How much you'll pay for a professional mover depends on several things. Are you moving locally or out of state? In ounces and pounds, how much stuff are you moving? Do you want the movers to pack and unpack for you? Load and unload?

For a local move with all the bells and whistles, you'll pay around $1,800. A cross-country move could cost five times that amount. Be ready to negotiate for the best deal with a reputable mover.

**Go on a fact-finding mission.** Start by calling three local companies. Check with a real estate agent for suggestions or use your phone book.

- Make an appointment to have an agent from each company do an in-home estimate. If a company won't come out, then cross it off your list. Companies within 100 miles of your home are required by law to give you an in-person estimate.

- Find out if the estimate is binding or nonbinding. A binding estimate includes all services, and it guarantees the price. A nonbinding estimate is what the mover thinks your move will cost. The final bill could be higher or lower than your original estimate, depending on how much your possessions end up weighing.

- While you have the agent's attention, ask about the moving team that will be assigned to your home. How much experience do they have? Did they pass a background check?

- Ask for each company's Department of Transportation (DOT) and Motor Carrier (MC) license numbers and write them down.

- Ask for recent customer references, and make sure you call them.

- Hop in the car and surprise the moving companies with a visit. Make sure they have an actual brick-and-mortar office. Although lots of reputable movers have websites, the consumer protection group *MovingScam.com* reports that nearly all of the complaints they receive come from people who found their movers on the internet.

While you're in their offices, ask more questions. How long has the company been in business? Are the trucks well-maintained? This would be a good time to get the company's contact information, including phone numbers and email addresses.

**Check licensing and insurance information.** Remember the DOT and MC numbers you wrote down? Go to *csa.fmcsa.dot.gov*, the Federal Motor Carrier Safety Administration's (FMCSA) website. Scroll down to the search field under the headline "Check Motor Carrier Safety and Performance Data" and type the mover's DOT or MC number or name. When the website returns with your search results, click on "Complete SMS Profile" under Tools/Resources. The full report information will appear and you can download or print a copy. Make sure the mover has an active license and insurance coverage. Is their license expired? Has their insurance lapsed? Both are red flags. Choose another mover.

Next, contact the Better Business Bureau and ask how many complaints have been filed against the company. You can also get a thorough complaint history by calling the FMCSA's national Consumer Complaint Hotline at 888-DOT-SAFT.

**Won't the mover's insurance replace that shattered TV?** Nope. The moving company is responsible for as little as 60 cents per pound for each item. And that's not much. Once you choose your mover, call your homeowners or renters insurance agent. Ask if they can add moving insurance to your policy for a small fee. If not, you may have to buy separate coverage from another insurance carrier, at a cost of $200 to $1,000. Choose a high deductible for a lower price. To get more information, and even calculate your own insurance costs, go to *MovingInsurance.com*.

When moving day finally arrives, be sure to take lots of pictures of your items. Video the packing process, too — just in case.

## Keep more cash with a DIY move

Dave chose PODS (Portable On Demand Storage) for his move from snowy PA to sunny FLA. He ordered three, 16-foot storage cubes for $3,000. Then he hired well-muscled men on both ends of the move to load and unload the cubes, adding around $600 to his price. The heavy lifters were worth the extra expense, though. "Loading PODS is not for the weak," he says. "It's very hard work."

Today, moving costs can shoot as high as $12,935 for a soup-to-nuts professional mover. That makes lower-cost options like PODS very appealing.

| | |
|---|---|
| Typical, long-distance move | $12,935 |
| Sample PODS move | – $3,600 |
| **Dave's savings** | **$9,335** |

The companies PODS, U-Pack, and 1-800-PACK-RAT all offer this popular moving service. They drop off a container at your home. You pack it up, then they pick it up and whisk it to your new home. To cut costs, Dave took advantage of PODS' 5-percent military discount. He also saved when a PODS truck, already headed south, had room for his containers.

These services aren't the only way to save money, though. Consider these out-of-the-box, DIY ideas.

**Round up a couple of friends and a big truck.** Still a popular way to go. Depending on the amount of stuff you're moving and how far you're going, this tried-and-true method might work for you.

Companies like U-Haul, Budget, and Penske have rental programs that include moving checklists, packing supplies, and even shipping and storage options. In-town moves can start as low as $19.95, but read the fine print to be sure you understand the mileage and fuel costs.

**Box it up and ship it out.** This is an inexpensive option if you're moving light. You can ship a 100-pound package for less than $160 on a Greyhound bus. That said, your shipment could take up to seven days to arrive, depending on the bus schedule and the amount of passenger luggage.

Ever thought about trains or planes? FedEx, Amtrak, Delta, and others offer shipping options, too. Visit their websites for rates and requirements.

# Remodeling

## Home improvements that make cents (and dollars, too)

You can get major home improvements, even additions and remodels, for half off or even free. That's because certain renovations literally pay for themselves by raising your home's sale price.

In their "2016 Cost vs. Value Report," the pros at Remodeling Magazine listed the four renovations that net you the biggest return for your fixer-upper bucks.

**1. Start at the top — insulate your attic.** Earn back as much as $1.16 for every $1.00 you spend when you add insulation to your attic. Blow in enough loose-fill, fiberglass insulation to raise your attic's R-value to at least 30. Fourteen inches of insulation should be just right. Visit *energy.gov/energysaver* for guidelines.

> Insulation is rated based on its thermal resistance (R-value). The higher the R-value, the better a product will insulate. Experts recommend different R-values depending on where you live. To see the suggested R-value for houses in your area, check the map at *energystar.gov*.

The average cost for you, the homeowner? It depends on the size of your attic, but usually about $1,200. The average return when you sell your home? A whopping $1,400.

**2. Add rock-solid curb appeal with manufactured stone veneer.** The priciest of the top four projects, this one can pay a hefty 93-percent return when you sell your home. For example, replacing 300 square feet of your old vinyl siding with new stone veneer will cost around $7,500. But when you sell your home, all that stone could yield a rockin' return of almost $7,000.

**3. Make it grand with a brand new garage door.** The pros behind "Cost vs. Value" say a midrange garage door replacement — an investment of about $1,600 — could net you a cool $1,500 return. An upscale garage door will cost around $3,000, but you can still expect a return of more than 90 percent. That's big bang for your buck.

**4. Lock up a great investment with a new front door.** Spend $1,300 for a new, steel entry door and you could pocket a $1,200 return when you sell. That's like getting back more than 90 percent of your original investment.

You may find a few surprising trends in recent remodeling payback estimates.

- Building on may not add up. A new high-end master suite could cost in the neighborhood of $245,000. When you sell your house, that master suite may only bring you a return of about 57 percent, or $140,000. That's $100,000 less than what you put into it. If you plan to stay in your home for a few more years, though, you may find that the luxury of your new suite makes up for the expense.

- But kitchens and bathrooms sell houses, right? They still can, but you may not get as much money back for your investment. For example, if you shell out $120,000 for a high-end kitchen remodel, you may recoup only two-thirds of that, or about $73,000. Upscale bathroom remodels fare even worse. Spend $57,000, and you stand to regain a little more than half of your investment.

For the best return on your dollar, spend your cash on smaller upgrades. Experts suggest capping kitchen improvements at $5,000 and bathrooms at $2,000.

## 7 IRS-approved upgrades that will slash your taxes

Did you make any of these home improvements in the past year? If so, give yourself some credit — tax credit, that is. Unlike deductions, tax credits shave actual dollars and cents off your tax bill. You can earn back as much as $500 of what you spent on certain improvements.

**Roof.** This credit covers Energy Star-certified metal and asphalt roofs. Spend $5,000 on a qualifying roof, not including labor, and you can cut your federal tax bill by $500.

**Insulation.** Earn back 10 percent of what you spend on typical bulk insulation products such as batts, rolls, and blown-in fibers, up to $500. You can't count the cost of installation, only the cost of materials. Weatherstripping, caulk, and canned, spray foam also qualify for this credit, as long as they come with a Manufacturer's Certification Statement saying they seal against air leaks.

**Water heater.** It'll keep you in hot water, and that's a good thing. Your Energy Star-certified electric water heater will net you a $300 tax credit.

**Wood-burning stove.** Also known as biomass stoves, they can be used to heat just one room or your whole house. Plus, that $300 credit is sure to warm your heart.

**Heat pump.** Pocket a comfortable $300 credit when you install an Energy Star-certified, air-source heat pump. Or install an Energy Star-certified geothermal heat pump and get back 30 percent of the cost.

**Central air conditioning.** This $300 credit will cool things down nicely. Just make sure your new air conditioner is recognized as an "Energy Star Most Efficient 2016" model.

**Windows, doors, and skylights.** Improve your view of the world through Energy Star-certified windows, doors, and skylights. The credit is for 10 percent of your cost, minus installation. The total amount of your credit cannot exceed $200.

Energy Star products are known for their efficiency and will definitely cut your utility bills, but not all of them qualify for these tax credits. Check before you buy. Keep your receipts and any manufacturer's certifications for all of these purchases. They'll come in handy if the IRS has any questions. Find the info you need on the manufacturer's website or with the product's packaging.

To claim your tax credit, you will need to file an IRS form 5695 along with your federal tax return. It's easy to download at *irs.gov*. Congress has to renew the Residential Energy Efficient Property Credit occasionally. Otherwise, it expires. Check with the IRS to find out if it's still in effect the year you plan to claim it.

# Yard smarts — ideas to save time and money

# Landscape design

## Plants prune your energy bill by up to 50 percent

Think landscaping can't save you big bucks? Think again. Shade trees in Pennsylvania cooled mobile homes enough to bring down their energy bills by 75 percent, compared to those baking in the summer sun. What's more, windbreaks meant some South Dakota residents reduced their heating bills by up to 40 percent. That's a terrific way to turn green into gold.

**Trees can grow your energy savings.** A 6- to 8-foot tree begins shading your home the very first year, and could grow to protect your simmering roof within five to 10 years. In fact, just one shade tree can pack the cooling power of 15 air conditioners. The best news is a tree "runs" for free. If this sounds like an energy-saving solution you'd be interested in, plant some trees on the sides of your house that receive the most sunlight — usually the west, east, or south sides. Choose deciduous varieties that will block summer rays, yet still allow sunlight to help heat your home in winter.

To save even more heating dollars, experts say to plant a line of trees where they can block the chilling winds of winter, most often along the north and northwest sides of your house. A windbreak like this can protect an area that is 10 times its height. So trees just 30 feet high can shield a 300-foot-wide area. A row of evergreen trees can cut heating costs by 10 to 50 percent a year.

Before you dig, though, remember this. "The biggest thing — when it comes to plants in the landscape — is to put the right plant in the right place," says Kim Toal, Fayette County Cooperative Extension Agent with the University of Georgia Extension Service.

Don't plant a tree any closer than 15 feet from your house. "Fifty years down the road," Toal warns, "it's going to be this massive tree right next to your home." And that spells all kinds of trouble. Roots can damage underground pipes or worm

> Tree-shaded neighborhoods can be 3 to 6 degrees cooler in summer than treeless areas. Plan your home's landscape with this in mind and slash your air-conditioning costs by 15 to 50 percent.

their way in through cracks in your foundation, leaves can clog your gutters, limbs or even entire trees can fall on your roof, and insects and rodents can gain easy access to your home.

**Shrubs shrink heating and cooling costs without touching the thermostat.** Azaleas with their springtime color, sweet-smelling gardenias, or even a formal hedge of boxwoods — shrubs are the mainstay of any landscape. Make sure you include some in your design, and with careful planning, you can trim some bucks off your energy bill.

- Plant shrubs 3 feet away from your air conditioning unit to shade it and improve its efficiency by 10 percent.

- Line dark, paved surfaces with shrubs to keep the concrete cooler, and you may lower the temperature of your yard and home, as well.

- Add insulation to your home without packing it into the walls. Plant shrubs 1 foot away from your exterior to create a cushion of still air that insulates your home and prevents heat from escaping.

**Divine vines offer cooling cover.** Take a stroll around your yard and inside your home during a hot summer day. Which windows are really baking in the sun? Notice that along with direct sunlight, they are letting in a lot of heat. Now build a temporary or permanent trellis around each one and plant deciduous vines. This simple step can reduce air conditioning costs by up to 50 percent.

Some utility companies may offer free trees or a home energy audit that includes ideas for landscaping. Call your gas or electric company, or visit their website to see what's available.

## Penny-pinching curb appeal: 3 ways to get more bang for your buck

Take your landscaping from ordinary to extraordinary and raise your home's value by as much as 10 percent with these three simple tips.

**Energize tired beds with an instant makeover.** "Fresh mulch or pine straw is a cost-effective way to make a landscape look new and improved," says Warren Elwell, Registered Landscape Architect for All South Lawnscapes, Inc. of Georgia.

If you're lucky enough to live in a wooded area, pine straw is free. Otherwise, it can run between $3 and $4 per bale in the southeastern states, but may cost as much as $5 or $6 in other parts of the country. If pine straw just isn't your thing, consider these other budget-friendly mulching ideas.

- Check your local garden centers or home improvement stores for torn bags of mulch priced at a deep discount. If the bags are mostly full, they could be a great bargain.

- Watch for tree trimmers in your neighborhood or call a local tree service to find out which ones are willing to dump their leftover wood chips in your yard for free.

- Team up with several neighbors to purchase mulch in bulk. A bigger order gives you more negotiating power, so call around to see who will give you the best discount.

**Make your front yard pop for less than $10.** "Annual flowers can keep your house looking fresh for a reasonable price," Elwell says. They are naturally showy right away, so you'll get an immediate impact. Choices like geraniums, vinca, marigolds, lantana, or impatiens are usually hardy, rampant bloomers, and require little maintenance in many parts of the country. Check with your cooperative extension agent or visit your local nursery to find out if one of these is right for your locale. Whether you fill a bed or border, or just put a couple of pots on your front porch, you won't be spending a lot of money. A twelve-pack of annuals may only cost around $10 — even less if you shop the sales.

**Rev up curb appeal with this simple secret.** "Good clean edges, and clean driveways and sidewalks go a long way in creating curb appeal," says Elwell. Whether you do it yourself or hire a service, he stresses that consistency is the key. Tackle yard maintenance regularly and you won't have to struggle with growth that's out of control.

"If the goal is to increase your home's value," Elwell adds, "remember, first impressions are everything."

## Light the night for less — DIY kits save you thousands

"Outdoor lighting is a landscape element people think is very expensive — and only for large expensive houses," says Warren Elwell, Registered Landscape Architect for All South Lawnscapes, Inc. of Georgia. "In reality, it is very affordable and easy to maintain."

Hire a professional and he can design and install a full package of quality lighting that includes path lights, accent lighting for trees and house features, and other specialty lighting. But that could cost between $3,000 and $4,000. Throw in motion detector lights and other accents, and the price tag could sky-rocket to $5,000.

**Save big by starting small.** The good news is you truly do not have to turn landscape lighting into a major production to get stunning effects. In fact, Elwell emphasizes that just a few fix-tures can make a big impact. "Lighting should be an accent to the landscape, not a runway for planes to land," he says.

With that in mind, consider a DIY path lighting kit that will let you "test drive" outdoor lighting without spending tons of cash. These kits can range from $80 to $150, and usually include a selection of lights, a length of cable, and a transformer. Besides that, they are a cinch to install.

"Lighting systems can also be planned to expand over a period of time," Elwell adds, "which can make it very economical." If you install lighting in stages, you'll spread the cost out over months or years. At each stage you can make new cost-saving adjustments.

**Smart tips help you roll back the darkness.** Here's how you can light up your night, but still save money, time, and trouble.

- If you plan to add extra lights to your design later, you may need a more powerful transformer or an extra one to support the new lights. Decide if starting out with a larger trans-former is more cost-efficient than replacing it down the road.

- DIY won't work for everyone, so read the directions very carefully before attempting to install your lighting kit. For example, you may want help from a pro if you need to run wiring under a concrete driveway, or if you don't have an out-door GFCI receptacle or GFCI breaker at the circuit panel.

- Unlike halogen or LED lights with replaceable bulbs, inte-grated LED lights are a single unit. These may be easier on your power bill, but they can be more expensive to repair or replace than other lighting.

- Solar lights may not require wiring, but they also may not last all night or be as bright as LED or halogen lights.

Whether you have simple path lights to welcome you home or a dramatic nighttime display, you can expect great benefits like these.

- A well-lit home is a safer home. Deter intruders by giving them fewer places to hide.

- Prevent accidents and falls with illuminated steps, driveways, and paths.

- Boost your curb appeal — and perhaps your home's value — with lights that accent your property's best features and add visual interest.

## Save $65 with DIY backyard bubbler

Formal English gardens, like the one at Blenheim Palace, birthplace of Winston Churchill, often include an elegant fountain — beautiful and soothing. Can you bring this little piece of luxury to your own backyard without breaking the bank? Sure you can.

While purchasing a small pot fountain could set you back as much as $100, if you have an eye for repurposing and recycling, you can make your own for around $35.

Pick up a fountain pump at your local home improvement store, then hunt around for an old glazed ceramic urn, cast concrete pot, or other type of waterproof container. You'll need a plastic liner or bucket and a few miscellaneous supplies listed with the pump directions. Check with friends, local restaurants or supermarkets, newspaper ads, and *freecycle.org* for some of these items. In no time at all you'll have your own charming water feature for a steal.

# Gardens

## Go green, not broke, with backyard composting

Maybe you can't spin straw into gold like Rumpelstiltskin, but you can turn your fallen leaves and kitchen scraps into money-saving "black gold" compost.

**You're spending more than you think.** Say you have a perennial bed that's roughly 100 square feet. Two inches of compost for this space equals 16 cubic feet and could cost as much as $300 to $400. Need compost for your trees, shrubs, the lawn, or other garden plantings? Then you'll spend even more.

**Cook up your own compost for free.** You don't have to kick into full pioneer mode just to build better garden soil. Composting is surprisingly easy. Start by saving your leaves, straw, and grass clippings, plus plant-based kitchen scraps like fruit and vegetable peelings, bread, tea bags, and coffee grounds. Pile all this yard and kitchen waste into a heap roughly 6 feet wide and 3 feet high. In three to six months you should have beautifully rich compost your plants will love.

For a slightly more structured look, use leftover hardware cloth, concrete blocks, or wood pallets to form an enclosure for your yard waste. Because this pile is freestanding, you can turn it over occasionally with a pitchfork or shovel, to help the compost develop faster. Just be aware that this easy access may also make it more attractive to animals and insects.

**Turn garbage cans into gold mines.** If you're handy with a drill, you can convert one or two plastic garbage cans into compost bins.

Drill rows of holes every 5 inches around the can, and add a few on the bottom for drainage. Fill with a 2-inch layer of sawdust or straw, then start adding yard waste and kitchen scraps.

You may get less compost in a can than with a large pile, but it's harder for pests to reach and easier to turn. Just fasten the can's lid on securely, and roll the garbage can on its side. What's more, your black gold should be ready in just two to four months.

**Tumblers make good long-term investments.** Maybe you're a little less DIY and little more citified. In that case, a compost bin or tumbler could be more your style. You'll pay, of course, for the convenience of a commercial unit — anywhere from $80 to $500 — but scout around for better deals. Some cities sell the bins for as low as $10, or you could pick a used one up at a yard sale. But for a devoted gardener, the math doesn't lie. Even if you buy a pricier composter, you'll still save hundreds of dollars in the long run.

## The easy weed-stopping solution that will save you money

Think twice before buying landscape fabric for your garden paths and walkways. Not only is it expensive — you'll pay as much as $2 for every 10 feet of pathway — but weeds can actually grow on top of it. When you cover your weed barrier with mulch, the wind and rain slowly add dirt, plant debris, and weed seeds to the mix. Eventually, you've got the perfect growing conditions for weeds, which rather defeats the purpose.

But you can get long-lasting weed protection for your paths without paying a dime. Simply lay down a line of recycled asphalt shingles. They won't harm your soil, but absolutely stop weeds cold. Just take a pass on shingles made from tar paper. They aren't good for your soil.

## Perennial power: save time and money with fabulous blooms

That showy flat of annuals is cheap and oh-so eye-popping —
just what you want for instant color and curb appeal with pow.
But a gardener in it for the long haul will save more money, and
get as beautiful a display, with perennials.

**Enjoy years of beauty for less.** Say you have two areas you
need to fill with flowers. In the spot near the porch, you plant
12 impatiens, at a cost of around $10. You fill the other bare
patch with five purple coneflowers and pay almost $30. The
annuals are so much cheaper, it sounds like a no-brainer,
doesn't it? But don't be fooled.

"Annual plants are a way to add seasonal color to your landscape," says Kim Toal, Fayette County Cooperative Extension
Agent with the University of Georgia Extension Service. "But
perennial plants add continuous color year after year." Even
though each annual costs less than a perennial, Toal is quick to
point out, "These plants will need to be replaced every year."

After seven seasons, you've spent about $70 to put in impatiens
every year. But you'd pay nothing beyond your original investment
for the purple coneflowers. "If you look at a cost comparison of
an annual versus a perennial," Toal says, "a perennial is much
cheaper due to the fact you're going to be seeing that same plant
year after year."

Planting perennials also means you've spent a lot less time and
energy every year clearing out the spent plants, digging, and
replanting. What's more, each perennial you buy can be a source
of additional plants, since some reseed and others can be divided
into more plants. Choose perennials wisely, and they can give
you years of beauty without requiring much care or cost.

**Save even more in the off-season.** Planting perennials in autumn can save you money three ways.

- Many nurseries run late-season specials on great perennials. Be sure to plant them six weeks before the first frost. Skip mums, asters, and other late bloomers, though, because they won't get established before winter.

- You're less likely to have pest and disease problems during cooler months so you won't need to buy remedies.

- You won't need fertilizer, since you don't want to encourage new growth during autumn.

# Lawn maintenance

## 2 lawn myths that steal money right out of your wallet

Don't get your lawn care advice while standing by the water cooler or your neighbor's fence. Chances are you'll hear some wild and weird ideas — like chewing gum gets rid of moles or you can just mow over crabgrass to kill it. Notions like these may not necessarily harm your lawn, but others can truly cost you money.

**Myth #1: You must water every day.** "Lawns require only 1 inch of water per week," says Kim Toal, Fayette County Cooperative Extension Agent with the University of Georgia

Extension Service. Soaking your grass frequently can cost you in two unexpected ways.

- "If you water too much, you increase your chances for disease," warns Toal. And that means spending extra money on remedies to cure the problem.

- In addition, overwatering can actually change how your grass grows. "Your turf could develop a shallow root system," Toal explains, "which will cause problems during drought periods."

So what happens if you stick to the 1-inch limit? Toal says you'll not only reduce your water bill, but you'll have a healthier lawn, to boot.

**Myth #2: Keep your lawn golf-course short.** Sure, you can mow your lawn low enough to roll a golf ball across it, but get ready to say hello to weeds, which will thrive in the extra sunlight. On the other hand, keep your grass around 2 1/2 to 3 inches high, and it will shade your soil enough to keep most weed seeds from sprouting. Experts also say never cut off more than one-third of your grass in one mowing.

Follow these tips and you'll mow less often plus spend less money on lawnmower fuel.

Many areas of the country get an average rainfall of 30 inches a year. If you collected and used every drop off a normal-sized roof, you could potentially recycle almost 32,000 gallons of free water — a savings of almost $50 off your water bill every year. Rain barrels can cost up to $400 each, so look for local programs that give them away or make your own.

# Make your home shine on a dime

# Cleaning

## 5 cleaning supplies that do it all — for less than $10

Window spray, shower scrub, stain remover. Do you really need all those special cleaners? If you're like most folks, you'll spend as much as $200 on cleaning supplies every year. Start using these five cleaning products, which you can buy for less than $10, and keep your house spic and span for cheap.

**Ammonia.** A half-gallon of this basic cleaner costs less than $1, and should last for ages.

- For example, to remove carpet stains for a fraction of the cost of a name-brand stain remover, mix 1 tablespoon of clear ammonia with a cup of water, then blot with a white towel. Just be aware that, if used improperly, ammonia can cause a color change in your carpet, so test this in an inconspicuous area. And never use ammonia on a wool carpet.

- Shine up your solid — not lacquered — brass, without buying a bottle of metal polish for $3 or more. Just rub the item with a soft brush dipped in ammonia, then wipe off. Be sure to wear gloves, work in a well-ventilated area, and never mix ammonia with bleach.

**Baking soda.** It's not just for baking. For around $2, you'll get a kitchen staple with many more uses throughout the house.

- Pour a bit on a damp rag or sponge, and use it to scour your tub, sink, and tile, rinsing well. It's just 3 cents an ounce, while Soft Scrub is nearly 12 cents an ounce.

- To freshen smelly carpets, sprinkle, let sit for 15 minutes, and vacuum. No need for costly carpet fresheners full of chemicals.

**Bleach.** When you need to disinfect, bleach should be your go-to choice — and a bargain at about $3 per gallon. Just remember, the same rules for using ammonia also apply to bleach — protect yourself and never combine the two. In addition, avoid using bleach on anything stainless steel.

- For a bleach-safe food prep surface — never use on granite, for example — mix 1 teaspoon of bleach into 4 cups of water. Surprise, this costs 10 times less than the same amount of a spray like Lysol.

- Do you like those pop-up disinfecting wipes? At more than 6 cents each, you better really love them. Make your own by mixing a tablespoon of bleach with 4 cups of water in a spray bottle. Spray a paper towel and use it to wipe down germy hotspots like refrigerator and microwave door handles, kitchen and bathroom faucets, toilet handles, TV remotes, phone receivers, light switches, and doorknobs. You'll need to make a fresh batch weekly because the bleach will lose potency.

**Rubbing alcohol.** A 32-ounce bottle costs around $2.50 and can replace multiple products.

- Cleanly remove sticker residue with alcohol instead of Goo Gone, which costs nearly $6 a bottle.

- Want to never scrub mildew again? Then use alcohol to keep your shower squeaky clean. Fill a 32-ounce spray bottle with a cup of rubbing alcohol, top off with water, and keep in your shower at all times. Spray the walls after each use, then squeegee off. No need for a special mildew spray.

**Vinegar.** It's an effective sanitizer, and at just $1.25 for a 32-ounce bottle, it's cost-effective, too.

- Spray surfaces with white vinegar, let sit for 10 minutes, then dry with a paper towel. For faster germ-fighting power, heat the vinegar to 150 degrees, spray, and leave on for a minute before drying. The smell will quickly fade.

- You can also get streak-free windows using a mix of 2 tablespoons of vinegar and 4 cups of water. Window cleaner can cost more than twice as much.

| | |
|---|---|
| Ammonia | $0.98 |
| Baking soda | $2.00 |
| Bleach | $3.00 |
| Rubbing alcohol | $2.50 |
| Vinegar | $1.25 |
| Total Cost | $9.73 |

## Clean your house for half the cost

One-stop shopping. It's so convenient to pick up bread, milk, a video rental, your prescription, and, oh yes, cleaning supplies, all in one place. But boy are you paying for that convenience. Cut your cleaning costs in half by thinking outside the supermarket.

**Dig for deals at the dollar store.** It's great for party favors, but the dollar store can also be the best place to buy basic cleaning supplies. For example, a pair of reusable latex gloves might cost $3 at your grocery store, so they're a bargain for just a buck. And if you need carpet stain remover, you'd pay almost 10 times more elsewhere.

Even though most carry a limited and ever-changing selection, you may be pleasantly surprised to find some of your favorite brand-name items on the dollar-store shelf. But even the off-brands are worth a try at that price.

**Bulk up at a warehouse club.** Sam's Club, BJ's Wholesale Club, or Costco can save you money on cleaning supplies if you don't mind buying big — sometimes really big — packages. That said, their house brands usually offer the best deals. For instance, buy the Sam's Club WindFresh laundry detergent bucket and save 50 to 70 percent, compared to several name brands they sell.

If you can't or don't want to carry those big containers home, check out the club's website. Sometimes they run online-only items on sale, and often there's free shipping.

The downside? Well, there is the cost of membership — at least $45 to $55 a year. Do some math to see if you'll recoup that expense through your savings. And then you might buy so much cleaner you can't use it all before it loses its effectiveness. While getting brand-name bleach at Sam's Club saves you about 24 percent, you have to buy nearly 3 gallons at one go. Since Clorox says bleach has a shelf life of just a year, can you say, cleaning party?

**Subscribe and avoid the heavy lifting.** It's easy. Go online, subscribe, and your cleaning supplies show up at your door when you need them. While that could make it harder to dodge the drudgery, you will save money. Subscription services such as Amazon Subscribe & Save, Target Subscriptions, and Boxed.com often have items at lower prices due to bulk packaging. They also offer discounts and free shipping.

Want a coupon for an item you buy all the time? Amazon has an array of digital coupons for subscription cleaning items. Or check out the gift cards Target offers when you buy multiples of an item.

Before you commit, however, make sure subscribing is not only a timesaver, but a money saver for you. Research the sizes and brands each service carries, and read up on how to cancel or change delivery frequency. Here's a quick rundown of the basics:

- Amazon Subscribe & Save offers free shipping plus 15 percent off each shipment if you subscribe to at least 5 items per month.

- Target Subscriptions gives you free shipping as well as 5 percent off subscriptions, and an additional 5 percent off if you pay using their REDcard.

- Boxed.com has free shipping for orders over $50. You also earn one point per dollar spent. Once you rack up 500 points, you get a $5 credit.

## The dirt-cheap secret to perfectly clean mirrors

Toss the glass cleaner and paper towels. Not only are they expensive, but they can literally ruin your mirrors. One day you'll finish spraying and wiping, spritzing and rubbing, and stand back to admire your handiwork. That's when you'll notice the scratches. And wait, what's that black stuff along the edge?

Blame the scratches on rough paper towels. They are meant to be abrasive — the better to scrub away stains and spills. Not so good for mirrors or glass, though. What's worse, a tiny drip of glass cleaner behind the mirror's edge can make the backing lift from the glass, leaving an ugly, dark rim.

The solution is cheap and easy. Clean your mirrors with a soft microfiber cloth dampened with warm water. Wipe and then dry quickly with another cloth for a streak-free shine. For stubborn spots, spray cleaner on the cloth — not the mirror — and avoid the edges.

## Homemade solutions replace high-priced cleaners

You don't need a special cleaner to make your granite countertops sparkle. Or a kit to keep your TV smudge-free. In fact, you don't have to buy many of the pricey cleaning products marketed especially for your big-ticket items. Make your own cleaning solutions and save.

**Keep your granite gleaming for pennies.** You'd be crazy to use just anything on your beautiful, but oh-so-expensive granite countertops. Ammonia, bleach, vinegar, or citrus can damage the sealant or even etch the surface. And guess what? Those are ingredients in most all-purpose or kitchen cleaners on the market.

But a cleaner that's specially formulated for granite will cost anywhere from $4 to $15 for an 18-ounce bottle. Even if it lasts you a couple of months, you'll be spritzing away a fortune over the course of a year.

How about a homemade granite cleaner, that, by the way, is also good for lots of other surfaces in your kitchen, but costs just pennies per use? What a smart idea.

For less than $3, buy 32 ounces of rubbing alcohol, then fill a spray bottle with half alcohol and half water. Notice, this ratio means you'll have enough rubbing alcohol to refill your spray bottle several times. Now spray the mixture lightly on your countertops and dry well with a soft cotton or microfiber cloth. That's it. You're left with a gorgeous streak-free shine and no soap buildup.

**Screen cleaning that won't kill your electronics.** What's the biggest problem with touchscreens? You touch them. Your kids touch them. The grandkids, neighbors, strangers, and sometimes even the dogs touch them. Pretty soon, no amount of dry wiping can remove the buildup of smears and blobs on your tablet, phone, laptop, or TV.

Before you start spraying the glass cleaner, wait one second. You'll probably damage not only any special coating on the screen, but the inner workings of your device, as well. Manufacturers say many cleaners are off limits because they will cloud or even ruin the screen, and negate most warranties.

But there is a product for everything, isn't there? Sure enough, a screen cleaner kit — containing a 16-ounce spray bottle plus a microfiber cloth — suitable for all types of displays and monitors, sells for about $14. Or you can make your own for around $6, including the bottle and cloth. The secret is distilled water and white vinegar. Don't cheat and use tap water, since it can leave streaks.

1. Unplug your TV or computer, or turn your mobile device off.

2. Mix the distilled water and white vinegar in a 1-1 ratio in your spray bottle.

3. Very, very lightly spritz your microfiber cloth. Never spray anything directly on the screen.

4. Gently wipe the screen from top to bottom.

5. Let the screen dry before you turn it back on.

The final word — don't guess when it comes to cleaning expensive electronics. Check the manual.

## Save $150 or more by showing your vacuum some love

How much do you love your vacuum? With a new one averaging $200 a pop, you should love it enough to give it at least a little TLC. For a year's worth of maintenance — around $50 — you'll keep your machine in tiptop form and save yourself from buying a new one — possibly for decades.

Terry Spencer, an expert technician at RepairClinic.com, says proper care and maintenance could easily extend your machine's five- to 10-year life span. Don't believe it? Stop by his house and he'll show you his 30-year-old vacuum cleaner that's still going strong.

The key to a happy machine, he says, is to keep it clean and periodically check that all parts are operating properly. Notice you're losing suction? That means you have a problem that's forcing your motor to work overtime. And that poor overworked motor will eventually overheat and burn out. To keep minor problems from turning into a major disaster like that, follow these tips.

**Empty the bags often.** This is your first line of defense. If you can't remember when you last emptied the bag or canister, now is the time. Look for a fill line, or empty it when it's half to three-quarters full. Check on it at least once a month. Most bags are cheap — just $1 to $2 each — even those guaranteed to filter out allergens.

**Don't forget to clean your filters.** These help keep all the finer pieces of dirt in the bag. Otherwise, loose dust can spew into the air or settle inside the motor. Check your vacuum cleaner's filter every two months. If it looks like a dust-bunny colony moved in, it's time to clean.

Clean paper filters by shaking them over a trash can outside. Plastic or foam filters can usually be rinsed or washed, but check the manual first. At least once a year, spring for new filters. They can range from as little as $2 for foam to $25 or more for a HEPA cartridge. Don't skimp here — without a good working filter all those nasty dirt and dust particles will just keep floating through the air.

**Inspect the drive belt.** This critical piece connects the motor to the brush roller. It can stretch out and snap, bringing the brush roller's spinning to a halt. That means your vacuum isn't pulling dirt out of the carpet anymore. Check the belt every six months, or you may get a nasty surprise.

"The belt will usually let you know when it's time to be replaced by producing a pungent burning smell that will have you opening the windows and lighting candles," warns Spencer. A mere $5 for a new belt will help you avoid the problem.

**Give the brush roller a trim.** It never fails. You check the roller and are shocked to see it full of hair and string. Where did it all come from? Doesn't matter, just grab the scissors and cut it off. All that debris can stop the roller from spinning and wear down the belt.

The next step is to check the bristles to see if they're worn down. Just like a well-used toothbrush, the brush roller occasionally needs to be replaced. This brush will cost you about $20, so fortunately you only have to do it every two to three years.

Spencer recommends occasionally removing and cleaning the brush-roll bearings as well. "That can substantially increase the life of the brush roll and belt," he says.

**Fix it or ditch it?** Spencer says most homeowners can replace the drive belt, brush roller, and wheels by themselves. To locate parts, contact the manufacturer, shop online, or check the Vacuum & Sewing Dealers Trade Association's website at *vdta.com* for local vendors. *Repairclinic.com* has both parts and instructional videos. Keep your manual close by to help with the basic DIY maintenance. If you misplace it, check *homeappliance.manualsonline.com* to see if you can locate one for your model.

Feeling overwhelmed or think you have a bigger problem? That's the time to take your vacuum to a repair shop. "If you feel the repair is too involved or complicated, it may be best left to a professional," Spencer says, noting the average repair could range from $30 to $90, depending on the parts needed. Still cheaper than buying a new vacuum cleaner!

If the motor does burn out, replacing it can be pricey. If this or any other repair is more than half the cost of a new, similar vacuum, it may be time to ditch your machine after all.

# Laundry

## Get a load of savings with a wash-day makeover

Your great-grandkids might love to inherit wedding china or a family pocket watch — but your favorite jeans? Maybe if they were 135-year-old "antiques" like the pair Levi & Strauss recently found near a Nevada mining town.

Your clothes may not last a century, but you can keep them for many years if you treat them right, plus save hundreds of dollars in repair and replacement costs. Here's how to do it.

**Keep darks dark and brights bright.** The average American spends $40 or more on a pair of jeans, but let's face it, that's one wardrobe staple that's worth it. At least, until they start fading. Want to keep all your colored clothes looking new, wash after wash? Three products for less than $25 will help do the trick.

- Wash dark clothing in a special detergent like Woolite Dark to lock in color. Turning the clothes inside out will help fight fading, too.

- Keep bright clothes colorful by using a detergent just for them, like Cheer.

- Color-safe bleach is another brightening agent for clothes. Check the label to make sure it works for that type of fabric.

**Take whites from dingy to dazzling.** Your white clothing and linens still look dirty after washing. The solution is to add chlorine bleach to the load, right? Not every load. Too much bleach can eventually turn whites yellow and thin fabric out, making holes more likely. Use it every few loads instead, or just for your dirtiest problems.

Ever wonder why your beautiful white towels have turned a dingy gray? It's all those frothy suds you wash them in. Soap buildup traps dirt inside the fabric that won't rinse clean. Try using half the amount of detergent, and boost its cleaning power with one of these laundry aids. Just $5 worth of products can revive all of your whites.

- Add 1/2 cup of borax with your detergent to get whites cleaner.

- Pour 1 cup of white vinegar in the rinse cycle to brighten and freshen up your whites.

- Wash white clothes in the hottest water that is safe for the fabric.

**Out, out, darn spot.** You bought a lovely dress at a fabulous price, then stained it the first time you wore it. Think it's a goner? Not if you have the right stain fighters on your laundry room shelf. Spend less than $11 on these products, and you'll save clothing and linens from stain-induced emergencies — and save money by not having to replace them.

- Chlorine bleach is a go-to remedy for stains on white cotton or polyester. Soak in a gallon of water and 3 tablespoons of bleach for five minutes before washing.

- Zap stains on color-safe washable laundry with an all-purpose stain remover like Shout. If you can't treat the stain right away, dab it with water. Use a little dish detergent for oily stains. Then treat it later.

- Blot protein stains like ice cream with a liquid enzymatic detergent such as Arm & Hammer Plus OxiClean, and let it sit for 15 minutes. Then wash using the hottest water safe for your fabric.

You may need to treat the stain more than once before it disappears, but don't put it in the dryer until then. The stain might set for good. For more stain removal tips, see the American Cleaning Institute's chart at *www.cleaninginstitute.org*. Click on Clean Living, then Laundry (in left column), then Stain Removal Chart.

# Simple ways to stretch your food dollars

# Grocery shopping

## Shop smarter: 6 simple habits save you more green on groceries

Three words strike fear into the hearts of shoppers everywhere: crazy coupon lady. And not just because she takes five times as long to check out. Her savvy skills seem to put your penny-pinching efforts to shame. But you can give that crazy coupon lady a run for her money without coupons — by adopting six simple habits that allow you to save more money than you spend.

**Map out meal time.** Thrifty shopper Penny Walker has been saving money for years with one easy habit. "I always plan meals beforehand," she says. "If I know there's going to be a sale on certain foods, I can organize my meals around those items and make my money go even further."

Planned meals mean fewer trips to the grocery store and less food wasted. For Penny, that also means spending less time and money in the long run.

**Shop with a list.** If you do nothing else to spend less money, always abide by this one simple rule: make a shopping list (and stick to it). If you see something you want, write it down instead of buying on impulse. If you still want it the next time around, get it then. You won't believe how much you'll save every time you shop.

Creating and sharing grocery lists is easier than ever, thanks to smartphone apps that can remember your list, organize it by aisle, and even help you find coupons. Check out these apps for starters.

- AnyList (for iPhones)

- Out of Milk (for Android devices)

- GroceryIQ (for iPhones and Android devices)

**Snap up sales at the right place.** Loyalty is a great quality, but, when it comes to shopping, you could be missing out on weekly savings if you always stick to one store. Scan the sales ads each week and shop where you can get the best deals.

Just need to pop in and grab a few items? Skip the convenience store. *Consumer Reports* recommends dollar stores for staples that could cost twice as much at drugstores.

**Eat healthy before you shop.** It's the golden rule of the grocery store: don't shop when you're hungry. That said, what you eat before you shop matters, too, according to a recent study.

When people ate an apple before shopping, they bought 28 percent more produce than people who munched on a cookie. Snacking on something healthy puts you in a healthier mindset and makes you more likely to buy good-for-you foods. So eat a healthy treat beforehand to help you resist the siren's call of the junk food aisle. Your wallet and your waist will be happier.

**Watch out for superstore sales schemes.** Have you ever grabbed a last-minute soda, magazine, or pack of gum placed conveniently by the checkout lane? Stores are banking on it. Keep your eyes peeled for other tricks like these.

- Stores encourage you to enter on the right and shop counterclockwise. Research shows you could spend $2 less by entering on the left and shopping clockwise, instead. Doing that once a week adds up to $104 a year.

- Foods at eye level are sometimes more expensive. That's because 40 percent of shoppers buy what's directly in front of them. Look high and low before you buy.

- End-of-aisle displays are prime real estate for flashy signs and misleading deals. These hotspots sell out eight times faster. Don't buy from end caps unless you know the price is actually a bargain.

- Grabbing a bigger shopping cart leads to longer receipts. Giving people shopping carts that are twice the normal size leads them to spend 40 percent more. Use smaller carts when possible. Really want to trim your grocery spending? Use a basket, instead.

**Buy in season.** The best way to bring down expenses in the produce aisle is to buy in season. That's when fruits and veggies are most plentiful, cost less, and taste better. Go to *seasonalfoodguide.org* to see what's in season where you live.

You can also get fresh produce at a discount when you buy local, especially if the produce is in season. Check out community-supported agriculture (CSA) programs, food co-ops, produce stands, and farmer's markets. Go to *LocalHarvest.org* to find the ones near you.

## Expert reveals top 10 ways to nab unbelievable deals

"The savings are everywhere," says Ted Booker. As a manager of a leading grocery chain for more than 35 years, he knows a thing or two about taking advantage of the best deals. Check out his expert advice on the top ways you can save big bucks on groceries.

**Stack the savings.** The number one thing Booker tells people to do is look for grocery stores that accept more than one coupon for a product. For example, Publix and Target let you combine a manufacturer's coupon with a store coupon on your favorite box of cereal, while Walmart limits you to one coupon per item.

**Join a club.** You can get super savings by signing up for rewards programs and online newsletters. "Even certain large food companies, such as Kellogg's, give you ways to save," says Booker. Just check out the website of your favorite brand and look for links to offers, promotions, or savings.

**Save it for a rainy day.** Your local grocery store wants your business so badly they'll give you a rain check on sale items that run out of stock. All you have to do is ask, and you'll get a slip of paper that allows you to buy that item later for the sale price. Many stores offer rain checks, but Booker suggests you ask a manager, not a cashier, about your store's policy. "Some companies train their employees so poorly that, if you go from cashier to cashier, you will get different answers."

**Request a substitution.** Another magic question you should ask is if the store offers substitutions. These are similar to rain checks, but instead of getting a voucher to use at a later date, the store lets you buy a similar item for the same sale price right then and there.

**Know the sales cycle.** According to *Consumer Reports*, you can sometimes get better deals by shopping Wednesday nights when stores mark down their perishable items. While this isn't true for every grocery chain, Booker confirms that some supermarkets run their specials on the same days every week. Why not ask around at your favorite store?

**Find the clearance rack.** You can often find all the marked-down food items in one place — the clearance section. "These are usually items that did not sell," says Booker, "and a push is being made to remove the item from the store." Ask a store associate for help if you have trouble finding the clearance area at your local market. And before you buy, check the expiration date.

**Learn the lingo.** Coupons may seem like the most obvious way to save money, but managers say people miss out on lots of bargains that are right in front of them. Just make sure you understand the deal. You may not have to buy multiples to score the sale price, for instance. Read the ad's fine print when you participate in BOGOs (buy one get one free) or 10 for $10 deals.

**Do your research.** Shoppers have more ways than ever to find deals and coupons, but you have to do the research, says Booker. When you shop, it helps to know the price you usually pay for staple goods. Make a list of items you buy frequently, like milk and eggs, and write down how much each normally costs. Pocket this list each time you go to the store, and check the "sale" prices against it. This way, you'll always know whether you're getting a good deal.

**Take your time.** Moving at a quick pace will get you out of the store faster, but slow down when you're browsing the sales ad and in-store deals, says Booker. "We miss so many savings because we are always rushing and just don't take full advantage of the deals."

**Don't be afraid to ask.** The store manager will know how to save the most money. If you ask questions while you shop, you'll not only get the best deals — you'll also save time at checkout.

---

### The secret to saving up to 60 percent on groceries

No gimmicks. No frills. No fancy services. No alluring displays. Discount grocery chains, like ALDI, Save-A-Lot, and Grocery Outlet, are as straightforward as it gets. And that's why you can save 40, 50, even as much as 60 percent every time you shop. For a couple, that translates into more than $3,500 off their grocery budget a year. A family of four will save even more, as much as $6,000 a year, just by shopping a discount grocery store every week.

If you want your favorite brands at half the price, check out salvage grocery stores. They offer consistently low prices on less-than-perfect brand-name and store-name goodies, like past-date foods, funny-looking fruits and vegetables, dented cans, and packages with misspelled or misshapen labels. Just be sure to avoid swollen or rusty cans and torn packages.

## Supermarket shopping mistakes: 3 ways to avoid paying top dollar

You've been roaming the supermarket since before you could walk. You know how to shop. Sometimes, though, you get into a routine, and sneaky savings slip right through your fingers. To get the most out of every shopping trip, watch out for these common mistakes so you never pay more than you should.

**Don't forget to price match.** Sometimes you just don't have time to shop around. The solution? Do all your shopping at a store that offers price matching. Walmart and Target are the main supermarkets with this service, but check around — you might find it in other stores, including retail.

Price matching is easier than ever with tools like Walmart's Savings Catcher. Download this app on to your smartphone, then scan your Walmart receipt. Or go to the website *Walmart.com/ SavingsCatcher* and type in your receipt number. Savings Catcher looks for lower advertised prices at stores all around town. If it finds your items for less somewhere else, it sends you an eGift card worth the difference. You can print this voucher and take it to the store or bring it in on your phone.

"I have gotten back as little as 10 cents and as much as $8.41 in one shopping visit," says savvy shopper Donna Barnett, who uses Walmart's Savings Catcher. She recommends shopping at Walmart on the days that competitors normally start their sales, so you can reap even bigger price-match rewards.

**Don't always buy in bulk.** You can often find items at a lower price per unit when you purchase a large amount. This lets you stock up on must-haves for less dinero than if you bought them individually. But bulk-buying also has a dark side.

- Most people waste more food than they think, says a study from Johns Hopkins University. If you buy a lot of perishable items you can't eat in time, you're throwing your money away. Avoid buying gigantic containers of stuff you rarely use, such as condiments, or items with a short shelf life, like fruits and veggies.

- Don't always assume you are snagging a better deal by buying in bulk. Check the unit price.

- Stashing more food in the house can encourage you to eat more, especially if you like to stock up on junk food.

**Don't overlook your loyalty card.** Some stores with loyalty programs inflate prices so they can give a discount to members. "It has the appearance of being a good program, but it usually is not," says the longtime manager of a leading supermarket chain. "Prices get raised in other areas to offset the balance of what was lost." That means every time you shop without swiping your loyalty card, you not only miss out on discounts and other incentives like fuel points, but you could also be paying a premium for everyday items.

Always pay attention to your loyalty program's policies. Many stores use loyalty cards to track your purchases. On the other hand, some use them to alert you when products you bought get recalled.

## Coupon clipping: the $1,000-a-year grocery savings secret

Clip and save. It looks so simple on extreme couponing TV shows when the pros buy four carts of groceries for just 10 cents. But who has the time and energy to become a real markdown master? The good news is, saving has never been easier. In fact, studies show that clipping coupons for just 20 minutes a week can help you save up to $1,000 on groceries every year. Use these smart tips to find the right coupons for you, and never pay full price again.

**Track down deals at all your favorite places — with the tap of a finger.** "You can get digital coupons all over the internet," says Ted Booker, longtime grocery store manager. Online clearinghouses and apps do the work for you, making it a piece of cake to rack up savings.

- Search for coupons online and print them at home with the websites *MyGroceryDeals.com* and *Savings.com*.

- Sign up at *SavingStar.com* to get cash back when you buy groceries at your favorite store.

- Browse coupons on your computer or smartphone at *Coupons.com*.

- Download the Grocery iQ or Shopular mobile app on to your smartphone or tablet, and you'll never have to deal with printed coupons again.

- Check your favorite stores' websites for apps and coupons you can use every time you shop.

"I hate couponing," says Nancy Hills. "But since I always shop at Publix, I signed up for their app." By creating an account with her email and phone number, she has access to all of their digital coupons. "I scroll through the coupons and electronically 'clip' the ones I want," she says. "At checkout, I punch in my phone number and any clipped coupons get deducted automatically." It's that easy.

**Surprise savings are in store for shoppers like you.** Apps are great, but if you focus solely on digital coupons, you could be missing out on spectacular deals right under your nose.

- On your way into the store, Booker recommends you grab the flyer that shows all the current sale items. Match these with your coupons to save even more.

- When you add items to your cart, check the packages for peel-off deals. If you rely on the cashier to do it for you, specials may get overlooked in the hustle and bustle of checkout.

- Watch for coupon dispensers in the aisles. They could be loaded with sneaky savings.

**Don't downplay old-fashioned paper ads.** Snail mail. That's how the first widespread coupons were distributed by none other than Coca-Cola back in 1887. Even with the rise in technology, 70 percent of people still use traditional paper coupons.

While clipping from the newspaper isn't as glamorous as using fancy apps, shoppers still get more than 92 percent of their coupons from newspaper inserts. That's a lot of savings you wouldn't otherwise find in stores.

---

### 12 healthy foods that cost under $1

Good nutrition doesn't have to cost a fortune. You can get more bang for your buck by choosing low-cost, unprocessed foods with high nutritional values. These wholesome choices are all under $1 per pound, so you can eat healthy for less.

- Bananas
- Brown rice
- Cabbage
- Canned kidney beans
- Canned tomatoes
- Cantaloupe
- Dry pinto beans
- Grapefruit
- Oats
- Potatoes
- Sweet potatoes
- Whole carrots

---

## Presliced and overpriced: how to save up to 60 percent on staple items

Time is money. Everyone knows it's true, but no one knows it better than the food industry. That's why you will find conveniently packaged foods with jacked-up price tags calling you from every aisle. Don't give in to temptation. Buy foods whole, instead of presliced and prepackaged, and save a ton on meat, fruits, vegetables, and more.

When prebagged produce is sold by the unit, the bag must contain at least the advertised weight. To avoid hiccups, most producers add a few ounces more. So if you need a 5-pound bag of potatoes, weigh several before making your selection. One might contain 4 more ounces than advertised.

Say you want to make a chicken sandwich. You have two choices. Crack open a package of precooked, presliced chicken breast; or cook and cut your own. The first option is awfully convenient, but buy a pack of raw, boneless chicken breasts, and you could trim 60 percent off your grocery bill.

Now suppose you make that chicken sandwich for lunch every weekday, using 2 ounces of chicken. Cooking and slicing the meat yourself would save you more than $3 a week — almost $170 a year that could go toward yummy ingredients to put on your perfect sandwich.

Check out the cost of some common items available whole or conveniently prepackaged or presliced. As you can see, you'll often pay double for a comparable product in a more convenient package.

| Food | Price per ounce | | Savings |
|---|---|---|---|
| | Convenience | Whole or bulk | |
| Oatmeal | 21.2¢ | 10.0¢ | 53% |
| Apples | 21.3¢ | 10.3¢ | 52% |
| Raisins | 33.0¢ | 18.9¢ | 43% |
| 100% Apple juice | 5.0¢ | 2.6¢ | 48% |
| Carrots | 10.5¢ | 5.5¢ | 48% |

If you don't mind the extra time and work it takes to slice, separate, and bag your buys, you could be on your way to huge savings. Plus, you'll avoid all the preservatives that manufacturers add during processing, which could mean big health benefits.

## Organic fare — when to splurge and when to save

Organic foods cost, on average, almost 50 percent more than your standard grub, which is why it pays to choose your food wisely. If you can't budge your budget, experts generally recommend you spend your organic dollars on fruits, vegetables, meats, poultry, and dairy. That's because they provide more nutrients and fewer harmful chemicals than their conventional counterparts.

**Pick produce with fewer pesticides.** You do have a little wiggle room with organic fruits and veggies. Thick-skinned produce you peel before you eat generally has less pesticide residue. That means you can buy conventional when shopping for avocados, pineapples, mangoes, papayas, kiwis, and cantaloupes. Instead of splurging on organic versions of these, put your money toward high-pesticide, hard-to-clean foods you often eat whole, like apples, peaches, nectarines, strawberries, grapes, tomatoes, and spinach.

Do you automatically make a beeline for products labeled "natural"? Those claims are currently unregulated by the FDA, which means natural foods can have sneaky ingredients, including artificial preservatives and coloring. Always check the ingredients list, and don't pay extra just because a product says "natural."

**Meat and dairy may be worth the cost.** Organic livestock is on a strict diet of 100-percent certified organic feed, no antibiotics, and zero added growth hormones. But these practices come with a price. For instance, you could buy three gallons of regular milk for less than the price of one gallon of organic milk. And organic ground beef costs about $3 more per pound.

You'll have to decide for yourself if the benefits are worth the extra cash. A recent study shows you'll get about 50 percent more omega-3 fatty acids in organically produced meat and milk, compared to the conventional variety. And that's good news for your heart, brain, and immune system.

**Stretch the savings by skipping processed products.** When it comes to processed foods — those that come in jars, bottles, cans, and boxes — don't assume you're eating healthy just because the label says it's organic. Up to 5 percent non-organic ingredients are allowed in products that tout an organic claim or the USDA organic seal. Think about your health, and remember, organic sugar is still sugar.

You can save over 30 percent by going conventional rather than organic on processed foods like these.

| Product | Price per ounce | | Savings |
|---|---|---|---|
| | Organic | Conventional | |
| Quaker Instant Oatmeal | 25.0¢ | 16.6¢ | 34% |
| Heinz Ketchup | 12.8¢ | 8.8¢ | 31% |
| Pam Olive Oil Cooking Spray | 70.6¢ | 57.2¢ | 19% |

# Beef up your savings by stretching your meat dollars

Given your grocery store receipt the once-over lately? If you're like most people, you spend more of your supermarket bucks on beef, poultry, and fish than any other food, including fruits and veggies. It's hard not to goggle when almost one-fourth of your grocery budget goes toward these foods. Why not trim the cost of pricey staples with just four frugal tips.

**Call in a substitute and save up to 77 percent.** People spend the biggest chunk of their meat money on beef. But you can still get the protein you need without the hefty price tag by subbing in beans. Each time you swap out ground beef for pintos, you save 77 percent. Do that every other week and pocket about $80 a year.

Beans aren't your only protein-packed alternative, though. Try nuts, seeds, peas, tofu, and eggs.

**Slash your spending with cheaper cuts.** Maybe you've got a meat-lover in the family. Keep him and your budget happy by buying cheaper cuts. For example, chicken thighs and legs are usually less expensive than chicken breasts, and chuck roast is less than tenderloin. Grill a sirloin instead of a T-bone to save a whopping $9 a pound.

You may have to adjust your cooking methods to make some cuts turn out juicy and tender, but a slow-cooker is ideal for the job.

**Give meat a supporting role, save $86 a year.** Shoppers usually spend $172 a year on poultry, but let other foods take center stage and you can get by with half as much. Use chicken in chili, stews, pasta dishes, and casseroles. Or make vegetables and healthy grains the star of your dinner table, and serve chicken on the side.

**Get canned for an ocean of discounts.** If you thought the price of beef and poultry was fishy, just wait until you shop for fish. Buy wild Alaskan salmon fresh and you're looking at $9 to $30 a pound — that could mean more than $5 for a 3-ounce serving. Canned salmon, on the other hand, is just as nutritious and could cost 90 percent less. Imagine a single serving that costs you just 49 cents.

## Save $39 a year with this simple trick

How would you like to get 5 cents back for every reusable bag you fill at the grocery store? That's what Target is offering with their sustainable living program. Bring 15 bags when you shop each week, and you could save $39 dollars a year.

And Target isn't the only grocery chain offering rewards for going green. Whole Foods gives back up to 10 cents at the register for each bag you bring in. Even some Ralphs stores like Kroger offer fuel rewards when you bring reusable bags. It's simple: go green and save green.

## Retailer secret knocks 30 percent or more off price tag

"Come on down!" It feels like you're on the latest episode of "The Price is Right." But in reality, you just walked into a grocery store, and you're seeing practically the same product with two different price tags — one at the usual cost and one at a deep discount. It's not a game-show trick. Your favorite places to shop often have big surprises in store for you — private-label versions of your must-have grocery items with deals too good to pass up. And that's how you can score first-rate groceries at discount prices without sacrificing quality.

Check out brands from crowd favorites like Walmart, Costco, Sam's Club, Target, and Kroger to cash in on the savings. For instance, you can save over 40 percent when you buy Walmart's Great Value brand of old-fashioned oatmeal over Quaker's more pricey variety.

Some people worry store brands aren't as good as brand-name products. And while that may be true sometimes, it doesn't apply to all products. In fact, 65 percent of shoppers in a recent *Consumer Reports* survey said they buy store brands whenever they can, and are rarely disappointed.

Here's another little retailer secret: many store-brand products are manufactured by the same companies that produce name-brand items — often with the exact same ingredients. The difference in price is usually a simple matter of marketing. Store brands don't spend loads of money on advertising, packaging, and primo spots on the store shelves. Fewer production costs allow them to sell at a lower price, which means more money in your pocket.

## Eat healthier for $955 less a year

It all began in 1999 when nutritionist Mary Flynn created the plant-based olive oil (PBOO) diet. What she didn't know then is that her diet would eventually prove you can eat cleaner without cleaning out your bank account.

New research shows the PBOO diet is actually cheaper than the MyPlate eating plan from the United States Department of Agriculture (USDA). According to the USDA, their average weekly food plan costs $57.13. But at $38.75 a week, the PBOO diet could save you a whopping $955.50 a year.

**Subtract meat for a cheaper eat.** The PBOO diet is pretty simple. Enjoy 4 tablespoons of extra virgin olive oil each day; eat more servings of vegetables, fruits, and whole grains; and cut down on animal protein.

MyPlate, on the other hand, calls for more dairy, and encourages most adults to get 5 to 6 ounces of protein daily from sources like lean meat, poultry, and seafood. And that's where it gets pricey. Studies show that animal products like meat can cost more than twice as much as vegetables and beans, and 60 percent more than fruit.

The PBOO diet is not only less expensive, but also thought to be healthier simply because it gives meat the brush-off. Remember, there's hard evidence that eating too much meat can lead to significant health problems, like obesity, type 2 diabetes, heart disease, breast cancer, prostate cancer, and colon cancer.

**Produce doesn't have to break the bank.** Don't let high prices in the produce aisle discourage you from trying this eating plan. Flynn's diet includes frozen and canned produce, which are often a lot cheaper than the fresh versions and just as nutritious. So don't be afraid to fill your cart with canned tomatoes and beans or frozen carrots and berries. You'll get tasty, nutrition-packed foods with a lower price tag.

## Groceries to go: how you can save time and cash

Betty had a hard time getting around and relied on her daughter for a lot of things, including groceries. It was a big blow to her independence until she discovered she could order from home and have groceries shipped right to her house.

**Arrange a front porch delivery.** Obviously, you'll save time and gas, but you really can save money, too. Just do your research to compare food prices. And don't forget delivery fees. They can range from zero to $10 or more, depending on where you live and how much you buy.

While popular services like AmazonFresh, Jet, NetGrocer, and Peapod are more common in major cities, search online or ask around to see if anyone offers grocery delivery in your area. And follow these tips to save.

- Do all your shopping at one time instead of buying items individually throughout the week. Often, the more you spend, the cheaper your delivery fee will be.

- Limit impulse purchases.

- Shop sales and use coupons when possible.

- Track your total to keep within budget.

**Never step foot inside a store.** Well-known retailers like Walmart, Whole Foods, Target, and Safeway offer delivery services for a fee in some locations, but Walmart and Target go one step further and allow you to order online and pick up at the store absolutely free.

It's simple. To use Walmart's pickup service, for instance, go to *grocery.walmart.com*, and enter your ZIP code to see if the service is available at a location near you. If it is, you can order your groceries online and schedule a time for pickup. When you arrive, a Walmart associate will load up your car for you. How easy is that?

---

### Canned and frozen: 60 percent cheaper, just as nutritious

Want to eat more fruits and veggies without blowing your budget? Then venture outside the produce aisle. You'll find fresh savings by rediscovering canned and frozen foods.

People used to think processing removed significant amounts of nutrients, but that's just not true. The American Heart Association says both canned and frozen fruits and vegetables are healthy choices if you're careful to avoid added sugar and salt. That's great news because these items are often cheaper than fresh produce. Take green beans for example — buy them canned instead of fresh and save a whopping 60 percent.

To keep it healthy, look for low-sodium labels, then drain and rinse to cut even more salt.

# Food storage

## Spoiler alert: 3 secrets to make picky produce last

You would never throw $600 into the trash, right? It sounds
ridiculous, but millions of Americans are doing this every year.
Researchers estimate that families toss out 15 percent of the food
they buy. And spoiled produce is a big culprit. Follow these storage
tips to cut down on costs and extend the life of tricky produce.

**Quench thirsty veggies with a splash of H2O.** Store asparagus
in a paper bag, and watch it go limp. Seal it in plastic, and you'll
find a slimy mess. So what do you do? Just like flowers in a vase,
you can extend the life of asparagus by trimming the stalks and
placing them upright in a jar filled with an inch of water. Cover
loosely with a plastic bag in the refrigerator and they will stay
fresh for about four days. Experts suggest this method for other
water-loving vegetables, too, like celery, fennel, green onions,
and leafy herbs — just not basil.

If you don't like the idea of a jar of water sitting in your
fridge, wrap these items in a damp towel instead, and place in
a plastic bag.

**Dry out water-weary produce.** Notice how some fruits and
vegetables seem to spoil in no time? That's because, for them,
moisture is the enemy.

Battle boggy berries and droopy greens by storing them in a
container with a dry paper towel in the bottom. When the towel
gets damp, change it out. Use this same trick on mushrooms, or
pop them in a paper bag.

**Some foods don't play well with others.** Maybe you've heard putting apples in the crisper with your lettuce is a no-no. But do you know why? Ethylene. It's a gas foods like apples, pears, peaches, avocados, and bananas produce as they ripen. Other foods, such as leafy greens, broccoli, asparagus, and mushrooms, are sensitive to this gas, and will ripen faster — even spoil — when exposed to it.

The best solution is to keep these foods away from each other. You can also invest in produce bags made to absorb these gasses. They claim to keep your veggies fresh up to 10 times longer.

## From store to storage — meat safety tips you can't afford to miss

Wouldn't it be nice if your hamburger had a label that gave you a warning, like "Eat in 2 days"? Futuristic-sounding — yes. Far-fetched — not really. Researchers at MIT are working on a sensor that will monitor your meat's shelf life, so you never have to dither over food freshness again. In the meantime, you can avoid waste and save money by following these tips for finding and storing the best meat.

**It pays to be picky when picking meat.** Make sure your meat is stored in a clean, cold case, and use your senses when choosing a cut. Steer clear if the meat or package has any of these characteristics.

- Slimy, sticky, or tacky texture

- Funky smell

- Expired use-by or sell-by date

- Leaky or torn wrapping

**Keep it cold, keep it safe.** The first rule of perishables is don't let them stay out of the refrigerator at room temperature for longer than two hours. Albin Krane puts this principle to work before he leaves the store parking lot. "I carry a cooler in my car when I shop," he says. "I pack my meat and cold stuff with ice, so I never have to wonder if it's still good by the time I get home."

**Practice smart freezer moves.** Refreezing is another storage issue that leaves people confused. In fact, it's one of the most commonly asked questions on the Food Safety and Inspection Service hotline. Experts say you can refreeze meats after both thawing and cooking as long as they were thawed and handled properly.

## Refrigerator rules: the right way to organize and save cold, hard cash

Think every nook and cranny of your refrigerator is going to treat your food the same? Believe it or not, the quality of fridge food is directly affected by where you store it. Follow these tips to make your goods go further, so you can save cold cash.

**Upper shelves.** As the warmest part of the fridge, the top shelves are best for ready-to-eat items like leftovers and drinks. They'll be at eye level, ideal for reminding you to gobble them up first.

**Middle shelves.** Those handy door bins seem perfect for dairy products like milk and eggs. But it's better to put these foods in the middle of the fridge where the temperature is more consistent.

**Lower shelves.** This is the coldest part of the fridge, which is why experts recommend it for fish, pork, beef, poultry, and other meats.

**Drawers.** The crisper drawers were made with fruits and veggies in mind. Store these items in separate drawers, however, to keep produce from ripening too fast.

**Doors**. Opening and closing your fridge all the time makes the temperature here go up and down. Put foods like condiments in door shelves because they are higher in preservatives and can handle the temp fluctuations better.

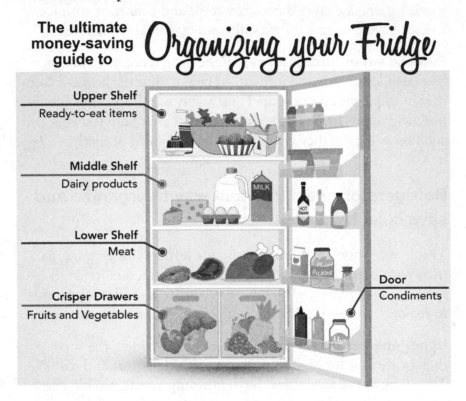

The ultimate money-saving guide to *Organizing your Fridge*

**Upper Shelf** — Ready-to-eat items

**Middle Shelf** — Dairy products

**Lower Shelf** — Meat

**Crisper Drawers** — Fruits and Vegetables

**Door** — Condiments

## 15 foods you should never refrigerate (and 7 you don't really have to)

To fridge, or not to fridge — that is the question. You bring a trunkload of groceries home each week. It's hard to keep up with what foods go where. The icebox seems like the universal food preserver. But storing certain foods in the fridge can actually ruin them, hurting your wallet in the long run.

**Fridge-fearing foods.** It's the cold hard truth: some foods just don't belong in the refrigerator. The cool temps and humid air can cause food to rot, change texture, and lose quality and flavor. The fridge also keeps some types of produce from ripening. So unless you've already sliced and diced your fruits and veggies, it's best to keep these guys in the pantry or on the counter.

| | |
|---|---|
| Basil | Onions |
| Bread | Potatoes |
| Coffee | Sweet potatoes |
| Fresh garlic | Tomatoes |
| Fresh ginger | Winter squash |
| Honey | Unripe avocados |
| Watermelon | Unripe bananas |

Unripe stone fruits, like plums and peaches

**On the fence foods.** Some foods will be perfectly fine out of the fridge, but won't be harmed by the frigid atmosphere either. For these foods, always check the package and follow the instructions.

| | |
|---|---|
| All-purpose flour | Nuts |
| Apples | Oils |
| Citrus | Peanut butter |
| Cucumbers | |

## Expiration dates: before you toss your food, read this

Half of Americans say they throw away food based on "best if used by" and "sell-by" dates. But most don't realize these actually refer to the quality of the product rather than safety. Before you toss another package, check out what these labels really mean.

**Use quality dates as guidelines, not deadlines.** If you're like most procrastinators, you want to know the last day you can eat a food before it starts to lose its freshness. Manufacturers recommend the "use-by" date for exactly that purpose. Foods with this label are often perishables like meat and milk. For this reason, the U.S. Department of Agriculture (USDA) suggests you don't purchase foods after the "use-by" date has expired. But if it passes after you've brought the item home, it's probably still safe to eat as long as you've handled the food properly, and it shows no signs of spoiling.

The "best if used by" date also refers to flavor and quality, and has nothing to do with safety. You'll often find it on canned goods, cereals, flour, sugar, and frozen foods.

**Get clued in with retail dates.** Manufacturers recommend "sell-by" dates to give retailers an idea of how long to display a product before removing it from their shelves. Never buy anything with an expired "sell-by" date. Then, once you unload your groceries, cook or freeze these perishables according to USDA guidelines:

- Poultry, ground meat, and sausage: within 1 or 2 days

- Beef, pork, and lamb: within 3 to 5 days

- Eggs: within 3 to 5 weeks

**Ignore packing codes.** Manufacturers use "closed" or "coded" dates — a series of numbers and letters followed by a date — to track their goods. These don't in any way reflect safety or quality, but are required on canned goods so manufacturers can rotate their stock and find items subject to recalls. Canned foods are safe indefinitely, as long as they are not exposed to temperatures below freezing or above 90 degrees.

# Dining out

## Dining on a dime: simple ways to save over $936 a year

Date night is Thursday evening for both the Smiths and the Johnsons. Between the nice restaurant and scrumptious meal, there's just one big difference. The Smiths save over $18 each date — a hefty $936 a year. How do they pull it off? It's simple. And you can do it, too.

**Feast on 53 percent savings with 3 tiny tweaks.** Switching to water alone as their mealtime beverage saves the Smiths over $200 a year. But they also trim their dinner check by sharing an appetizer and an entrée instead of buying two separate entrées. What's more, a sweet treat to finish off the evening can be pricey. So when the Smiths go out, they skip the $6 dessert and drop by the store on their way home to pick up an entire cheesecake of their own. They end up paying only a couple quarters per slice.

|  | Smiths | Johnsons | Savings |
|---|---|---|---|
| **Beverages** Water vs other drinks | $0.00 | $4.00 | $4.00 |
| **Meal** Shared appetizer and entrée vs 2 entrées | $15.98 | $19.98 | $4.00 |
| **Dessert** Store-bought vs restaurant cheesecake | $1.08 | $11.98 | $10.90 |
| **Total** | $17.06 | $35.96 | 53% |

**7 more ways to tuck into dining deals.** Munch on these money-saving tips to keep your cash where it belongs.

- The early bird gets the worm — even when dining out. You can sometimes get discounts by eating around 5:30 instead of your usual 8 p.m. These specials are more popular with older folks and families with young kids, but the savings are available for everyone.

- Go where kids eat free. Don't you hate it when you order an $8 meal that ends up on the floor? Save big bucks every time you eat out on a kid's night. "Atlanta Bread Company offers kids-eat-free night — our family loves this!" says bargain hunter Tara Christian. Some restaurants offer free meals when you order an adult entrée, while others give you a discount.

- Be on the hunt for midweek specials. Restaurants often use these to encourage people to come in on their slow days. For instance, go to O'Charley's on Free Pie Wednesday and get a complimentary slice when you order an entrée.

- Score restaurant rewards. You can get coupons plus free food and drinks when you sign up for a membership card. Loyalty also comes with perks during certain times of the year. "If I register my email with a restaurant, I can get a free meal or dessert for my birthday," says Tara. "It comes in handy when I want to eat out for a birthday celebration."

- Every special isn't special. Don't assume all specials are good deals. Restaurants may be testing new recipes, trying to get rid of surplus food, or highlighting a popular menu item. Ask about the price and compare it to other items on the menu before ordering.

- Don't double tip. Some restaurants add gratuity to your tab. Pay attention to your receipt, especially when eating at fancier restaurants or with a large party.

- Consider the coupons. "I always check the Sunday newspaper for restaurant coupons," says Tara, who has discovered deals at Ruby Tuesday, Applebee's, LongHorn Steakhouse, Chili's, and even Olive Garden. You never know what you'll find.

## Brew up coffee savings with this 20-second trick

Don't pay $4 for a designer brew. Take just 20 extra seconds and you could have the best-tasting cup of coffee ever. Right from your own kitchen.

According to coffee specialists, disposable filters affect the quality of your cup of joe. Make java the regular way and you may notice a papery taste. But if you rinse the filter with hot water before you brew, you'll get rid of that unpleasant flavor and warm up the coffee maker. Baristas do this all the time, and coffee experts say the improvement will be worth the extra seconds.

Adopt this method when brewing at home and you won't mind skipping your local coffee shop. Try it just two days a week and you could save around $400 a year.

## 6 ways to score local dining deals with the tap of a finger

Wouldn't it be nice if you could shop for restaurants online like you shop for shoes? The good news is resources are already all over the internet for the latest dining deals, steals, and comparisons. Don't miss these super sites for checking out all the discounts available in your area. Most have their own apps, so you can take your savings on-the-go.

**Restaurant.com** (*restaurant.com*). This savvy site allows you to search for the perfect restaurant and read reviews by past customers. Then select a certificate denomination — usually anywhere from $5 to $100 — which is basically a discounted gift card. For example, you can buy a $25 Partners Pizza gift card for just $10. That's a 60 percent savings! The restaurants often require minimum purchases, but your certificates never expire.

**SeniorDiscounts** (*seniordiscounts.com*). Pay less for everything — just because you're over 50. This website finds hidden deals at restaurants in your neighborhood, providing info like where to go to score savings and how old you have to be. Basic Registration, which is free, allows you to search their database of deals, but you can't always see specific details. Upgrade to Premium Membership for about $13 a year and get access to thousands of members-only discounts.

**OpenTable** (*opentable.com*). Available in larger cities, OpenTable helps you find restaurants and make reservations online. Become a registered member, and when you book a table through their website or through their mobile app, you earn Dining Points. Once you get a certain number of points, you can redeem them for an Amazon gift card or a Dining Rewards gift at any participating restaurant.

**Out to Eat with Kids** (*outtoeatwithkids.com*). "Load up your crew, eat great food, and save some money." That's what this resource promises with their database of more than 15,000 participating restaurants where kids eat free or at a discount. Search by city or ZIP code to find sweet deals within your area.

**Zagat** (*zagat.com*). This popular service allows you to search by location and food type, then compare ratings, reviews, and prices of restaurants in your area. You can filter results by how much you want to pay and what kind of service you're looking for.

**LocalEats** (*localeats.com*). Search for restaurants by cuisine or restaurant name. Then filter results based on price category, features, and awards, so you can get the best deals while still enjoying local hotspots.

## Save up to 50 percent at almost any restaurant

You can shave your bill in half and still check out the best restaurants in town with a simple tip most diners forget. Skip the dinner menu markups and save 25 to 50 percent wherever you go.

"If I do lunch at my favorite Chinese restaurant, I can get a combo meal that includes a main dish, soup, egg roll, rice, and crab rangoon for $6.50," says Kimberly Lewis. "If I pop in after the dinner menu starts, the main dish and rice will cost me $9.95."

No coupons necessary. By just going in for lunch instead of dinner, Kimberly saves 35 percent each visit. And lunch meals don't always have smaller portions. You may find out you're not missing anything — especially money in your wallet.

# The kitchen garden

## Save $1,200 with seeds and turn your garden into a grocery store

Who says you can't grow money? A study by Burpee Seed Company found just $50 invested in seeds and fertilizer can produce

$1,250 worth of groceries each year. Think about this. At the supermarket, a single pound of spinach will set you back $3.83. But for less than a dollar, you could buy seeds and grow up to 6 pounds of spinach. Check out these expert tips to learn how gardening from seed helps you cash in on crops.

**Planting seeds can be dirt cheap.** "These days, it's expensive to go out and buy your own transplants," says consumer horticulturist Robert Westerfield. The little plants you find at the store then transfer to your garden are easy to work with, but Westerfield warns, "You're paying sometimes a couple of dollars for a plant that you could have produced on your own for a few pennies."

**Go to seed for free.** The easiest way to get free seeds is to save some from a previous harvest. For best results, you want true-to-type seeds, or ones that will produce new plants exactly like their "parent." That means you should avoid gathering seeds from any hybrid plants you may have in your garden.

You can also snag seeds for next to nothing by participating in seed exchanges. Some are free and some require a membership fee. Contact local gardening clubs or organizations, or search online to find programs available in your area.

"Hybrids are crosses from one plant to another to get a certain color fruit or certain growth habit or disease resistance," says Melinda Myers, nationally known horticulture expert and host of TV and radio's "Melinda's Garden Moment." "When you save and grow from those seeds," she says, "you're not going to get exactly the same

**Start seeds right and watch your savings bloom.** "In general, most of the cucurbits — squash, cucumbers, melons, gourds, and pumpkins — are easy to grow by direct seeding," says

Westerfield. "You take the seeds at the proper time of year, plant them in the garden, and blooms are going to sprout and develop into a bearing plant."

However, solanaceous crops, like tomatoes, peppers, and egg-plants, grow best if you start seeds indoors about six weeks prior to the planting season, then transfer the sprouts to the garden. "Don't try to direct seed them," he explains, "because they are very susceptible to temperature changes as well as some soil diseases — things that cause them to fizzle before they ever get to size."

## Shop your backyard for high-priced produce

"I've seen bell peppers at the grocery store selling anywhere from $1 to $1.50 a piece," says Robert Westerfield, Horticulture Extension Coordinator for the University of Georgia. "But a pepper plant, even if you buy the transplant, costs about $2. By the time it's said and done — with nutrition, fertilization, and water — you've got about $8 in that plant." However he's quick to point out you won't get just one pepper from your plant, but as many as 50. "It's going to put out peppers as long as the plant's happy," he says. That's up to $75 worth of peppers from your $8 plant — quite an impressive payback.

"Just about any herb you can think of will be expensive to buy in stores, but relatively economical to grow at home," adds horticulture educator Jennifer Nelson. Of course, not all home-grown foods save you loads of money. Vegetables like potatoes, cabbage, and onions are already pretty cheap at the supermarket. But check out the savings you can sprout by growing pricey produce like tomatoes, squash, leafy greens, peppers, green beans, and berries.

# Pricey produce you can grow dirt cheap

**Beefsteak tomatoes**

**Summer squash**

**Store price:** $3.16/lb
**Grow your own:** One plant can produce up to 20 pounds of fruit, but will cost just pennies if you start from seed.

**Store price:** $1.64/lb
**Grow your own:** Buy 100 seeds for $4, and pick fresh squash every 1-2 days during harvest season.

**Romaine Lettuce**

**Bell peppers**

**Store price:** $1.84/lb
**Grow your own:** Buy 250 seeds for $3, and harvest until the weather gets too hot.

**Store price:** $2.06/lb
**Grow your own:** You could get $75 worth of peppers from a $2 plant.

**Green beans**

**Raspberries**

**Store price:** $2.14/lb
**Grow your own:** Start from seed and harvest about 6 pounds of beans for under $1.

**Store price:** $6.98/lb
**Grow your own:** Buy a plant for $14, and get 1.5 quarts of fruit every year for up to 12 years.

**Blackberries**

**Blueberries**

**Store price:** $5.77/lb
**Grow your own:** Buy a plant for $15, and pick fruit every 2-4 days during harvest season for 12 years.

**Store price:** $4.73/lb
**Grow your own:** One plant costs about $14 and yields 4-6 quarts of fresh blueberries for 20-30 years.

## Perennial power: buy once, harvest every year

Every backyard gardener bears the same burden — year after year, you have to start all over again. Wouldn't it be nice if your vegetables came back each season like your perennial flowers? Well, the word perennial doesn't just refer to pretty blooms. You can grow vegetables, fruits, and herbs that make a comeback every year. Gardening expert Melinda Myers shares the best part of growing perennials. "Once established," she says, "you've got decades of harvest without investing in more plants, just weeding and maintenance." That means less time and money you have to put into your garden and more tasty treats you get to harvest.

**Grow $40 of this crowd favorite every year.** One of the most popular perennials is asparagus. "If you grow them properly and cultivate good beds, asparagus plants can last 20 to 30 years," says consumer horticulturist Robert Westerfield. Still, he's quick to remind that, in most cases, asparagus plants take two years to start producing. "The first year, you let all the energy go back into the plant, and it's from the second year on that you can begin the harvest."

This is a real money-saver, since fresh asparagus might cost $3.21 a pound at the supermarket. Buy 25 plants for $16.95 and, once they start producing, you could get more than 12 pounds, or about $40 worth of asparagus every year. Over the lifetime of your plants, that adds up to at least $1,100 you get to trim off your grocery bill.

**Plant pleasing perennials for a garden that keeps on giving.** Like all produce, your success with perennials will depend on where you live. Check out these popular plants that will return every season for years to come, and see if you can grow them in your gardening zone.

- Veggies: Jerusalem artichokes, scarlet runner beans, radicchio, rhubarb

- Herbs: shallots, garlic chives, bronze fennel, German thyme, sorrel, spearmint

- Fruits: blackberries, blueberries, strawberries, raspberries

- Fruit trees: apples, peaches, plums, pears

## Small space, big harvest — 4 ways to get more out of your garden

Don't let a tiny growing space cramp your garden plans. While fancy trellises and vertical garden towers will make more room for your favorite veggies, they usually come with a hefty price tag. Save more green by following these low-cost tips to produce a generous harvest while keeping your plants in tip-top shape.

**Prevent plant problems with perfect partners.** You may have heard you should plant tomatoes with basil, asparagus, or marigolds. But do you know why? Companion plants like these may help neighbors thrive, particularly by keeping away pests. Plus, some gardeners say placing basil near tomatoes, for instance, just makes the fruit more tasty since the two plants share nutrients.

Science has yet to weigh in, but some gardeners swear by combos like squash and nasturtiums, mint and cabbage, onions with lettuce, and summer savory alongside beans.

**Grow more greens every single season.** Save space, produce more, and harvest a greater variety by growing one crop right after the other — all in the same season. It's called succession planting, and gardeners have been doing it for years.

"I'm a huge believer in succession planting," says Melinda Myers, author and host of The Great Courses series "How to Grow Anything: Food Gardening for Everyone." She explains,

"Start out the season with cool season crops, like lettuce. When the heat hits, you plant beans or cucumbers. When those are done, and the cool weather's back, you throw in some radishes — something short-season. Depending on where you live, you might get two or three crops out of one row."

**Double your space, slash your weeding time.** You can also get more out of your garden space by using a technique called interplanting. The trick is to find two different vegetables that can be planted close together without interfering with each other's growth. For example, speedy growers like radishes, lettuce, spinach, and beets can shade the ground and prevent weeds while they grow. So if you plant them among slower growers like broccoli, carrots, cabbages, and corn, they help keep the soil weed-free until the slow growers appear.

"By the time you're ready to harvest that short-season crop, the big plants are going to fill in that space," says Myers. "You've grown something where you might have grown weeds instead. You get two harvests. It's just a great way to maximize your space."

**Keep plants superbly healthy and robust for cheap.** It sounds simple, but you need to make sure your plants have enough nutrients throughout the growing season.

Tomatoes, for example, need consistent water and calcium. Without these, they can crack and develop blossom end rot. Myers says to water thoroughly to encourage good, deep roots and reduce any moisture imbalance that can lead to a calcium deficiency. Some gardeners also add clean crushed eggshells to the soil for extra calcium to help prevent blossom end rot. And that won't cost you a single penny.

## Reap more benefits with raised beds

"Raised beds don't have to be expensive," says consumer horticulturist Robert Westerfield, who has taught many programs on the subject. People balk at the idea when they consider the price tag — you could easily spend over $100 on a raised bed kit. But you don't need to splurge on pricey materials or pre-made sets. In fact, you can purchase low-cost supplies at your local home improvement store and build a 4-foot by 4-foot raised bed for under $20.

And think of it as a long-term investment. "When you build a raised bed," Westerfield says, "you're looking at getting 10 to 12 years out of it." That means your expenses come out to just $2 or less a year.

Even if you do end up investing a little more in your raised beds, these elevated plots have many benefits that outweigh the initial cost of getting your garden off the ground.

- They make planting simple and weeding easier. "With raised beds, a couple of hand tools is about all you need for maintenance," says Westerfield. Plus, they're convenient for gardeners who have a hard time getting around.

- "By bringing your garden off the ground, you've improved the drainage," he adds. In places where waterlogged roots are common, raised beds can literally save your crops.

- Get a head start on the season, and grow more produce. "The soil in a raised bed typically warms up quicker," Westerfield explains, "so you can get the crop in the ground a little bit sooner."

# Today's tech at yesterday's prices

# Cellphones and Carriers

## 'Unlock' the secret to cellphone savings

Raise your hand if you've signed yet another two-year contract with your cellphone carrier. Yep, they'll get you every time. But there's a way to avoid signing on the dotted line that can actually cut your cellphone bill in half. It's a simple solution to saving money your service provider won't suggest.

What's the secret? Getting an unlocked phone and shopping around for an alternative carrier. A locked phone has software on it that only allows you to use it with a specific carrier. An unlocked phone is one you can use with other carriers. When you sign up to pay off a phone with a two-year contract, odds are you have one that's locked.

What cellphone companies don't want you to know is that more and more phone manufacturers are selling reasonably priced, unlocked phones directly to the public. Google, for instance, sells unlocked Nexus phones for $350, and OnePlus offers the remarkable OnePlus One for $300.

Of course, you have to buy them up front instead of making payments, so it may seem like a lot of money. But whether you realize it or not, you're paying that much or more when you stretch payments out over two years. You'll save money in the long run because you can shop around for the data plan and rate you want. Plus you can change carriers anytime you want.

"My wife and I were paying nearly $150 a month for two phones on a big network," says Grayson Bell, founder of the blog Debtroundup.com. "After our contract ended, the last one we've had, we moved to Straight Talk Wireless, which cut our bill in half. We then tested out Walmart Family Mobile, Cricket Wireless, and now Republic Wireless.

"Now we pay $55 a month for our two phones," he says. "The key is making sure you have an unlocked phone that can be used on different carriers."

When you start shopping for a new service provider, Bell suggests pitting carriers against each other. "Don't forget to include the smaller carriers that just resell service. They typically can give you a much better rate while still using the same network."

Here's a look at a few smaller carriers and their basic plans.

| Carrier | Talk/text | Data | Network | Price per |
|---|---|---|---|---|
| Cricket | Unlimited | 2.5 GB | AT&T | $40 ($35 with auto pay) |
| Freedom Pop | 200 minutes/ 500 texts | 500 MB | Sprint | Free |
| Metro PCS | Unlimited | Unlimited | T-Mobile | $30 |
| Republic | Unlimited | 1 GB | Sprint (when Wi-Fi not available) | $25 |
| StraightTalk | 1500 minutes/ unlimited texts | 100 MB (50% more data with auto-refill) | Sprint, AT&T, T-Mobile, Verizon | $30 |
| Walmart Family Mobile | Unlimited | Unlimited | T-Mobile | $30 |

If you have a phone you love and want to keep, all is not lost. Once your contract ends, ask your current carrier about unlocking your phone. As long as you meet the company's requirements, they should share a code with you to unlock it.

Check to make sure your phone will work with your favorite low-cost carrier's network. If so, simply pop in a new subscriber identification module — known as a SIM card — and you'll be in business.

## 3 new and improved ways to keep in touch — and they're all free

Phone calls are so last year. Video chats make it easy for you to see your loved ones while catching up on the latest. Try these three free chat apps on your smartphone, tablet, or computer, and say hello to the 21st century.

- Google Hangouts. Lets you make video calls with up to nine people. You can also share photos, call phone numbers, and send text messages. You need a Google account and the latest version of the Hangouts plug-in installed on your device.

- Skype. Make one-on-one or group video calls. You can also send video messages and share your computer screen with the person you're talking to. Visit *skype.com* to download.

- FaceTime. Comes already loaded on iPhones, iPads, and Macs. Lets you switch from a phone conversation to a video chat in the middle of a call simply by tapping the FaceTime icon.

## 5 ways to slash the cost of your next cellphone

Albert Einstein once said, "The definition of insanity is doing something over and over and expecting a different result." Take buying a cellphone, for instance. You want to save money, but you get sucked into your carrier's latest promotion every time.

It's time to stop the cycle and slash the cost of your next cellphone with these tips.

**Buy your cellphone used and unlocked.** That's the best way to save on cellphones, says Grayson Bell, founder of the blog Debtroundup.com. You can find deals on eBay and Amazon, but buying from individuals could be risky.

Bell recommends websites dedicated to buying and reselling electronics. "Sites like Gazelle are great for used phones that work," he says.

**Don't finance the trendiest phone with a two-year contract.** "One of the biggest mistakes is to finance a phone in order to get the latest and greatest," says Bell. "These finance plans tend to be costly, and you can end up paying way more than the phone is worth.

"On top of paying more," he says, "many don't realize you have to pay the remaining balance if you want to leave the carrier. This can lead to some sticker shock."

**Go for a model from a previous generation.** "Just like a car, don't buy the newest phone," Bell advises. "Find an older model and save upwards of 40 percent. This is especially true when a new phone model comes out. Retailers will discount the older model to get them off the shelves."

**Look for certified preowned phones.** Before a phone is classified as "certified preowned," it gets a thorough checkup. T-Mobile makes sure you know that with a humorous note on its website. "To be called T-Mobile Certified, each device must pass a rigorous and thorough exam — and we do not grade on a curve."

These deals can save you $100 or more. T-Mobile lists a certified Samsung Galaxy Note Edge for $370, while a new one costs $550. And a certified Samsung Galaxy S6 lists for $480 compared to a new one at $580.

**Ask your carrier about trade-in programs.** They may buy back your old phone, and you can put the money or credit toward the purchase of your next phone.

Just remember when you're dealing with a major carrier, they may try to sell you a new phone and a contract. If they do, here's your go-to response — "don't call us, we'll call you."

## Never face a shocking cellphone bill again

That moment when you open your cellphone bill and see it's hundreds of dollars higher than usual. After you pull yourself up off the floor, you look over your bill and realize your costly mistakes — you went over your plan's data limits, plus you roamed outside your network. Here's how to head off those problems so you never face astronomical charges again.

**Watch your location to avoid roaming.** Roaming fees kick in whenever you travel outside your cell provider's service area. Even if you turn off data roaming in your phone's settings, you may still find yourself in trouble because of apps running in the background. Here's how to play it safe before you leave for that fabulous trip to Europe.

- Call your wireless provider and ask them how to disable international data roaming. Or ask if they have an international calling plan. Some companies offer special discounts for calls made during overseas travel.

- Turn off cellular data in your phone's setting. And while you're at it, turn off special features like location services, push notifications, and background app refresh.

- Sign up for Skype or the Google Voice app. Then switch your smartphone to airplane mode to disable its text and data. You'll still be able to make and receive calls with Skype or Google Voice when you're connected to Wi-Fi.

- Get a special subscriber identification module (SIM) card for your phone with prepaid minutes for the country to which you're traveling. You can get one for as low as $20. Check with your carrier to be sure you have an unlocked phone that will work on the GSM network.

- Make sure your wireless carrier is set to send you automatic usage alerts if you're traveling abroad and don't have an international plan. The major providers have agreed to do this for free per an agreement with the Federal Communications Commission (FCC).

- Take a break and leave your phone at home. After all, you're on vacation.

**Adjust your settings to escape overage fees.** Spent too much time listening to Pandora on your phone? Spend five minutes making these adjustments, and you should never go over your data limits again.

- On Android — go to Settings then Data Usage to set limits. Also, tap "Alert me about data usage" to get advance warning before you go over.

- On iPhone — go to Settings, then Cellular, and scroll to the bottom. Make sure you reset the counter at the beginning or end of each billing period by tapping Reset Statistics. Then check your usage periodically to see when you're getting close to your limit.

- Ask your carrier to send you an alert when you're about to reach your data limit. Most will give you a heads up when you've reached 75 percent and 90 percent of your usage. In

Save up to $10 a month on your phone service with Lifeline, a program for low-income residents. If you participate in programs like Medicaid or Federal Public Housing Assistance, you may qualify for Lifeline. Contact your landline or cellphone company to apply, or visit *lifelinesupport.org* for more information.

fact, your carrier should alert you automatically and for free thanks to an agreement with the FCC.

- Get an app like My Data Manager for iPhone or Android. Not only will this handy app keep track of your data, it will manage data usage across multiple devices including anyone on your shared plan. Plus it will let you know which of your apps uses the most data.

Now that you've taken care of stamping out future charges, what can you do about your current bill? Call your carrier and negotiate. Many will work with you to help slash those extra fees.

## Talk is cheap with these home phone plans

If you're paying more than $15 a month for your home phone, you're paying too much. Switch gears to Voice over Internet Protocol (VoIP) and you'll save a bundle. It's the new way to talk with friends and family all over the country via your high-speed internet connection.

|  | Ooma | MagicJack | Vonage |
|---|---|---|---|
| Setup | Ooma Telo device, $99.99 | MagicJack device, $39.95 | free |
| Annual cost | $0 | $0 first year, then $35 ($99.75 for 5-year plan) | $120 ($9.99/month) |
| Minutes per month | 5,000 outgoing | unlimited | 300 outgoing, unlimited incoming |
| Current number | keep for one-time fee of $39.99 | keep for one-time fee of $19.95 | free |
| New number | free | free | free |
| Website | www.ooma.com | www.magicjack.com | www.vonage.com |

*Federal fees, plus state and local taxes, are not included in pricing.*

# Computers and Tablets

## Surprising way to find the best computer deals

Every now and then, a computer dies. After you've said your good-byes and laid it to rest, you're tempted to run to your local big-box store and replace it with a newer, shinier model. Don't do it! You'll spend way more than you need to.

Here's how to pay the rock bottom price on everything you buy, including electronics. It's easier than you think.

Many popular manufacturers have outlet or clearance websites for everything from refurbished computers to scratch-and-dent tablets. These labels may sound scary, but when you buy directly from the manufacturer, you get a device that's undergone rigorous testing.

Hewlett-Packard's website says its refurbished products can't be distinguished from the new ones, except for possible blemishes or scratches. And Lenovo states their products are certified to meet Lenovo's new-product specifications, and any cosmetic wear and tear will not affect performance or quality.

Not convinced? Then check these sites for brand-new, discounted devices. Dell has a clearance section on its website with new merchandise slashed by $100 to $250 from its original prices.

Other perks include free shipping from Apple and Lenovo, and limited warranties like Apple's one-year and Dell's 100-day coverage.

Just take a peek at a few of the deals you can snag and where to find them.

| | Apple | Dell | Hewlett-Packard | Lenovo |
|---|---|---|---|---|
| **Website** | apple.com, search for "refurbished products" | dellrefurbished.com | hp.com, search for "refurbished products" | www3.lenovo.com |
| **Product example** | Refurbished 13.3-inch MacBook Air | 14-inch Dell Latitude E5430 | EliteBook Folio 9480m | ThinkPad Helix |
| **Retail price** | $1,099 | Clearance price $359 | $1,199 | $1,933 |
| **% off retail** | 15%+ | 25% to 40% off clearance prices | 25% to 50% off | 25% to 35% |
| **Discounted price** | $929 | $252 | $617 | $649 |
| **Savings** | $170 | $107 | $582 | $1,284 |

## Don't pay another penny for software programs — use these for free

Some of the best things in life are free — and they're just a few clicks away on your computer. So if you're tempted to buy a software program at your office supply store, tap into these free apps and programs first. They may meet your needs and save you hundreds of dollars.

**Enjoy top-rated word processing programs.** You could spend from $50 to $200 on word processing software, but why bother when you can access these exceptional programs that don't cost a cent.

- Pages. Mac computers come preloaded with this program that helps you create documents, flyers, newsletters, tables, and bar graphs.

- TextEdit and Notes. These Mac apps are great for making quick lists, saving website links, dragging in files like photos and videos, creating folders and checklists, and saving directions from your Maps app. Both apps store everything to the cloud so you can access them from multiple devices.

- Microsoft Word. You may get a free trial of Word on a new Windows computer, but after the trial is over you'll have to pay for it. Instead, sign up for Office Online and tap into a free version of Word for documents, newsletters, resumes, and flyers. The only catch is that your documents will reside on the cloud, so you'll always need an internet connection to access them. The plus side is you can start a document on your home computer, work on it at the office, and finish it on your tablet at your favorite coffee shop. Plus you can invite others to work on your document in real time.

- Google Docs. This online word processor lets you create text documents, collaborate with other people in real time, review previous versions, and translate them into 100 different languages. You'll need a Google account to get started.

- Jarte and OpenOffice. Jarte is an easy-to-use program based on Microsoft Wordpad. OpenOffice is a free software suite that includes word processing and works on all computers. Check them out at *jarte.com* and *openoffice.org*.

**Take advantage of fee-free spreadsheets.** Spreadsheet programs can also cost you a pretty penny, ranging in price from $20 to $300 or more. Try these and you'll never have to pull out your wallet.

- Excel. Sign up for Office Online to get the web version. Use it for accounting, billing, budgeting, and tracking, plus working with others on a project in real time.

- Numbers. If you've got a Mac, try this spreadsheet program for personal or business computing and for creating colorful graphs and tables to illustrate your data.

- Sheets. Google's spreadsheet app offers some of the same features as Excel and Numbers. It's free with your Google account.

**Fill your calendar without emptying your wallet.** Are you still using a day planner, the kind you write in and lug everywhere you go? When you're ready to throw it out and join the digital age, you'll find time management programs starting at $10. That's not much, but better yet, play around with these cheap dates.

- Mac's Calendar app. Add events and locations to your heart's content. Calendar connects to your map and email apps, sends you reminders via the alerts feature, and shares events with other users.

- Office Online's Calendar or Google Calendar. PC users can stay on schedule with these apps. Both calendars sync with your email accounts, send you reminders, and allow other users to share your calendar.

**Freebie ways to fix and frame your photos.** Unless you're a serious photographer, you don't need to spend hundreds of dollars on photo software.

- Apple's Photos app lets you organize your pictures and create photo books, cards, calendars, prints, slideshows, and albums.

- Most PCs come with a photo program built in, like Lenovo's Photo Master 2.0, which makes editing and organizing a breeze.

- Google's Photos app lets you access shared albums, movies, and videos. It also comes with built-in facial recognition to help you identify your subjects, and a location finder to help you remember where you snapped your shots. Feeling a little artsy? Google Photos serves up ways to create collages and short animation videos.

---

### Secret to saving up to 75 percent off your next computer

If you're on the hunt for the best tablet or computer deal, check out these websites, too.

Newegg.com and TigerDirect.com sell refurbished devices for up to 75 percent off. Plus, Newegg features dozens of daily deals online while TigerDirect emails a daily deals flyer, loaded with new and used merchandise.

Apple reseller MacMall.com offers both new and refurbished Macs for $100 to $240 below retail as well as iPads for $5 to $100 less. Gazelle.com is best known for buying used electronics and reselling them at a discount. You'll find certified pre-owned iPads and MacBooks there at a savings of $40 and up.

One last site to consider is Rakuten.com, which boasts a large array of new and reconditioned devices for discounted prices. Just make sure you get one that can support the current operating system.

## Learn the ink-onomics of printing and save

Fine champagne. Expensive perfume. Luxury items like those are probably way out of your price range. Yet you wouldn't think twice about buying pricey inkjet cartridges for your printer. And that ink can cost up to a whopping $75 an ounce, says *Consumer Reports* — way more than those luxuries you only dream of buying.

You can buy a brand new inkjet printer for less — and that's the idea. Companies sell printers cheap because they know they'll make more money off the ink you'll buy over their lifetime. Beat them at their own game with these tips to print more for less money.

**Extend the life of your cartridge.** You just spent an arm and a leg to replace your ink cartridge, and it's already low. Head for your bathroom — yes, your bathroom! — for an easy way to give ink a second life.

The secret weapon is your hairdryer. Take out the ink cartridge, and hold the dryer over the nozzle on low for about two minutes. You could get months more ink out of the cartridge just by doing this one time. Try printing while the cartridge is still warm to see how well it works.

Another tip — don't believe your printer when it says it's low on ink. The cartridge could still be as much as 30 percent full. Keep on printing until you see the ink fading.

Get the coolest "print anywhere, from any device" service. It's free and takes less than five minutes to set up. All you need is a web-connected printer and a Google account. Sign in and search for Google Cloud Print. Once it's set up, you can print to that printer from anywhere in the world.

**Print smarter and use less ink.** The font you use to print makes a difference. Some standard fonts, such as Garamond, use less ink simply because they print smaller. If you want to save 20 to 50 percent on ink, invest in Ecofont software that prints your words in standard fonts with tiny holes. Don't want to spend the money? Set your printer to print at lower quality, and consider printing in draft mode, too.

**Seek out deals on ink.** Brand-name ink cartridges cost a fortune, but is it worth it to buy refurbished ones? Refilled ink cartridges can work just as well in many cases, for less.

For instance, HP brand 61 xl black cartridges sell for about $36 on Amazon, but LxTek sells a remanufactured one for about a third of the cost. Read reviews before you buy, and ask questions of the vendors if possible, because not all refurbs are created equal.

**Get rewarded for recycling.** When you've wrung all the ink you can out of your ink cartridge, don't toss it in the trash. Some big-box stores will reward you for bringing in your used cartridges.

If you spend $30 on ink at Staples, for example, you'll get $2 back for each cartridge you return, up to 10 per month. At Office Max/Office Depot, you'll get 200 reward points for each cartridge you recycle after spending $10 on any purchase that month. When you reach 1,000 points, they award you a $10 certificate. Every little bit helps!

**Buy a more efficient printer.** Cheap printers are a dime a dozen, but if you want to save on ink, maybe it's time to consider a top-of-the-line machine. The Epson EcoTank printer starts at $279.99 at Staples and comes with two years' worth of ink, assuming you print about 300 pages a month. The cost of refilling the tanks ranges from $13 for color bottles to about $20 for black, and each prints up to 6,500 pages.

Print only on occasion and only in black? A laser printer may be the way to go. You can get a monochrome laser printer for as little as $80. Replacing a high-yield toner cartridge may cost you almost as much, but it will print 2,600 pages at a cost of 2 cents per page.

# Internet service

## 7 amazingly easy ways to tap into free Wi-Fi

Tired of paying the high price of Wi-Fi? Pay no more. Here's a look at how and where you can get Wi-Fi for absolutely nothing.

**Rediscover dial-up.** NetZero has the plan for you if you only check your email and browse the web occasionally. The free dial-up plan offers 10 hours of internet access. You only pay your telephone company's monthly charges.

You can either use your own device like a phone or tablet or order one of theirs, like a NetZero 3G stick for $14.98 or a 4G LTE Hotspot for $39.95.

Sure, dial-up is slower than high-speed internet, but if you're a casual browser and have the patience of Job, why not try it for free?

**Find free Wi-Fi on the go.** Before you hit the road, check the website *wififreespot.com* for a listing of free hotspots at hotels, motels, and mom and pop shops en route and at your travel destination.

The website also lists airports, RV parks and campgrounds, and vacation rental properties with free Wi-Fi. Keep in mind that discount bus companies like Megabus and Boltbus offer free Wi-Fi, as does Greyhound on limited routes.

**Pinpoint a park with perks.** Communities like Santa Monica in California now offer a host of free hotspots at places like Palisades Park and the Third Street Promenade. As more cities jump on the bandwagon, don't be surprised to find hotspots at local parks, community centers, and shopping strips near you.

**Mix business with pleasure.** When Annie works out, she connects her smartphone to her fitness center's free Wi-Fi so she can listen to her Pandora stations. Smart move.

"I like to listen to about 30 to 40 minutes of music on my iPhone while I work out," she says. "Using the gym's free internet connection keeps me from using up my data."

Then, when she stops at her favorite supermarket, Annie taps into the free Wi-Fi there so she can get a head start on dinner. "I like to look up recipes while shopping," she says.

Chances are the places you love to hang out probably have free Wi-Fi, too. Ask before you start using up your data.

**Let an app find it for you.** Yes, there's an app for that. In fact, multiple apps. WiFi Map shows you where to find a free connection in more than 5 million hotspots around the world. Users share passwords and add comments about their experiences at each locale.

The app Wefi let's your phone automatically find and hook up to the strongest free network available. Both apps are available for iPhone and Android.

**Visit your local library.** It's not just a storeroom for great books. Stroll into your local library, and you're likely to find the password for free Wi-Fi posted on a wall. And if it's not, just ask a librarian. They know everything!

**Connect with your cable company.** If you get home internet through a cable company, you may be able to connect to your provider's free internet around town.

Search your cable company's website, and look for a map of hotspots with instructions on how to access them. Or see if your internet company has an app like Time Warner Cable's TWC WiFi Finder.

## Simple way to pocket up to $100 a year

Pesky fees — your internet bill is loaded with them. But there's one fee you can stop paying once and for all. Simply buy your own modem.

That's what Wes did. He paid $70 for his new device and cut out his $7-a-month rental fee. The modem paid for itself in less than a year.

"I bought mine at Best Buy, but they're available at electronic stores and online," he says. "I looked at reviews to help make my decision."

If you go this route, check your bill carefully. Some cable companies drop your rental fee but then add an "internet gateway fee" to your monthly bill.

If one of these crops up on your statement, challenge your provider. They should remove it. If they don't, you may have to invest in a router for $30 to $40 to avoid the extra charge.

# Network and Cable TV

### Stream on: ditch cable and stash loads of cash

Cord cutting. It's all the rage. And, no, you don't literally take scissors to your electrical cords. This is about severing ties with your cable company or your satellite dish. Costs for both keep going up and up. But switch to a streaming plan, and you could be on your way to snipping your bill in half. No wonder it's so trendy. Here's what one man did to slash his viewing tab by over $700 a year.

Tech-savvy consumer Wes got fed up with paying over $90 a month for what he calls a "middle-of-the-road" package from his satellite company. That was more than $1,000 a year to basically watch HGTV and "The Big Bang Theory." So he decided to check out online streaming, a service that allows you to watch television programming over the internet, instead of paying for a cable or satellite package. Simply pick a service based on your preferences.

**Sling TV.** Wes read about Sling, and one phone call later, started getting 20 channels for 20 bucks — including HGTV, AMC, CNN, TBS, and ESPN. For an extra $5 a month, he added a kids package for his two daughters.

Sling offers other pricing tiers — think more channels, more options — as well as different add-on packages like Sports Extra and Lifestyle Extra. If you're into premium channels, $10 more a month gets you Cinemax, and for $15 a month you can stream HBO. Call Sling for more information at 888-291-5217 or find them online at *sling.com*.

Making the switch saved Wes $780 a year. "I was really happy with it," he says, "until I discovered PlayStation Vue."

**PlayStation Vue.** Don't let the word "PlayStation" turn you off if you're not a gamer. This entertainment powerhouse offers their live streaming service on a month-to-month basis with no contract. Now Wes uses a PlayStation 4 and an Amazon Fire TV to stream Vue, but you could also use Google Chromecast, a PlayStation 3, Roku, iPhone, iPad, or Apple TV.

Their introductory package has over 55 channels for just $29.99 a month. That's more than you'll pay for basic Sling, but you get almost triple the number of channels. Plus, PlayStation Vue offers premium channels like Showtime for a standalone fee of $10.99 a month or added to a package for $8.99 a month.

Want even more channels? Check out Vue's Core Slim package with 70 channels for $34.99 or Elite Slim with 100 channels for $44.99. Note that pricing and channels may vary by ZIP code.

"PlayStation Vue is great for someone who does a lot of TV watching and needs lots of channels," says Wes. Get all your questions answered online at *playstation.com*.

Finally, don't forget about Netflix, Hulu, and Amazon Prime Video, especially if you're a movie lover. They are perfect for streaming movies and original series plus TV shows and full seasons of your favorites.

---

### What your gaming device can do — for free

You may already own a Microsoft Xbox or Sony PlayStation (PS), but only pull it out when the grandkids come to town. If so, you're missing out on a great entertainment option. Did you know these consoles do more than just support video games? They can stream your favorite TV shows, classic movies, and even new releases, through dozens of video service apps like Netflix, Amazon Video, and Hulu.

Don't race out to the store if there's not a game system in your closet, however. New consoles can be pricey — anywhere from $200 to $500. Go for a refurbished or preowned unit, which will set you back only about $180.

---

## Get instant entertainment without spending a dime

Internet streaming services you pay for, like Netflix, may offer a wide range of choices. But before you pile on the subscriptions, take a quick peek at these free online options for watching movies and more:

- Crackle (*crackle.com*)

- Popcornflix (*popcornflix.com*)

- Snagfilms (*snagfilms.com*)

- tubitv (*tubitv.com*)

These may not have as much variety as the paid services, but if you're looking for a quick fix, they'll do the trick.

And don't forget about network websites like *abc.go.com*, *nbc.com*, *cwtv.com*, and *cbs.com*. You probably won't find entire seasons of TV shows, but if you miss an episode, you can often watch it on the website within a few days. Some even allow you to view broadcasts live, depending on your location. Here's the catch though. Not all networks have apps that will stream to your TV, so you might have to watch on your tablet or computer. But hey, you can't argue with free.

| The low price of streaming (it's cheaper than you think) | | |
|---|---|---|
| Ready to start streaming? You're going to need a streaming device. They come in all shapes and sizes, and prices start as low as $35. Take a look at these popular devices and their best movie and television apps. | | |
| Apple TV (3rd generation) | $69.00 | Netflix<br>Hulu Plus<br>YouTube |
| Amazon Fire TV Stick | $39.99 | Netflix<br>Hulu<br>Amazon Video |
| Roku Stick | $39.99 | Netflix<br>Hulu<br>Amazon Video |
| Google Chromecast | $35.00 | Netflix<br>Hulu<br>YouTube |
| Streaming Blu-ray Player | $59.99 and up | Apps vary by device |

## Trim $200 a year off your cable bill

Here's a secret your cable company won't let you in on. You don't have to pay every month to rent their set-top boxes. Instead, purchase your own.

A high-definition, recording (HD-DVR) cable box sells for about $175. Compare that to the $232 most households spend a year just on cable-box rental fees, and you can see how fast this purchase pays for itself. Shop for one online or at your local electronics store.

You'll want a box that is CableCARD-ready or -compatible, which means it needs a credit card-size device called a cableCARD to access your channels. Your cable provider will either give you one or charge a very small monthly fee for it — most likely a couple of dollars. The Federal Communications Commission (FCC) says your cable company must provide one along with instructions on how to install it.

## The return of the rabbit ears: home antennas save you money

You hear the word "antenna," and probably think of those fiddly rabbit ears people used to place strategically around the house. But antennas have received a major upgrade since those days. Now young money-savers, like roommates Maureen and Suzi, are kicking cable to the curb and switching to this much cheaper option.

How much cheaper? The women bought their antenna for only $30 from Amazon, although you could pay as much as $100. "We just looked for something that didn't cost a lot," says Maureen. The flat, square antenna attaches to the wall behind their TV and picks up about 15 stations.

"We like it because we can watch all our local channels," she says. In fact, you'll be amazed at what you can pick up on today's small but high-powered antennas. You get most of the big broadcast channels such as ABC, NBC, CBS, Fox, CW, and PBS, plus independent channels. Your location determines if you're a good candidate, however. Go online to *tvfool.com* and enter your address. The website will let you know which channels you're likely to receive.

Streaming isn't for everyone. If you want to keep your cable service but pay less, try a chat session via the company's website. That's what Annie did. She told her cable company's customer service rep her bill was too high. So they knocked off $15 a month and didn't change her plan.

To round out their viewing experience, the roommates invested in an Apple TV. "We use it to stream movies and other TV shows through our subscriptions to Netflix and Hulu," says Maureen.

Their bottom line? They went from paying $75 a month for cable and internet, to paying $45 for internet only. That's a savings of $360 a year.

## 5 places to rent DVDs for next to nothing

Your taxes paid for it — use it! One of the most neglected public resources is loaded with benefits. It's your public library, and many are chock-full of classic movies, documentaries, and even new releases.

Can't find what you're looking for? Then check into other low-cost sources. They offer affordable plans for those of you who like to rent an actual DVD and slip it into your player.

| Redbox | • 35,000 locations nationwide<br>• $1.50/night rentals (plus tax in some places)<br>• Sign up for weekly deal and coupons<br>• Play Pass rewards program<br>• New releases available immediately |
|---|---|
| Netflix | • Reserve online, receive by mail<br>• Plans start at $4.99/month<br>• Keep as long as you want<br>• First month free<br>• Free shipping<br>• Cancel anytime |
| Public library | • Need library card<br>• Free for one to two weeks<br>• Classic movies, documentaries<br>• Some newer titles<br>• Reserve online |
| Local DVD stores | • Limited locations<br>• Movies as low as 99¢/night<br>• New releases available |
| 3D-BlurayRental.com | • Rents 2D and 3D Blu-ray discs<br>• Reserve online, receive by mail<br>• Plans start at $6.99/month<br>• Pay-per-rental option, $3.99+ for 7 days<br>• Must have Blu-ray player |

## The 'ultra' cool way to watch your favorite flicks anytime, anywhere

Don't you hate it when you buy a DVD but can only view it at home? Well, a new kind of movie watching has come to town, and everyone is giving it a warm Hollywood welcome. It's called Ultra-Violet. And though it's ultramodern, the concept is pretty simple.

**Go digital, go mobile.** When you buy DVDs and Blu-ray Discs with the UltraViolet logo on the box, you also get a redemption code inside for a digital copy of your purchase. Create an Ultra-Violet account at *myuv.com*, then use the code to add the movie or show to your account — at no extra charge. UltraViolet stores all your digital copies in the cloud, so you can watch them anywhere and at any time.

Now say you want to watch your movie on your favorite device, like your tablet or iPad. You will need to sign up for a streaming service that works with UltraViolet, such as Flixster, Vudu, or CinemaNow. You may end up using more than one because not all services are supported on all devices. It's easier than it sounds to manage several accounts, since you can link them and use just one password.

The downside is UltraViolet is not available for all movies and shows. Some studios and distributors, including Disney, don't currently support UltraViolet. That means some of your DVDs will have to wait.

**It's time to kick the disc habit.** Here's an UltraViolet added bonus — you can eliminate purchasing a hard copy of the DVD entirely, and just buy the redemption code at *myuv.com*.

**Convert your library without spending a fortune.** So now, what to do with the hoards of DVDs you already have? Don't worry, you don't have to buy new digital copies. Use a disc-to-digital service like Vudu to convert them. Do it yourself by going online to *vudu.com* or, for the technically challenged, Vudu has partnered with Walmart to make the process more convenient. There's a small fee per disc, but you can often get a bulk discount.

# Home theater

**Think 'inside' the box to save on home entertainment**

They're like puzzle pieces — all the components you need to create a killer home entertainment system. The problem is, you don't even know where to start or how to put them all together. And what about a budget?

Rest easy. A home theater-in-a-box (HTIB) may be just what you need to deliver that movie theater experience in the comfort of your own home.

**What's in the box?** Starting at $200, HTIBs are an affordable way to take the guesswork out of putting together a system from scratch. They come jampacked with these components.

- at least five speakers, three for the front of your room and two surround-sound channels for the back

- subwoofer for deep bass and low-frequency sounds

- cables, some with color-coded ends to match their plug-in points on a receiver

- audio/visual receiver

- CD/DVD player, a DVD recorder, or a Blu-ray disc player, included in some packages

**What to look for?** Stick with a basic setup and avoid high-end systems, suggest tech experts. Extra features usually mean more money, and if you don't need them or don't know what they do, you could be throwing away cash.

Consider these features instead. If you want a gratifying visual experience, upgrade your television to the best high-definition flat-screen TV (HDTV) you can afford.

On the other hand, if you'd rather hear every sound effect clearly or enjoy your music collection, then look for an HTIB with highly rated speakers.

**What's the catch?** An HTIB sounds great for the money-conscious, non-techie consumer. But prepackaged systems have one major problem — they limit your ability to upgrade later.

If you buy a single receiver and build your speakers and DVD player around it, you can easily swap out elements you no longer want for better ones down the road. That's harder to do with a kit where the components work best together.

Before investing in an HTIB, do some research and read online reviews to figure out the best system for you.

Confused about the wide range of prices for HDMI cables? Save your money and go with the cheap ones. Tech experts say there's no difference in picture or sound quality between those and pricier cables.

## Bust battery myths and charge up your wallet

Let's take a little stroll through your home. Watch. Alarm clock. Book light. Razor. Radio. Remote control. Remote control. Remote control. We haven't even gotten to the kitchen or garage yet and notice how many battery-operated items are part of your life. Most households have about 28. That's a lot of batteries. Which means that's a lot of money spent on replacing batteries, especially if you subscribe to some notions that are, quite frankly, just plain wrong.

**Myth: Immediately toss batteries that die.** Hold on. Those AAA's may still have some juice left. Buy a tester — which you can get for less than $10 — and in seconds you can see the power left in everything from button batteries to 9-volts. A battery that's less than 100 percent may not be able to power a digital camera anymore, but it could still keep a low-drain item like an alarm clock going.

**Myth: Rechargeable batteries aren't worth the expense.** It's true they cost more up front, but when placed in high-use gadgets, where they'll be recharged often, they can definitely save you money over time.

For example, each Energizer Recharge Power Plus AA battery could set you back $2 to $3. However, they'll last three to five years and take anywhere from 700 to 1,500 charges. Disposables like Energizer Ultimate Lithium batteries cost around $2 each, but in a high-drain item you'll have to replace them frequently.

Even when you throw in a $10 charger, this type of battery could save you money faster than you can say, "Where's the remote?"

**Myth: Name-brand batteries are best.** Not always. Generics can be just as good, especially if you're putting them in a low-drain gadget like a flashlight. They can also cost up to 60 percent less. The Dollar Tree, for example, sells AA Sunbeam alkaline batteries in a four-pack for just $1. Get the best deal by checking the cost per battery.

**Myth: All batteries are the same.** You've got choices. Learn the differences so you pay for the right amount of energy to meet your needs.

| Type | Pros | Cons |
|---|---|---|
| Rechargeable | Saves money with high-use items | Costs more at startup |
| Lithium | Best in high-drain items | Most expensive disposable |
| Alkaline | Routinely priced at least 50% lower than lithium; lasts up to 7 years on the shelf | Disposables that need frequent replacement in high-drain items |
| Zinc carbon or Carbon zinc | Least expensive; works well in low-drain items | Disposable with the lowest power |

# Clever ways to guard against danger

# Frauds and Scams

## Cheap ways to safeguard your data and your dollars

Every two seconds identity fraud claims a new victim. If it hasn't happened to you yet, there's a good chance it will. The best ways to lock down your personal information and your money involve the major credit bureaus, Equifax, Experian, and TransUnion. Using them, here are three easy and inexpensive things you can do to protect your identity.

**Give your credit reports a once-over.** In addition to your name, where you work, and where you live, credit reports contain information about your bill payment history, loans, current debt, and other financial information. They show whether you've been sued, arrested, or filed for bankruptcy. They impact whether or not you get that loan and what interest rate you'll pay. On top of that, credit reports are one of the first places you'll find fraudulent accounts opened in your name. You can see why it's vital everything is correct.

Review each of your credit reports regularly, and notify the credit bureaus of inaccuracies. Watch for new accounts you didn't open, incorrect financial or contact information, wrong account balances, or other errors. You can order one free copy of your credit report from each of the major credit bureaus every year. Just visit *annualcreditreport.com* or call toll-free 877-322-8228. If you request from a different bureau every four months, you'll get a pretty good annual overview.

**Place a fraud alert — it's fast and free.** If you ever lose your wallet, credit card, or Social Security card, or if your information has been stolen in one of the more than 5,800 data breaches since 2005, don't stop at calling your bank, credit card company, and the police. Set up a fraud alert on your credit report immediately. This tells credit card companies and lenders to check with you before approving any new line of credit. And it's your first line of defense against identity theft.

While a fraud alert lasts only 90 days, you can renew it repeatedly. Submit a police report and affidavit showing you're an identity theft victim, and you can sign up for a 7-year extended fraud alert without having to renew.

To make the process easier, you only have to notify one of the major credit bureaus, and by law the others are alerted.

**Stop swindlers cold with a credit freeze.** Experts say this is the #1 way to protect yourself from identity theft. A freeze locks down your credit report so creditors can't see it — and without a credit report, most won't open new accounts. So even if someone applies for a credit card in your name, it shouldn't go through. On the other hand, a credit freeze does not affect your credit score or any existing credit cards or loans you may have.

It's a little time-consuming, but you have to apply for a freeze with each credit bureau. If you're a victim of identity theft or over the age of 65, it may be free. Otherwise, each credit bureau will charge a small fee — $3 to $10 depending on where you live. And when you're ready to lift the freeze, say to apply for a new loan, you'll have to pay again, anywhere from $2 to $12. Just remember, there's no price tag on peace of mind.

| Bureau Name | Website | Toll-free Numbers | |
|---|---|---|---|
| | | Fraud alert | Credit freeze |
| Equifax | Equifax.com | 888-766-0008 | 800-685-1111 (800-349-9960 in NY) |
| Experian | Experian.com | 888-397-3742 | 888-397-3742 |
| TransUnion | Transunion.com | 800-680-7289 | 888-909-8872 |

## Credit monitoring: how to get powerful protection without spending a dime

"While doing a routine online check of my main credit card account, I noticed a large charge to somewhere I haven't shopped in years — and I would certainly never spend that amount of money there," said Terry C. "I contacted my credit card company's fraud department, and they were very swift in reversing the charge."

Terry was smart to keep an eye on her finances. Because she was on top of things, she limited the damage. The longer fraudsters can use your identity, the bigger the financial tangle you'll find yourself in, and the more harm they can do to your credit history and score. Credit monitoring — paying a company to check your credit report for possible fraud — has become big business. But is it really something you have to spend money on?

**Monitor finances yourself.** It's not hard to do, it just takes some organization and a little time. Like Terry, you'll want to look at your credit card, bank, retirement plan, and other financial statements regularly — as often as twice a week — for questionable transactions. To make it easier, ask how you can securely monitor your accounts online and whether you can receive phone, email, or text alerts regarding irregular charges or withdrawals.

"I received a call from my bank about suspicious activity on my debit card," said Angelica Jones. "Just small amounts that I didn't notice." After going over each of the charges, she determined three were fraudulent. She's very relieved her bank had an alert system in place.

**Take advantage of free credit monitoring.** Some banks, credit unions, and other organizations offer limited — but free — credit monitoring if you have an account or credit card with them. You can also get free monitoring of one bureau's credit report from *creditsesame.com* and *creditkarma.com*. Visit their websites for details.

The bottom line is, if you're offered free credit monitoring, there's no reason to turn it down. Just be aware of its limitations. It may only last a short time and there are often strings attached. In addition, many companies will use their free basic service to try and sell you their pricier premium service.

**Professional credit monitoring offers detection but no protection.** It's like finding out your house was on fire after it burned down. If you'd been notified at the first spark, you might have prevented disaster. That's how many experts feel about professional credit monitoring.

You'll pay anywhere from $9.99 to $19.99 or more per month for a company to track at least one major bureau's credit report and alert you if it's updated or if your FICO score changes. Because you're informed after the fact, you can't always prevent identity theft. The best you can do is limit your losses. Even worse, if the service doesn't monitor credit reports at all three major national credit bureaus, it may not detect a fraudulent account opened in your name. So you're shelling out anywhere from $120 to over $200 a year for something you can do yourself for free.

## Top places to check right now for hidden identity theft

Could you be a victim of identity theft and not know it yet? Most companies take several months to detect data breaches — a few take years — so don't wait to find out. Check your credit reports first, then look into these specialized resources. You can request one free report each year from most of the businesses listed.

**See banking reports most people miss.** If someone writes a check from your legitimate bank account or any other account opened in your name, you want to know. Check and bank screening services track your history and other financial data that may detect this kind of fraud.

| ChexSystems | ChexSystems.com | 800-428-9623 |
|---|---|---|
| Certegy Check Services | AskCertegy.com | 800-237-3826 |
| Early Warning Services | EarlyWarning.com | 800-325-7775 |

**Dig deeper with supplementary credit reports.** Specialty credit reporting agencies gather information on real estate transactions; lien, judgment, and bankruptcy records; details on professional licenses; historical addresses; and other details that affect your credit report. Experts use this info to spot fraud, and so can you.

| Innovis | Innovis.com | 800-540-2505 |
|---|---|---|
| LexisNexis Risk Solutions | PersonalReports.lexisnexis.com | 888-497-0011 |

**Look into your rental history.** You suspect you're a victim of identity theft, but you need proof. See if there's wrong or bogus information in your rental history by ordering a tenant screening report from CoreLogic SafeRent. Visit *CoreLogic.com*, type "SafeRent report" into the search box, and select the Request Form option. Or you can call toll-free 888-333-2413.

**Did a data breach put you at risk?** The Identity Theft Resource Center tracks data breaches that could lead to fraud. To be sure you haven't missed a data breach notification from a store or business you use, visit *idtheftcenter.org*.

## 3 scams that scare the dollars out of you

"Three of the top four scams scare people with threats of arrest, lawsuits, or other frightening actions," says Mary E. Power, president and CEO of the Council of Better Business Bureaus. Con artists contact you claiming to be government agents, lawyers, debt collectors, or police officers, she explains, hoping to use terror to take your money. Get wise to the most common intimidation schemes, and learn which clues may mean the scare is just a scam.

**The fake tax man cometh — with threats.** In just two years, Americans lost about $29 million to scammers claiming to be from the IRS or Treasury Department. Experts call this the IRS tax scam, and here's how it works.

Crooks call saying you owe back taxes or penalties. They threaten to arrest you or take legal action if you don't wire money or pay by prepaid debit card or certified check.

"Taxpayers should remember their first contact with the IRS will not be a call from out of the blue, but through official correspondence sent through the mail," says IRS Commissioner John Koskinen. "A big red flag for these scams are angry, threatening calls from people who say they are from the IRS and urging immediate payment. This is not how we operate." He advises people to hang up immediately and contact the Treasury Inspector General for Tax Administration (TIGTA) at 800-366-4484 or the IRS at 800-829-1040.

> Scammers that repeatedly call your smartphone are not only annoying, but can cost you in many ways, including potential fraud. Block specific numbers or add them to a reject list through your Phone or Contacts app. Just be aware some carriers may charge for certain call-blocking features or for blocking too many lines.

**Bogus experts aim to bamboozle.** Be suspicious of "tech experts" claiming to be from Microsoft, Apple, or a security company, who say they've just spotted a virus or serious security problem on your computer. Pay a fee, and they'll log in to your computer and fix the problem remotely. Unfortunately, they will also steal passwords or install malware. One version of this tech support scam cost consumers over $120 million before it was shut down. Signs it's all a swindle include:

- You've had no computer problems, yet you're asked to pay for a computer fix.

- The caller asks for remote access to your computer without trying other solutions first.

**Beware of shifty debt collectors.** A scary caller says you haven't paid a debt, and threatens jail time, wage garnishments, or lawsuits, if you don't pay immediately. This may be a scam if the caller:

- refuses to give you their debt collection company's name, phone number, and address.

- insists on payment by the end of the day, often by credit card over the phone.

- threatens you with arrest.

## Good news gone bad: 4 ways fraudsters trick, cheat, and steal

Florida-based scammers made $28 million just by tricking people into believing something too good to be true. "This outfit promised huge prizes," said Jessica Rich, Director of the FTC's Bureau of Consumer Protection, "but never paid out a dime." Four of the top money-stealing cons use similar "good news" tactics. Once you understand how these rip-offs work, you can build up a healthy skepticism to protect yourself.

**You may already be a loser.** In this sweepstakes racket, a call, letter, or email claims you've won a prize, but must pay delivery, processing, or insurance fees. "If someone says you have to pay to claim a sweepstakes prize, assume it's a scam," warns Rich.

**Make $379 a day from home.** Con artists made this false promise to consumers, but FTC lawyers finally caught up with them. "This case halts a massive scam that bilked consumers out of millions for useless work-at-home kits and business coaching services," announced Rich. "The defendants duped consumers into thinking they could earn thousands working from home."

Steer clear of online ads offering an unusually high salary for at-home work like shipping packages, stuffing envelopes, or posting ads. Also, be wary if some other reward of the job is too good to be true. Investigate the company to make sure it's legitimate before providing money or personal information.

**That lottery from sunny Jamaica is shady.** Like the sweepstakes scam, this swindle starts with a call, email, or letter declaring you've won a foreign lottery. You may even receive a small check — which will turn out to be bogus. Most lottery scams say you must:

- pay the taxes, insurance, and fees to get your winnings.

- forward the money from depositing a check or accepting a wired payment.

**"Free" government grants are not so free.** If a caller promises you've qualified for a free grant to help pay for school loans, home repairs, home business expenses, or unpaid bills, rest assured, they're trying to pull a fast one. Keep these points in mind.

- You never have to pay fees for a true government grant. Even the lists of grant-making institutions are free.

- You'll never get a grant you didn't apply for.

- The government simply will not call you out of the blue or send unsolicited letters or emails to offer you "free" money.

Remember, never give bank account or other personal information to unfamiliar people or businesses — no matter how good the news.

## How to guard against credit crooks, lying lenders, and bogus buyers

"Hi, this is Tiffany from Card Services. You're now eligible for a lower interest rate, but only if you act today. Press 2 to speak to a live representative." If this sets off alarms in your head, you're on the right track. Scammers love to use credit cards, loans, and checks to steal your money. Here's how they put this to work in three of America's most successful scams.

**"Card Services" is robocalling you.** Typically, a computerized autodialer is delivering a prerecorded message from Tiffany. If you choose to speak with a representative, they will say to qualify for that lower rate, they need your credit card number, security code, or other sensitive information to "confirm your identity." The rest, as they say, is identity theft history.

**This loan ad is brought to you by scammers everywhere.** Imagine you spot an attractive ad for a loan in your newspaper or mailbox. Maybe you visit a loan website. Sending in an application can trigger something known as the advance fee loan scam. Swindlers email or call, promising you'll be approved for the loan once you pay a processing fee, security deposit, or insurance fee. Hint: You never get the loan after paying the fee.

The Federal Trade Commission (FTC) advises you to be leery of lenders who:

- offer a loan by phone.

- don't need your credit history.

- require fees up front.

- ask you to pay or wire money to a particular person.

- aren't registered with your State Attorney General's office. Visit *naag.org* to find contact information for your state office.

**That overpayment may be underhanded.** Let's say you're selling something online for $200, and the buyer sends a money order or check for $500. You're asked to deposit the payment and wire back the difference. Your bank may accept the check at first, but it bounces sooner or later. And you're out $300. The Better Business Bureau warns that fake checks can be used for any type of scam, so never write a check against a deposit until it clears.

---

### Spot the top 10 money-stealing scams before they rob you blind

1. Tech support scam

2. IRS tax scam

3. Debt collection scam

4. Sweepstakes or prize scam

5. Work from home scam

6. Lottery scam

7. Government grant scam

8. Advance fee loan scam

9. Credit card scam

10. Overpayment scam

---

## 3 dangerous habits you must stop now

Do you write your PIN on your debit card? Have you ever left your smartphone unlocked? Would you throw your bank statements in the trash without shredding them first? Of course not. But nearly half the people worldwide do engage in at least one risky behavior that increases their odds of financial fraud. Here are three surprising habits you need to change so you won't become a victim.

**Don't swipe your debit card in untrustworthy places.** Watch out for ATMs at convenience stores, hotels, bus stations, and other places that aren't banks. Some of them may be fake. What's more, thieves may install hard-to-see skimmers on these ATMs to record your PIN and account information. Most business owners don't monitor the machines and aren't trained to spot this kind of tampering.

This is a growing problem, as, according to the credit-scoring firm FICO, the number of skimmers on nonbank ATMs during the first four months of 2015 was up 317 percent compared to the same period in 2014. The good news is your risk of being skimmed may be lower if your debit or credit card has an EMV or smart chip.

**Don't give your ZIP code to a cashier.** Some stores note the name on your credit card so they can submit it along with your ZIP code to data brokers. That's all those brokers need to find tons of information about you for the retailer's tracking and marketing. What's more, data brokers can sell information about you to various companies. That's how data breaches at businesses you never use could still put you at risk of identity theft.

**Don't become a target for scammers.** It's not always about how you handle your money. You may be upping your risk of fraud when you sort your mail, watch TV, or talk on the phone. Avoid these actions to stay safer at home.

- Don't listen to sales pitches from callers or others you don't know.

- Don't leave documents with personal information lying around. Shred all your junk mail, old bills, financial statements, and canceled checks.

- Don't attend a free seminar if it comes with a free meal or hotel stay.

- Don't enter your name in drawings.

- Don't call the 800 number mentioned in TV ads to "learn more".

## 7 smart ways to keep hackers out of your email

If a hacker gets into your email account, he can block you from using it. Then, he can follow the links to your bank accounts, credit cards, health records, and more. Take these steps to stop a hacker in his tracks.

**Use a password that would take four centuries to guess.** Experts recommend a complex password that combines upper- and lowercase letters, numbers and symbols. Why? Estimates suggest it could take up to 400 years to crack a password that tricky. But don't stop there. Make it long enough — at least 13 characters — so hackers get frustrated and move on to someone else's account. And change it from time to time.

To help keep your accounts protected, never use the same password for more than one account, and never email your password to anyone.

**Don't answer security questions honestly.** Where were you born? What's your mother's maiden name? A recent Google study found security questions with answers that are easy to remember are also easy for hackers to guess. If your email provider offers password reminder questions or security questions, don't choose answers anyone can easily find on the internet, in public records, or by trawling social media accounts. And remember, if you give false answers, avoid choosing ones other people are likely to pick.

**Double your protection with two-factor authentication.** After you turn on this setting, every login attempt to your email account triggers a message to a phone number or email address you've chosen. That message contains a one-time code. Even if a hacker snatches your password, this extra step means he probably won't have enough information to hijack your account. Check Help or Settings for instructions to turn two-factor authentication on.

**Frustrate a community hacker.** Always log out of your email completely when using a public computer, like those at a library or school.

**Regularly check your email settings.** Make sure they haven't been changed. For example, hackers may insert their own email account in your mail forwarding settings. That means all your emails will wind up in their inbox.

**Don't make hacking easy.** Never open emails you don't recognize. Keep financial and personal information out of emails in free accounts.

**Secure your devices like Fort Knox.** Use anti-virus, anti-spyware, and anti-phishing software plus a firewall on your personal computer, smartphone, and other internet-connected devices. Keep your security software, browser, and operating system software up to date.

## Sidestep sneaky spammer traps and still save money

Your web search turned up dozens of sites offering free stuff, but that may mean you're one click away from a tidal wave of spam flooding your inbox. Some freebie sites are just a way to get your email address or other information, so hucksters can spam you back to the Stone Age. This doesn't mean you must give up freebies forever. Instead, boost your spam defense system and take smarter paths to freebies.

**Build your anti-spam fortress.** Spammers constantly change their tactics, so you'll need a variety of precautions to keep spam from sneaking in.

- Create an email address you only use for freebies.

- Find out if your mail program includes a tool to block or filter spam. If not, try anti-spam software.

- If you get spam email, don't respond to it. Instead, check your email Help files to learn how to block the sender's domain name — that part of the email address after the @ sign.

- Turn on the email setting to block images. Spammers often hide programs inside images that will notify them of live addresses. You can still choose to view images embedded in emails you decide are safe.

- Be picky about freebie sites that require your email address. Check out comments and reviews on sites like *TheKrazy CouponLady.com*, *MoneySavingMom.com*, or other bargain sites. Then decide which freebie sites make providing an email address worthwhile.

- Before signing up for freebies, read the privacy policy to find out how your email address will be used. Also, consider reading the disclosure policy, user agreement, or terms of use, if available. These notices may tell you how to opt out of mailing lists, advertisements, or other annoyances from the site or its advertisers. Take every opportunity to opt out.

**Become a savvy site selector.** Three kinds of sites can help you find the real free stuff online while avoiding spam and scams.

- Manufacturers. Start with the websites for products you already use. If you don't find offers at first, check back frequently. Promotions change and supplies run out quickly. When you do find free samples, you may hit the jackpot and score valuable coupons, as well. Experts say sites like L'Oreal, Gillette, or Proctor & Gamble are good choices. Before you sign up for freebies, just make sure the URL in the address bar includes the name of either the company or the product.

- Freebie aggregators. These sites, like *HeyItsFree.net* and *Hunt4Freebies.com* find the freebies for you.

- Preferred retailers. Visit the websites for your favorite retailers like Walmart, Sephora, or Target. Search for "free samples" or check their customer loyalty programs.

# Home and Auto security

## Sound the (burglar) alarm for hundreds less

Homes without any kind of alarm system are as much as 300 percent more likely to get burglarized than alarmed homes. That's incentive to invest in security, isn't it? And while experts may recommend professionally installed and monitored systems, these Cadillacs of home security come at a wallet-crushing price. Installation and equipment costs range from $300 to $1,600, and third-party monitoring could set you back anywhere from $15 to $60 every month, depending on your plan. Still, you can protect your home without spending wads of cash. Systems you install and monitor yourself are available now, and they're expected to spread like wildfire over the next few years — largely because they save you big bucks.

**DIY and hang on to your cash.** Order an alarm kit for around $200 from Amazon, and you get a keypad, door and window sensors, and even motion sensors similar to those found in more expensive systems. That's a savings of up to $1,400 since you'll install the kit yourself. Plus, because you also do the monitoring, you'll save $180 to $720 in monthly fees during the first year alone.

These systems are wireless, so they are easier to install than the wired variety. What's more, they are great for renters who can take the whole shebang with them when they move.

Roughly 65 percent of all home burglaries occur during the day.

**Make intruders panic for less than $100.** For an even cheaper option, buy standalone door and window alarms priced as low as $11 a pair. That means you could put alarms on 14 windows and two doors for under $100. They attach with adhesive pads, and sound off loudly if a door or window is opened. Since they run on batteries, they will work even during a power outage. Just don't forget to change the batteries.

When you do it yourself, it's important to remember these points.

- Self-monitoring means no one else is watching over things while you're busy or asleep.

- You are the one who must call the police if anything happens.

- You'll have to handle any repairs, problems, or upgrades on your own.

## Smartphone, smart home: cut security costs with your own digital watchdog

Thanks to a smartphone app, one Florida woman spotted burglars entering her home and scared them away — while she was at work across town. See how pairing your smartphone with economical smart gadgets could make your home safer without breaking the bank.

**Turn your doorbell into a virtual doorman.** A "smart" doorbell, like Ring or SkyBell, does more than just chime. Whether someone presses the button or merely skulks within a few feet of your door, the bell will ring and send an alert to your smartphone. Tap the alert, and you'll see a live video feed of your doorway area via the built-in wireless camera. Doesn't matter if you're at home or miles away, still using your phone, you can speak with the person at the door. That's brilliant because you're able to fool burglars who knock just to see if the house is empty. You can appear to be at home in Iowa, even if you're really in Miami.

You'll spend less than $200 on one of these gadgets, but to get it going you'll need a smartphone, a wireless home network, and an internet connection.

**Keep an eye on things when you're away.** Pair a wireless camera with your smartphone and monitor not only the doors and windows, but the kids, the dog, the refrigerator — whatever you need to keep tabs on. Features vary, but here's what many home camera systems offer:

- an app that connects to your smartphone for monitoring and receiving alerts

- night vision

- alarms or sirens

- real-time streaming video

- free cloud storage for video

- motion-activated recording

- easy installation

- no monitoring fees

The price for basic security camera units from companies like Piper, Canary, or Nest are right around $200.

## Cops and robbers: 3 expert tips shut down home heists

Can you afford to lose $2,229? Of course not. But that's the average value of property stolen in home burglaries last year. Sgt. Brian Eden, a police Community Outreach Coordinator, says there are easy — and cheap — things you can do to protect yourself and your home.

**Foil porch pirates and box burglaries.** As more people order products online, porch pirates have begun stealing packages left outside. If you can't be home, Eden recommends you have your purchase delivered to your workplace or picked up by a neighbor who's around during the day. "That way," Eden says, "it's not just sitting there enticing somebody to take it."

And don't leave the box for your new high-definition flat-screen at the curb for trash pickup, he cautions. Take the evidence of expensive purchases to a dumpster. You don't want to advertise to thieves you have something worth stealing.

> Never post information online about a current or upcoming vacation — or anytime you plan to be away from home, for that matter. "Bad guys use this information to know when it's a good time to break in," says Sgt. L.D. White, a property detective supervisor with the Cobb County Police Department.

**Lock the one door everyone forgets.** Think about it. If a bad guy gets into your garage — either he breaks in or steals your remote control — there's nothing standing between him and all your possessions but that interior door. What's worse, Eden warns, once your garage door is closed, no one will have a clue he is there. He can walk into your house and spend as much time as he needs.

While you're at it, check that all your doors and windows are closed and locked. "So many times we go to a scene where somebody had their vehicle broken into or their home burglarized, and we find out that their car or house was not locked," says Eden. In fact, about 30 percent of home burglaries start with an open or unlocked door.

**Bolt the door on crime.** Buy a heavy-duty, solid wood or steel entry door and you're sure to stop robbers cold. Right? Not if you used the itty, bitty screws included to attach your strike plate, says Eden.

This metal plate fastens to your door's frame, and includes a hole so the bolt for your doorknob can keep the door closed. A burglar may try to kick his way in, but that sturdy door won't break. "Instead, it just comes right out of the frame," says Eden. All because the little screws can't hold up. "Replace those with longer screws that go all the way into the stud," he advises.

Your local Red Cross or fire department may offer free home fire safety checks or free fire extinguisher training. Some even install discounted or free smoke alarms for people with limited incomes or physical disabilities. Look up your city's fire department at *firedepartment.net* and get Red Cross chapter contact information at *redcross.org* or by calling 1-800-RED CROSS.

## 6 items you should never leave in your car

Is your car window like a Macy's display for thieves? "We see people leaving cellphones, iPads, computers, and things like that out all the time," says Sgt. Brian Eden, Community Outreach Coordinator for an Atlanta-area police department. In the hands of a criminal, these items put your financial and personal safety at risk. Cellphones, in particular, may contain information that could be used for identity theft. Eden urges people to take all electronics, and other valuables, out of cars completely or at least put them in a locked trunk. For added protection, hide accessories like your phone charger.

In addition to electronics, the following items are not only valuable, but can reveal personal details about you. Never leave them in your car and perhaps you'll frustrate thieves.

- Important ID. Your Social Security card and passport are major sources of information for identity theft.

- Your mail. Is that a bank statement on your floorboard? Mail can give thieves your home address and other personal or financial information.

- A GPS unit. If you have programmed in your home address, thieves not only have the GPS, but now they know where you live.

- Credit cards. These, along with debit cards and gift cards, are like an ATM for thieves.

- Your garage door remote control. If unsavory characters have your garage remote and your home address, they can easily steal items from your garage — then rob your home.

## Keep thieves out of your driver's seat

A New York Times reporter glanced out his kitchen window and saw teenagers point a small device at his locked vehicle, open his car door, slide in, and prepare to drive away. He was able to foil the would-be thieves, but was stunned to learn they used his keyless entry key fob — while it was sitting on his kitchen counter — to manage the break-in.

The first keyless entry fobs had you press a button to unlock your car from nearby. Newer fobs bypass the button and automatically unlock your vehicle as soon as you carry the fob within range. Investigators say thieves are now using amplifier devices to boost your key fob's signal and trigger your door locks, even when your fob is as much as 300 feet away. And that's how you, and your key fob, can be in your kitchen, while criminals are unlocking and stealing your car from your driveway.

So how do you protect yourself? By insulating your key fob from the amplifier. Lock your car, then slip your fob into a pouch made of aluminum foil. Once you seal the pouch shut, try to open your car door. If it stays locked, your pouch is working. Keep your fob sealed in this pouch whenever you're not using it. For a more elegant solution, search *Amazon.com* for an inexpensive "key Faraday bag."

---

### Home safe home: 5 cheap ways to stop a thief

"Most burglars choose the path of least resistance," says Sgt. White, a property detective supervisor with an Atlanta-area police department. "So homeowners have to make it as difficult as possible for a burglar to even attempt to break in." Don't worry, you don't have to spend a lot of money to turn your palace into a fortress.

- Trim away overgrown shrubs and trees that block the view of your property.

- Know your neighbors. "There is nothing more effective in deterring a criminal element than a 'nosy' neighbor," says White.

- If your exterior door has decorative glass near the lock, install a deadbolt that requires a key from both sides.

- Make sure outdoor lights work, so you — and others — can see your yard clearly at night.

- Don't leave ladders or tools outside that burglars can use to break in.

# Awesome ideas to get there on a budget

# Car buying and selling

## Let's make a deal: expert ways to spend less on a new car

Want to pay rock-bottom prices for your next car? Then get your motor running with these smart tips you won't hear from any auto dealer.

**Steer your way to a better new car loan.** "Financing is what gets most car buyers into trouble," says Jeff Ostroff, CEO of CarBuyingTips.com, a consumer advocate website for everything related to car buying, leasing, financing, and avoiding dealer scams. He warns that shoppers need to have all their finances in order before they start shopping. "Too many suckers find out the hard way — in the finance office — that they have poor credit and cannot get approved," he says. "Or they get stuck with a super-high APR."

A few months before you even start applying for a car loan, check your credit score and find out if you need to clean up your credit report. "Otherwise," Ostroff says, "dealers will rake you over the coals." (See page 176 for how to check your credit score and report.)

Before contacting any car dealer, get pre-approved for an auto loan with a bank, credit union, or other local lender. And find out what interest rates you qualify for. Only consider a dealer's financing offer if it's better than offers you already have.

**The #1 secret to landing your best price.** Negotiate from a position of strength. You'll need to do a little research to amp up your bargaining power, but Ostroff says this is one of the most important things that will allow you to pay bottom dollar for a new car. "You must know all the factory incentives available to the dealers and every consumer rebate," he says.

Next check the prices your preferred car sells for on websites like *truecar.com* and *edmunds.com*. Pay close attention to the sticker price, the wholesale or factory invoice price, actual prices paid, and incentives. Knowing these may help reduce your final price.

Finally, get more information about offers from local dealers by visiting manufacturer and dealer websites.

**Haggle a great bargain on the lot.** The factory invoice price is not a car dealer's true cost, say consumer experts. Over the years, and with the explosion of internet-based car-shopping sites, invoice prices have become bloated. To come up with a fair offer, Ostroff says to ignore the invoice price and instead figure an amount that is about 3 to 5 percent above the dealer's real cost of the car plus all the options.

Unfortunately, it's not always easy to calculate the dealer's cost. Ostroff's website says to start with the invoice price, then subtract out the factory holdback and factory-to-dealer incentives. If all that math has your head spinning, just go to *carbuyingtips.com* and look under New Car Invoice Pricing for a spreadsheet that will help crunch the right numbers for you.

Dig deep for any additional new-car discounts, like these:

- Military bonus

- USAA member bonus

- Future Farmers of America discount

- Student or recent college graduate discount

- Police officer discount

- Loyalty discount

- Competitive conquest discount (to entice you from a competitor)

- Aged inventory dealer bonus (to help sell leftovers from previous years)

Bring your calculations, the price, and any finance information you've gathered to the dealer's lot, and parley like a pro.

**Use email to negotiate the best deal on wheels.** Find several dealers who have the car you want. Send an email to each dealer's internet sales department, describing the make and model, your must-have options, and the total price. Ask if they can beat that, and say you'll be ready to buy in a few days.

Compare offers and confirm the winning dealer has the car in stock, verifying that the price and fees won't change. Make an appointment to sign a contract and pick up your new car.

---

### Which colors sink your car's resale value?

Don't buy a teal car just because it's your favorite color. You'll regret it come resale time when that not-so-trendy hue reduces its value by up to $500. Neutrals like black, white, silver, and gray are the safest bets because they're all very popular. In fact, white is the way to go if you buy a minivan, SUV, or truck. On the other hand, people most associate silver with luxury cars. If you simply must have some color, medium blue ranks consistently in the top five most popular.

Just be careful about novelty colors like fuschia, yellow, purple, orange, or pink. These are more likely to cost you during resale, particularly if that color is discontinued. Darker colors can also be a problem if your car has scratches or paint damage, because these flaws are easier to see against a dark background.

---

## Skip costly dealer fees and save thousands

"Most people let down their guard when they enter the finance office," says Jeff Ostroff, CEO of CarBuyingTips.com, a consumer advocate website. "But all they did was go from the frying pan into the fire." Once you've agreed on a price for your gorgeous new car, you think you can relax. But Ostroff says most of the financial damage is done during the hard sell on the extras, like extended warranties, rustproofing, and more. In fact, you're looking at more than $5,000 in potential fees and add-ons.

"The best way to avoid some fees is to confront the dealer about the real cost, and get them to remove them or cut them in half," says Ostroff. "My brother-in-law was given about $1,000 in fees a few months ago on a new Ford. I told him to haggle with the dealer, and they did indeed remove 50 percent of the fees."

Here's the scoop on 11 different pricey add-ons.

**Documentation fee.** The U.S. average for this fee is $276, although your state could be higher or lower. To see your average and find out whether this fee is capped where you live, visit *edmunds.com*. If the dealer's fee is much higher than the average, negotiate it down.

For example, the average in Illinois is $160, with a limit of $166. So if the Finance Manager is hawking a $600 fee, speak up. Dealers also charge sales tax on this fee, so you may save more than you expect.

**Tag and license fees.** These are legitimate, but you can still be overcharged. Visit the online Car Payment Calculator at *carmax.com* or your state Department of Motor Vehicles website for estimates. Use this to help negotiate bloated fees down to a sane level. After all, why pay $300, if your actual cost is around the U.S. average of $153.

**Electronic filing fee.** Many dealers outsource this job to third parties, and pay $20 to $40 — or less — for them to electronically register your new car with the state. "They charge $100, but should ask for no more than $20," says Ostroff.

**Dealer prep fee.** "This dealer service fee is a rip-off," says Ostroff. He explains that the dealer could charge you $700 or more for removing seat protectors, vacuuming the car, installing fuses, and checking the liquids. Since manufacturers often reimburse dealers for the labor involved in preparing a car for sale, it's perfectly legitimate to ask that this fee be waived or reduced.

**Tire and battery fees.** Most states impose fees to offset the environmental impact of new tires and batteries. Ostroff says the actual fee in Florida is $7.50 but you often see charges of $8.50 to $10 or more. Check with your state's Department of Revenue for the amount you should pay. The difference may only be a dollar or two, but it all adds up.

**Extended warranty plans.** A recent *Consumer Reports* survey says automobile extended warranties average around $1,200, but can go as high as $2,200. Most people in the survey said they paid more for the warranty than they saved in repair bills. So turn down the plan, and hang on to hundreds of dollars.

**Ding protection.** Pay for this and the dealer will repair small dents and scratches for free for a couple of years. Skip it, and you could save as much as $650.

**VIN etching package.** Putting the car's Vehicle Identification Number (VIN) on the window can cost as little as $25 if you buy a kit and do it yourself. That could save $175 over the dealer's $200 VIN package.

**Splashguards and bug shields.** Before you make an offer on a car, visit *autozone.com* or *weathertech.com* to see how much these accessories, tailored to your chosen vehicle, might cost. Prices for bug deflectors could range from $45 to $140, and splashguards from $20 to $150 if you buy them yourself, but the dealer may charge several hundred, even for the cheaper ones.

**Fabric and paint protection.** Experts say today's automotive paint and interior materials are advanced enough — and usually of such high quality — that you don't need to pay for extra protection. Decline the $200 or $300 "protection package" and take care of spills yourself.

**Rustproofing.** Dealerships charge anywhere from $200 to $1,200 for undercoating or rust protection, even though automakers already apply this at the factory. Just say no.

## Car loan madness: low payments steal $5,000 from your wallet

Are you willing to pay $5,000 extra dollars for that snappy new car? That's exactly what you're doing if you agree to a long-term auto loan. More people than ever are now borrowing money for six, seven, even eight years to pay for their new cars. And while the budget-friendly monthly payments make long-term financing seem attractive, they come with alarmingly high hidden costs. Not only are you charged a higher interest rate for a longer loan term, but you owe more to the bank than your car is worth as soon as you drive it off the lot. Heaven forbid you total your car during the first few years, since it's unlikely your insurance payout will cover what you owe. Take a look at this typical example:

| $29,550 car loan | Interest rate | Monthly payment | Total interest paid |
|---|---|---|---|
| 3-year | 3% | $859.35 | $1,386.59 |
| 7-year | 6% | $431.68 | $6,711.35 |
|  |  | Extra interest paid | $5,324.76 |

## Going, going, gone: bid for bargains with care and luck

That used Ford Expedition may sell for $13,000 on a well-known auto website, but you could get it for the low, low price of

$9,000. And who wouldn't love a 5-year old Chevy Impala for just $205? How can you get deals like these?

**Find goods galore at Uncle Sam's auctions.** Check these three government websites for cars — and just about everything else.

- *govsales.gov.* Think of it as one-stop shopping because this is where approved federal agencies can sell cars and trucks, often at amazingly low prices. Search through available items, click on the one you're interested in, and register at the seller's website to buy or bid on it.

- *govdeals.com.* Here you'll find public surplus or confiscated items that government agencies put up for bid. Browse through the more than 90 categories including Automobiles, Vehicle Parts, and Motorcycles.

- *treasury.gov.* The U.S. Department of Treasury auctions off seized property or items forfeited by people who have broken federal law. Cars, boats, planes, and more are sold at 300 auctions around the country every year. On their website, search for Auctions under Services.

**Follow these 4 tips so you don't get fleeced.** For best results, make sure you do your homework before shopping at these auctions.

- Research prices before you buy, so you'll know whether or not you're getting a good deal. And find out if the auction charges a buyer's premium. "Don't bid market value for a car, and then have to pay 10 percent on top of that," says Jeff Ostroff, CEO of CarBuyingTips.com, a consumer advocate website for everything related to cars and car-buying.

- Read the help pages, FAQs, and other information pages on the auction websites. Learn about the different types of auctions to make sure you can get the best deal. Sit in on a few without bidding, to see how they work and plan your strategy.

- No financing is available for expensive items like cars, so be ready to pay the full price in cash or have your loan already approved.

- "You can't test drive the cars," warns Ostroff. And you may not get a chance to inspect them well either. Since vehicles are usually sold as-is, without guarantees about their condition, Ostroff says, "It is truly buyer beware." However, if you can get the car's VIN number, he suggests you order a vehicle history report from CARFAX (*carfax.com*) or AutoCheck (*autocheck.com*) to find out if the car has ever been flooded or had other serious problems. If you attend an auction in person and can inspect the car, some experts recommend bringing a mechanic or auto expert with you to help steer you away from lemons.

## Don't miss out on additional steals and deals

Government auction websites sell a wide variety of items beyond vehicles — including jewelry, computers, and even collectibles. For example, at *treasury.gov*, you may find electronics, boats, and real estate. What's more, *govdeals.com* is where unclaimed packages from the U.S. Post Office eventually end up, so you may be astonished at the wide variety of items available.

If you need discount luggage and maybe even some vacation clothes to go with that new car, one interesting place to get great deals is the Unclaimed Baggage Center in Scottsboro, Alabama. They accept lost luggage and unclaimed freight from airlines after all attempts to reunite the property with its owners have failed. Call them at 256-259-1525 or check them out online at *unclaimedbaggage.com*.

## Show and sell — how to get top dollar for your used car

You've traveled hundreds of miles together, shared wheel alignments and oil changes. But now it's time to "kick the tires and light some fires," as they say. So when you finally turn the keys over and move on to something a little newer, don't leave money on the table.

You could raise the resale value of your faithful old car by $2,000 or more, experts say, just by paying attention to these few details.

**Drive the best deal with a value that's on the money.** Check *cars.com*, *kbb.com*, and *nadaguides.com* online to determine the real value of your car. But don't stop there. For a competitive price, search used car listings in your area to see how much your exact make and model is selling for. You can also solicit trade-in offers from local car dealers. Get copies of these offers so you can use them as evidence of what your car is worth if you decide to sell your vehicle privately.

**Shift into top gear with a little spit and polish.** Get your car thoroughly detailed for around $100, and you'll not only make that money back, but raise your resale value by as much as $500. Also, don't forget often-overlooked resale boosters like topping off the fluids and replacing any blown-out bulbs or fuses.

**Turn secondhand blues into money-making news.** If your car needs a lot of repairs or a few very expensive ones, determine which costs more, the repairs themselves or the drop in resale value if you don't do them. Some repairs may not be worthwhile. On the other hand, repairs like these may pay off:

- Worn tires. A buyer may pay $300 to $700 less for the car if they think they have to replace the tires right away.

- Body damage. If you can repair a big dent in your car for $200 or less, you may make at least five times your money back.

- Squealing brakes. This will scare off even the most interested buyer. Bite the bullet and replace them.

- Cracked windshield. Ask your car insurer what they cover. You may pay very little for the repair, but get hundreds more on trade-in from a car dealer or in cash from a private buyer.

**Don't forget to fine-tune your tune-up.** If your car is due for a major maintenance package, skipping that could lower the value of your car by several hundred dollars.

**Cash in with valuable paperwork.** Reassure potential buyers by providing documents that show your car has been taken care of. Include as many of these as you can:

- records of maintenance and service

- the car's manual, title, registration, and insurance information

- a vehicle history report to show that your car has been accident-free

# Car care

## Gas smarts: small ways to save big at the pump

No matter how high or low gas prices go, filling up at the pump will always put a painful pinch on your wallet. But here are some driving tips that will help you ease that pain.

**Don't pay to idle.** Have you done any of these today?

- Warmed up your car in the driveway or parking lot?

- Let the car idle while you put on your seat belt, made a quick call, or put things in order?

- Idled at a train crossing or while waiting for someone at a school or airport?

- Used the drive-through at a restaurant or ATM?

Idling costs 1 to 2 cents per minute, the Department of Energy reports. Doesn't sound like much, but since Americans average 16 minutes of idling daily, over the course of time, it can really add up. "Idling makes no sense because there's no work done," says Joe Thomas, Director of the National Center for Automotive Science and Technology. "You're throwing away gas money out the tailpipe."

> A Central Massachusetts University study found that each car at a McDonald's drive-through idled for about six minutes.

Even if you only reduce idling by four minutes a day, you can save $29.20 a year.

- Don't warm up your car for more than 30 seconds. Modern automobiles no longer need extra time to get primed. Driving moderately as you start out does the trick.

- Turn off your engine if you're waiting or delayed for more than 10 seconds. Idling for longer uses more fuel than turning off and restarting the engine. Just try not to restart more than about 10 times a day, and allow at least one minute between turning off the engine and restarting.

**Life in the fast lane is overpriced.** When a light turns green, do you floor it so you can reach the next stoplight and zip through before it turns red? Doesn't always work out, does it? Often you get to the light and have to slam on the brakes. If jackrabbit starts and hard stops are part of your routine, you may be using up to 40 percent more fuel — raising your gasoline costs by an eye-popping $554 in one year. Try slow-and-go driving instead.

- Increase your speed more gradually and you'll save up to 2 miles per gallon, or as much as $141 a year.

- Keep your car at a steady pace as you approach a light. It can take 20 percent more gas to accelerate from a full stop than from 5 miles per hour.

You're off to a good start, so why not double or possibly triple your savings with more gas-saving ideas.

| How to save $450 a year on gas EVERY YEAR for the life of your car! | Potential Annual Savings |
|---|---|
| Haul less cargo. Reduce what you carry inside your car and trunk by 100 pounds and save 2¢ per gallon. | $12.48 |
| Use the recommended motor oil to save 4¢ a gallon. | $24.96 |
| Reduce the amount of time you spend idling every day by 4 minutes. | $29.20 |
| Keep tires inflated to the correct pressure and save up to 7¢ a gallon. | $43.67 |
| Keep your engine properly tuned and save 9¢ a gallon. | $56.15 |
| Switch to slow-and-go driving. Gain 2 mpg by ditching jackrabbit starts and hard stops. | $141.33 |
| Limit your speed. Every 5 mph you drive over 50 mph is like paying an extra 16¢ per gallon. Travel 50 instead of 55 for just 10% of the miles you drive, and save a bundle. | $148.49 |
| *Savings based on gas price of $2.22 per gallon and 13,476 miles driven per year. | TOTAL POTENTIAL SAVINGS $456.28 |

## 5 maintenance rip-offs your car doesn't need

When do you feel most like an idiot? For many, it's when your mechanic starts spouting gibberish about fan assemblies, valve cover gaskets, and exhaust manifolds. And then comes the tricky part — do you pull out your wallet or take your car and go home?

Experts say the smart thing to do is spend some time reading your owners manual before you go in for service, to see which checks and changes the manufacturer recommends. Technology is improving so quickly that you may find many tried-and-true rules about car maintenance have become outdated myths. Unfortunately, some mechanics, for whatever reason, still recommend maintenance too frequently. What your mechanic doesn't want you to know could save you as much as $400 this year.

| Service | Mechanics may suggest | Experts say | You save |
|---|---|---|---|
| Oil change | every 3,000 miles | every 6,000 miles or more | $21 |
| Fuel injector cleaning | randomly | never, unless your check engine light is on or your car is running rough | $65 |
| Air filter | replaced at every oil change | every 12,000 – 15,000 miles | $77 |
| Coolant | flush twice a year | newer cars may only need flushing once every 2 years | $109 |
| New spark plugs | every 50,000 miles | every 100,000 miles | $149 |

Do a lot of stop-and-go driving? Often drive on dirt roads? Live in a very hot or cold climate? You may need to step up your maintenance schedule. Follow the recommendations for severe or extreme driving in your car's manual to help keep it running longer.

## Solve the check engine light mystery for less

It's alarming yet puzzling. Ominous but unclear. The dratted check engine light.

It flickers on when certain things go wrong with your car. Then stares at you like some evil eye. But what does it mean? You could pay a mechanic anywhere from $80 to over $100 to plug a special scanner into your car's onboard diagnostic port, fetch the error or OBD code, and diagnose your problem. Or you could face down the beast yourself — and save some money.

- First, if the check engine light blinks or flashes, don't mess around. The problem is an emergency. Pull over as soon as you can, and call a mechanic. In some cars, the light doesn't flash, but turns red in case of an emergency and yellow or orange for less severe problems. Check your owner's manual to be sure.

- In the case of non-emergencies, try this. Remove the gas cap, put it back on, and tighten until it clicks three times, or whatever number is printed on the cap. Wait for the light to reset. If it turns off after a few drives, you may have solved your problem. If not, you'll need more information.

**Crack the OBD code for free.** If you don't have a friend with an OBD scanner you can borrow, call a local auto parts stores. Some offer free readings or will loan you a scanner to do it yourself. At least one auto parts chain reads the code for free, but charges a big fee for additional information to diagnose the problem. Find out the store's policy when you call.

Some scanners will just interpret the problem as a code, such as P0135, then leave you guessing. For an explanation, try an internet search using the make, model, and year of your car along with the code. For example, you might type in "Honda Civic 2008 P0135."

Other scanners include a semi-helpful description — maybe something like "oxygen sensor heater circuit malfunction." If this stumps you, look it up online or call your local mechanic for a translation.

**Buy your own OBD scanner.** You can find hand scanners that read and decipher OBD codes at places like Walmart, auto parts stores, and on Amazon.com. Prices range from $15 to over $2,000.

Be sure to choose one that is right for the year, make, and model of your vehicle. Cars made before 1996 may use the older OBD I codes instead of the now-standard OBD II. Some cars even have special codes tailored to their make and model.

## 4 tips to keep your car running (almost) forever

You're not crazy if you expect ol' Betsy to keep on chugging long after she reaches the 200,000-mile mark. In fact, one in three car owners already have at least 100,000 miles on the odometer, a recent AutoMD survey found. This means instead of spending money on a new vehicle — with higher insurance rates — you're keeping more dough in your pocket.

But, you've got to do your part if you want your car to last for decades. Make it happen with this mix of time-tested advice and simple tricks you've probably never even heard of.

> "With proper routine maintenance, the typical car should deliver at least 200,000 miles of safe, dependable, efficient, and enjoyable performance," says Rich White, executive director of The Car Care Council, a non-profit organization dedicated to educating motorists about the importance of regular vehicle care and repair.

**Save up to $260 and a lot of hassle.** Key rings weighted down with house keys, work keys, and other attachments can wear out your ignition switch. And when that dies, you not only can't turn the key, but may not even be able to insert it in the ignition. To avoid replacing the switch, do this and save $178 to $260 in repairs. Put your car key on a quick release ring, so you can detach it from the heavier keychain before driving, then easily reattach it when leaving the car.

**Drive long enough to prevent sludge problems.** Your car hates it when you drive a couple of miles to the store and come right back, especially in winter. Short trips don't give your engine enough time to reach a temperature that burns off extra fuel in the oil and exhaust system, or water in the engine. Over time, this mixture of excess water, oil, and fuel turns into a sludgy mess in your crankcase and spells all kinds of trouble for your car. Avoid this by combining errands so you drive at least five miles per outing — more in the winter.

**Perform the weekly "LOOK-LISTEN" test.** Catch problems early and you'll not only dodge excess wear and tear, but also help keep repair costs from skyrocketing out of control. Once a week, use your senses to save money and boost the life of your ride.

- As you pull out of your parking spot, LOOK for evidence of leaks left on the pavement.

- As you drive, turn down the radio for a moment and LISTEN for unusual vibrations, squeaks, or other noises that could mean trouble.

Explain anything odd as accurately as possible to your mechanic.

**Become car care aware.** Small decisions can make a big difference in your car's lifespan, so use these hints to keep it in top condition longer.

- Regularly clean out your car and trunk to help your suspension last and to limit gasoline consumption. Your interior will also look and smell new longer.

- Many experts say synthetic motor oil is better for your engine and gets you better gas mileage. You'll pay more for these advantages, so talk to your mechanic the next time you change your oil.

- If road salt is often used in your area, choose ridged, rubber floor mats to keep salty slush from soaking through the carpet and damaging electrical parts below.

- Drive less aggressively to reduce wear and tear on your engine and brakes, and help your car live to a ripe old age.

# Auto insurance

## Save a fortune on your car insurance

Only 16 percent of Americans have asked their auto insurers for common discounts, reports insuranceQuotes.com, an online consumer resource. What are you waiting for? Reduce your premiums by as much as 20 percent if you've been accident-free and ticket-free for several years, for example. That's a potential savings of $168 a year. And maybe you didn't know you qualify for a discount if:

- you own a hybrid or electric car.

- you are married.

- you work in certain fields, such as teaching, nursing, or accounting.

- you are a member of an organization like AAA, a sorority, or the Farm Bureau.

That's free money you're letting slip through your fingers. Check with your insurer to learn what discounts on this necessary expense you're eligible for and the requirements.

| | *Discount | **Potential |
|---|---|---|
| **Senior specials** | | |
| Complete defensive driving course | 15% | $126 |
| Turn 55 years old | 10% | $84 |
| Have low annual mileage | 10% | $84 |
| **Payment perks** | | |
| Pay policy premiums annually | 10% | $84 |
| Go paperless | 10% | $84 |
| Pay by automatic withdrawal | 5% | $42 |
| Pay on time for last 12 months | 5% | $42 |
| **Car safety boosters** | | |
| Passive restraints like airbags or motorized seatbelts | 30% | $252 |
| New car | 30% | $252 |
| Anti-lock brakes | 10% | $84 |
| Anti-theft device | 10% | $84 |
| **Loyalty benefits** | | |
| Multiple cars insured with same provider | 25% | $210 |
| Life, homeowners, or renters insurance with same provider | 22% | $185 |

*Discounts may not be available in all states or from all insurance companies
**Based on national average insurance cost of around $841 for one vehicle

## Traffic ticket? Put the brakes on a rate hike

You're an excellent driver. But sometimes things go wrong — terribly wrong — and you get a ticket. Boy, will you pay for it down the road, in the form of higher insurance premiums. A single traffic ticket for a moving violation could raise your premiums as much as 94 percent. Thank goodness not all offenses trigger that kind of increase.

| Ticket category | Average hike in annual car insurance premium* |
|---|---|
| Drunk Driving (DUI or DWI) | $793 |
| Speeding at least 16 mph over the limit | $234 |
| Speeding up to 15 mph over the limit | $178 |
| Failure to stop | $163 |
| Driving without a license | $139 |
| Not wearing a seatbelt | $48 |

*Based on national average insurance cost of $841.23 for one vehicle

Even though rates typically go up for several years after you receive a moving violation, Laura Adams, senior analyst at insuranceQuotes.com says, "There are ways drivers can save money."

- "Taking a defensive driving course to remove points from your record is a smart strategy," says Adams. Check with your state's Department of Motor Vehicles to make sure your chosen course is approved for this.

- For minor traffic violations, see if you can plea bargain at traffic court for a lesser offense that won't have as big an impact on your record.

- Ask your insurance agent if the company "forgives" first-time or minor traffic tickets.

- Shop around for a reasonably priced policy that has similar coverage, but doesn't demand as high a penalty for your particular traffic ticket.

Note that premium hikes won't start until your insurance is up for renewal, so you may have time to fend off rising rates. Finally, drive very carefully to avoid a second traffic ticket that would cause your premiums to skyrocket even more.

> Yearning for that snappy little red car, but terrified of what it will do to your insurance premiums? Roughly 42 percent of people think car color affects rates, but that's just not true. Insurers consider the make and model of your car, but never the color.

## Avoid a $387 mistake

You could be saving $387 a year on car insurance, says a J.D. Power survey. That's the average amount pocketed by people who switch carriers. While comparison shopping for auto insurance may be about as much fun as a root canal, it's pretty obvious, not shopping around is a costly mistake.

**Loyalty is overrated.** The average driver has stuck with their same car insurance company for more than a decade. But a lot has changed during that time. Being true blue may not be getting you the most green. Here's why.

- Your insurer may no longer fit your needs. Different companies have different risk preferences, with different premium ranges. Perhaps you've moved into a new category. For example, some insurers offer better rates for single drivers with one car, while others give super deals to families with multiple cars.

- As of 2006, insurance companies use credit scores to set premiums, but each insurer uses the data in a different way. If your credit score has changed significantly, you may find a better rate with a new company.

- Loyalty discounts vary among companies — some give little or no price break when you continuously renew your policy. So why are you staying?

- You may even be penalized simply because you are loyal. Sounds crazy, but it boils down to a practice fairly new to the insurance industry called "price optimization." Insurers gather all kinds of data on you to set your rate — some of it completely unrelated to your driving risk, like how you've responded in the past to price hikes for other services. They plug that information into computer programs to predict the highest fee you'll tolerate. Price optimization is why people who occasionally switch insurance companies may pay less for the same coverage. "Most Americans are required by law to buy auto insurance," says J. Robert Hunter, Director of Insurance for the Consumer Federation of America, "and it is terribly unfair and entirely illegal for insurance companies to vary premiums based on whether or not they are statistically likely to shop around." While price optimization is banned in several states, some companies may still charge you less if you're a proven "shopper."

**5 secrets to comparison shop like a pro.** For best results when looking for a new insurance company, start with these tips.

- Talk to your current insurer first. The easiest way to get a better rate or discount is to ask for it.

- Visit your state insurance commissioner's website for information about rates in your area. Check for complaints against specific insurers while you're there, or get similar information from the National Association of Insurance Commissioners online at *naic.org*.

- Get quotes from online aggregators and independent agents. Good websites include *CarInsurance.com*, *Insure.com*, *insuranceQuotes.com*, and *Insurance.com*.

- When comparing quotes, make sure you're looking at the same level of coverage.

- Start hunting for a new policy well before your old one is due to expire. And don't cancel your current coverage until you've locked down a new one.

## Financial crisis — use this loophole to fight rising rates

Your credit score tanks due to something completely unexpected, like a catastrophic illness or identity theft. To add insult to injury, your insurer sends out a rate-hike notice because of that slumping credit score. Don't panic. Instead, ask your insurance agent for an "extraordinary life circumstances exception." You're a good candidate if your finances and credit were damaged by factors you couldn't control, such as the death of a family member, involuntary unemployment, military deployment, divorce, fraud, or medical bills. If your request is approved, they will take these unexpected life events into account and recalculate your insurance score.

# Airfares

## Up, up, and away: booking tips nab sky-high savings

Frequent fliers know the key to grabbing a great deal on airfare is to book your flight on the right date, at the right time. Book it too soon? You pay too much. Book it too late? You still pay too much. It's no wonder today's travelers have reservations about flying the friendly skies. Clear up the plane nonsense — and land the fairest fares — with proven tips from travel pros.

**Book on a Sunday and pocket the savings.** Bet you thought you'd get a better price on Tuesday or Wednesday, right? The experts at Airlines Reporting Corporation (ARC), a tech firm that provides the U.S. travel industry with statistics on airline ticket transactions, say no.

The average price of a domestic flight, according to ARC, is $495. But buy your ticket on a Sunday, and you'll typically save anywhere from $50 to $110. The average cost for booking a flight on Tuesday through Friday tops off at almost $500.

**What's the cheapest day to fly?** That one's sort of up in the air. Most travel experts agree that Tuesday and Wednesday are the least expensive days to fly. Some travel gurus also include Thursday, and a few even recommend Saturday.

**Flexible fliers can save more.** Try sites like *onetravel.com* and *cheapair.com* to explore low-cost options if your travel dates are flexible. You'll find the lowest-priced flights for the dates you enter, but you'll also see some alternative dates that could save you money.

Closest may not be cheapest when it comes to choosing an airport. Name your departure city — not your nearby airport — when booking online. Most sites will show you prices for flights in and out of several nearby airports. You may be surprised to find the best deal is just a short commute away.

**Book in the zone.** The experts at CheapAir.com say you'll get the best deal if you buy your ticket during these time periods.

- Front Runner: You'll get your pick of flight times and seats, but your ticket will cost an average of $50 more if you book your flight between 335 and 197 days before you plan to travel.

- Early Bird: This zone covers days 196 to 113 before you fly. Some flight options will still be available during this period, but your ticket's price tag jumps up around $20.

- Prime-time Buyer: This is the experienced traveler's sweet spot. Book your flight between 112 and 21 days before you travel, and you'll get the best overall prices.

- Long Shot: Fares change daily in this zone, from 20 to 14 days before your trip. You may be able to find a super deal depending on how full the flights are. But you may end up paying a whole lot more than you expected if you're planning to travel during peak seasons.

- Down-to-the-wire Flier: You plan to book at the very last minute, hoping to grab a great rate. And you might. But you may spend an average of $75 more if you wait to book 13 to 7 days out. Even worse? Your cost could soar by over $200 if you purchase your ticket less than a week before you travel.

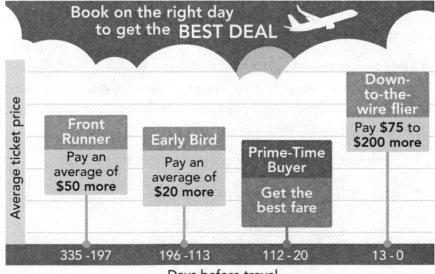

## 4 ways to land budget-friendly discounts

Remember when a little silver in your hair and a few wrinkles around your eyes came with a hefty airfare discount? Southwest and United Airlines may still cut you some senior slack, but the days of cheap seats for the over-60 crowd are just about gone with the wind.

Don't give up, however. Anyone of any age can still soar into the wild blue yonder for bargain-basement prices. Here's how.

**Travel with the pack, save a few bucks.** Airlines like United, Southwest, and Delta offer special pricing for groups of 10 passengers or more. Or book a group of 30 passengers with Southwest's Group Travel Program and one in your party flies free.

**Join the club.** Organizations like AAA and AARP offer special travel perks that may include lower airfares. For example, AARP touts a whopping $400 discount on select British Airways tickets. Go to *britishairways.com* for details.

**Give it the old college try.** Check with your alumni association for great package deals through their travel programs. Whether you're a Wildcat from Kentucky or a Michigan Wolverine, that sheepskin you earned way back when might score you a win to somewhere new and interesting.

**It pays to be true blue.** An airline loyalty program could be your ticket to low-cost travel. But which one is best? The experts at *U.S. News & World Report* evaluated 10 frequent flier programs using six criteria:

- How easily you can earn free round-trip flights

- Extra benefits they offer like free checked bags, cabin upgrades, and hotel discounts

- How many routes are offered by each airline and its affiliates

- The number and variety of award flights you can purchase using few points or miles

- How many daily flights the airline offers

- The airline's quality rating score which takes into account how often their arrivals are on time, how frequently they lose or mishandle baggage, and consumer complaints

The top three scorers were Alaska Airlines Mileage Plan, American Airlines AAdvantage, and Southwest Rapid Rewards. See where other airlines landed in the rankings at *travel.usnews.com.* Click on Rewards.

---

### Promo code mojo: how to bring down unfair airfares

You're ready to purchase your airline ticket online. But as you scroll down the page, you spot a box marked Promo Code. So what's that all about?

Airlines must pay a commission when you buy your ticket through third-party websites like Orbitz or Travelocity. To encourage customers to book on their websites instead, airlines send promo codes — worth up to 50 percent off regular fares — to members of their frequent flier programs.

To join a program and take advantage of these discounts, register at the airline's website and provide an email address. Quick as a wink, you'll find promo codes landing in your inbox. Type in the code when you pay online, and away you go on your discounted flight.

A word to the travel savvy — don't waste your time with websites advertising promo codes for airfare discounts. Go straight to the source and speed up your savings.

## Fix travel troubles on the fly with this airline secret

You're stranded in snowy Omaha while your luggage is winging its way to Miami. As you slog through endless airport lines, you notice some passengers typing furiously on their smartphones. Within minutes, they smile, step out of line, and stride happily off into the sunset. What just happened?

Perhaps they were simply watching the latest cute puppy video, but more likely, they quickly and easily solved their transportation nightmare by using Twitter.

This online messaging service is the newest way airlines are staying in touch with their passengers — and how passengers are bypassing traditional, and often frustratingly jammed, customer service avenues.

Most airlines, including Delta, United, and American, have trained staff monitoring their corporate Twitter accounts. They are on standby 24/7 to help solve the problems travelers post in Twitter messages. Delta, for example, receives about 3,000 of these messages, called tweets, every day from Twitter users.

Depending on your predicament and your airline, tweeting can resolve issues much faster than a phone call, especially when you either can't get through to customer service, or can't get them to give you a straight answer. Tweeting is particularly good for those little hiccups so common during travel — like missed connections, delays, cancellations, or baggage mix-ups. Imagine tweeting about a problem while your plane is in line for takeoff, and discovering that everything's straightened out by the time you land.

All you need to use Twitter is an internet connection or mobile phone and a free Twitter account. You don't have to be an expert to get great results, either. But knowing the right way to tweet can help a lot.

**Address your airline directly and accurately.** Since there are 1.3 billion registered Twitter users, each with a unique username, you don't want to fly by the seat of your pants when it comes to connecting with an airline account. Here are just a few you might find helpful:

- @AmericanAir

- @AlaskaAir

- @Delta

- @FrontierCare

- @SouthwestAir

- @united

- @VirginAmerica

**Make tweets count.** Tweets are limited to 140 characters, but may also contain photos, videos, and internet links. Follow these tips so your airline has enough information to understand and solve your problem.

- Be specific about what you need and how urgent it is.

- Ask for help politely.

- Only include facts, not opinions.

- Fit your problem and help request into as few tweets as possible. Use common abbreviations like "min" for minutes, and substitute the three-letter airport code for the city or airport name. ATL stands for Atlanta and LAX is Los Angeles, for example.

- Be sure the airline knows which passenger, flight, and so on is involved with the problem by including information like your flight number, departure date and airport, and arrival airport.

- Don't tweet any information that could be used for identity theft. You have another way to pass confidential details to the airline.

**Go private when it matters.** Tweets are publicly available to anyone on the internet, but Direct Messages (DM) are private — only seen by you and the recipient. Keep your initial tweets public for high visibility that gets the airline's attention. Then switch to DM if the airline requests it or if you're sending sensitive information, such as your frequent flier number, passenger name record (PNR), or reservation code.

Visit *support.twitter.com*, Twitter's help page, for details.

**3 reasons you shouldn't tweet.** Sometimes, this strategy is not a good idea. Don't tweet when:

- you want to file a complaint. The complaint forms on the airline's website will get better results.

- the problem is something the airline can't change, such as bad weather.

- your tweet is a threat that could be misinterpreted as something a terrorist or hacker might say.

Before making a reservation, check your airline's past tweets to see if they reply straightaway to customers or not. Many are quick on the draw, but a few don't respond rapidly or well to Twitter.

Finally, keep in mind, You may see slower responses during off-hours or bad weather.

# Big style — bigger savings

# Personal care

## 4 ways to snag freebies without leaving home

Lancôme Visionnaire Nuit Beauty Sleep Perfector. Sounds expensive, doesn't it? Well, it is. A 1.7-ounce jar runs $88 at a high-end beauty store. Or you can get a sample completely free. How is this possible? Companies will go to great lengths to get you to try their products — even giving them away, if it gets you hooked. And now that the world has gone digital, tons of free samples from your favorite beauty brands are just a click away.

**Sites that love to give you goodies.** "The best sites to get free stuff are, in my opinion, *BzzAgent.com* and *PINCHme.com*," says beauty and fashion blogger Sissi Nuthman. They give you the chance to score free products and give feedback. But Nuthman also recommends sites that don't require you to set up an account.

- *Freebies.org*
- *TheFreebieBlogger.com*
- *FreeStuffFinder.com*
- *MySavings.com*
- *FreebieShark.com*
- *Hunt4Freebies.com*

Just enter the URL into your web browser's address bar and press Enter. Be on the lookout for tabs that say beauty, personal care, freebies, or samples.

**Online freebies from your favorite brands.** Sure, you can find things you love on sale, but what's better than rock bottom prices? Free stuff. It's easy to get free samples straight from the source — if you know where to look. Go to your brand's official page and look for a tab that says something like freebies, free samples, or offers.

For instance, you can go to *Dove.us*, click Offers, and sign up to become a Beauty Insider. The perks: beauty tips and tricks, exclusive content, special offers, and free samples.

**Get free stuff when you buy other stuff.** The biggest mistake you can make when completing a purchase on a beauty brand website is forgetting to check for giveaways. While many stores offer free samples when you purchase online, they may not advertise it. Here's a little tip — type "free" or "free stuff" into the site's search bar and press Enter. You'll get a list of all the deals and learn exactly what you need to purchase to get certain freebies. Check out:

- *Sephora.com*
- *Ulta.com*
- *BareEscentuals.com*
- *Nordstrom.com*
- *Origins.com*

**Score free samples just by being social.** If you have a Facebook account, the easiest thing to do is search for your favorite brands and click the Like button on their page. Sometimes you'll get coupons and freebies for just doing this. Other times, you must wait until they post a freebie. Many of the previously mentioned freebie sites have their own Facebook page. Just go to the site and click on the Facebook icon.

You can also sign up with ThePinkPanel, a Facebook group from the consumer research firm The Benchmarketing Company. They give you free samples in exchange for your feedback on products. Go to *Facebook.com/thePinkPanel* and click the Join tab to "like" the page and receive updates, then fill out the quick survey.

You'll find a dazzling array of free offers right on Twitter, as well. Search for a brand, click Follow to add your favorite beauty line to your feed, and stay up to date on any freebies they may offer. Be sure to check out these handles:

- @Hunt4Freebies
- @FreeStuffFinder
- @HeyItsFree
- @FreebieShark

**Play it safe on the internet.** Generally, you have to give up a little info to get access to free samples — your name, your shipping address, and a valid email address. Why not create an email account for freebie subscriptions and keep it separate from your personal email?

Also, look for signs that the offer is legit, and never give out personal information you aren't comfortable sharing. If it sounds too good to be true, it probably is. Your safest offers are those coming from a brand's official website.

## Don't pay top dollar — know where to go for beauty bargains

Think toiletries cost the same everywhere? They don't. You can actually snag certain items for more than 30 percent less by dodging the drugstore.

Take an 18-ounce bottle of Aveeno Daily Moisturizing Lotion, for example. CVS and Rite Aid have the highest prices, while supermarkets Walmart and Target come out on the lower end. Unless you favor drugstore brands or dig into the sales papers frequently, you may want to stick with superstore sales for your beauty buys.

**Aveeno Daily Moisturizing Lotion (18 oz.)**

| Store | Price |
|---|---|
| CVS | $12.99 |
| Rite Aid | $12.49 |
| Walgreens | $10.49 |
| Walmart | $9.26 |
| Target | $8.99 |

## Save 13 percent in the beauty aisle with this insider trick

You toss a few toiletries into your cart and try not to look at the tags. These items are so pricey. But if you just took a few more steps down the aisle, you could save over $5 on four items alone. How? By purchasing products marketed to men.

**Bypass the secret "tax" you didn't know you were paying.** That's right, according to a recent study conducted by the New York City Department of Consumer Affairs, it costs to be a female. Some call it the "gender tax," the "woman tax," or even the "pink tax." But no matter what it's called, it's still money you could be saving.

The NYC study analyzed products advertised for men and women with similar branding, ingredients, appearance, and construction — both online and in stores. Across five industries, including personal care products, clothes, and senior health care items, women's goods cost an average of 7 percent more.

Personal care items — shampoo and conditioner, razors and razor cartridges, lotion, deodorant, body wash, and shaving cream — had the highest price tag for women, a steep 13 percent more than those for men. Over the course of a year, this could add up to more than $80 in extra costs. Haircare products, specifically, had the biggest gap in price and could cost women a whopping 48 percent more.

**Shop smart to sidestep gender pricing.** Of course, you'll find some product differences — packaging, color, and fragrance are the most obvious. But you don't have to pay extra when there are fresh scents and huge savings in the men's aisle. Here's how you could save more than $5 on a single shopping trip.

| Product | Women's aisle | Men's aisle | Savings |
|---------|:---:|:---:|:---:|
| Gillette shaving gel (7 oz) | $6.45 | $3.51 | $2.94 |
| Gillette disposable razors (18 ct) | $12.97 | $11.77 | $1.20 |
| Nivea body wash (16.9 oz) | $10.47 | $9.77 | $0.70 |
| Suave 2 in 1 Shampoo and Conditioner (28 oz) | $2.97 | $2.50 | $0.47 |
| Total | $32.86 | $27.55 | $5.31 |

## Soak up 75 percent savings at bath time

Which would you rather do? Take a nourishing, ultra-pampering bath for a top-of-the-line price, or take a nourishing, ultra-pampering bath for just pennies? It's a no-brainer. And by swapping out pricey bath soaks for classic tub therapy, you can be thrifty and feel like a million bucks.

**Take a warm mineral bath and save over $5 in cold cash.** Ready to unwind and let the tension fall away? A stress-relieving Bath and Body Works Eucalyptus Spearmint Bath Soak could cost you almost $7 every time you fill the tub. But if you nix the expensive mineral salts and go for Epsom salt, a single soak would run about $1.75. That's a 75 percent savings.

Two cups of these magnesium sulfate crystals added to your bath will gently exfoliate and smooth your skin as the stress melts away. You can also add your favorite calming scents like eucalyptus or lavender oil to really set the mood.

What's the difference between a $7 bath and a $2 bath? Nothing, except five bucks you could spend somewhere else.

**Refresh for half the cost of other soothing treatments.**
Show your body a little TLC by soaking in a warm bath mixed with a cup of baking soda. This tried-and-true spa treatment exfoliates to leave you with brighter, softer skin. Dermatologists also recommend it for relieving the itch of skin irritations like poison ivy.

A calming Aveeno Soothing Bath Treatment runs about $1.24 per bath. But buy baking soda in bulk to save 49 percent on each soak.

## Youth in a bottle? Experts reveal why you're paying too much

Shameless. That may be the best way to describe the cost of many anti-aging products. Countless companies market luxurious brands with big promises and hefty prices. But the "quality" anti-aging products you're spending an arm and a leg on may not be any better than the inexpensive brands.

**Don't be a sucker for overpriced beauty buys.** It's natural to think that the more expensive a product is, the better your results will be. But according to the American Academy of Dermatology (AAD), that just isn't true.

"In many cases, expensive products have more fragrance or maybe a prettier package," says Dr. David Harvey, board-certified dermatologist and cosmetic surgeon at the Dermatology Institute for Skin Cancer and Cosmetic Surgery. "I stress to my patients that just because they pay more for something doesn't mean they are getting a greater benefit. Sometimes, the simpler and less expensive a cream the better."

Luckily, dermatologists have shared a few of their anti-aging secrets, so you don't have to overspend trying to track down the fountain of youth.

**The most effective anti-aging products you can buy.** You love to bask in the warm glow of the sun. But be warned, its ultraviolet (UV) rays can actually speed up the aging process, causing wrinkles and sun damage. That's why dermatologists regard sunscreen as one of the best wrinkle repellers of all time.

Titanium dioxide and zinc oxide are perhaps two of the most protective broad-spectrum ingredients, which means they shield you from both ultraviolet A (UVA) and ultraviolet B (UVB) radiation. Harvey recommends anti-aging products with these FDA-approved ingredients because they're strong enough to protect your skin from the sun, yet rarely cause allergic reactions.

And never forget your moisturizer. A good one will plump up your skin, minimizing fine lines and brightening your complexion.

**Get fresh-faced with the right anti-aging ingredients.** "Skin becomes damaged after repeated ultraviolet light and pollution exposure," says Harvey, who recommends you scan ingredient lists looking for antioxidants such as retinol, vitamin C, vitamin E, CoQ10, or coffee berry. These destroy molecules called free radicals that cause skin damage and aging, get rid of toxins that penetrate your skin, and help create collagen, which gives your skin strength and flexibility.

Alpha hydroxy acids (AHAs) — including glycolic acid, lactic acid, and malic acid — are also common ingredients in anti-aging products. They remove old, dead skin cells, which helps even out your skin tone and reduces dark spots. AHAs can be irritating or cause sun sensitivity, so make sure you read the directions and wear a good sunscreen if it's not already included.

**Save a bundle when you comparison shop.** Put products, ingredient lists, and prices in a head-to-head matchup online before you buy. And don't count out generic options. They may work just as well and have a slimmer price tag. For example, Walmart's Equate Rejuvenating Micro-Remodeling Cream costs less than $16, while Olay Regenerist Micro-Sculpting Cream Moisturizer has a recommended retail price of $33.99.

Want to save even more moola? Harvey suggests you use a product every other day to make it last longer, clip local beauty store coupons, and stock up when your favorite skin product is on sale.

## 5 things you should never buy at the dollar store

Play it safe and don't buy these items at a dollar store. Their poor quality makes them either dangerous or a waste of money.

- Toothpaste. An antifreeze ingredient was found in dollar-store toothpaste around the nation in 2007.

- Vitamins. No-name discount brands may not contain the nutrients they claim or dissolve properly once swallowed.

- Batteries. They're usually made from carbon zinc and won't last nearly as long as alkaline batteries.

- Holiday lights and other electrical products. They are so poorly made they may pose serious safety hazards.

- Kids' toys and jewelry. These Chinese-made goods are more likely to contain lead.

## Money-saving secrets for hair color that lasts

"You're not getting older," declares a 1960s Clairol beauty ad, "you're getting better." Sure it sounds nice, but frequent trips to the salon, never-ending touchups, and the drain on your bank account have you wondering, when exactly is coloring your hair supposed to get better?

Normally, you would spend $50 to $150 or more each time you stop by the salon. But you can spend less and look amazing by following these tips from color experts.

**Extend your touchup timeline and save $100 a year.** The easiest way to save money on hair color is to go to the salon less often. But anyone who has sported the "skunk" look knows that comes with a price of its own. So how do you get a little wiggle room between touchups without looking like your natural shade is trying to make a comeback?

Experts recommend you choose a color that's no more than two shades away from your natural color. "Don't go too far astray, and it will help you manage your cost a little bit," says Jacklyn Stewart, Atlanta-based color specialist known as The Color Goddess. "If you have a lot of gray hair and you don't have a lot of money to spend on it, opt for a lighter color." The same two-shade rule works if you have mostly dark hair and you want to lighten it up. "If you don't go a whole lot lighter, you'll have less contrast between the light and the dark."

A trip to the salon every six weeks could cost more than $450 a year. But use this trick and stretch your visits to every eight weeks, and you could trim that by at least $100 a year.

**Save 84 percent when you follow the golden rule of hair care products.** You picked that color for a reason. The last thing you want is to strip or fade it with the wrong products. When it comes to choosing the right shampoo and conditioner for color-treated hair, Stewart has a go-to standard. "If the company that makes the shampoo has a hair color line," she says, "you're pretty much golden." In other words, they won't make a product designed for color-treated hair that would jeopardize their color.

Both Aveda and L'Oréal make products that claim to keep your hair color vibrant longer. Yet, ounce for ounce, Aveda Color Conserve Shampoo costs 84 percent more than L'Oréal's Advanced Haircare Color Vibrancy Shampoo. "You don't have to have the most expensive one," Stewart is quick to point out. "You just have to find the one that works the best for you."

# Clothing and Accessories

## Swap and save — how to shop till you drop and spend nothing

Everyone loves a good shopping spree. That's probably why Americans spend over $1,700 a year keeping up their wardrobes. But what if you could go shopping with friends, come home with stuff you want, and spend nothing? Sounds impossible, but people are doing it all over America.

**Swap your way to the top and spend zero bucks a pop.** Want to get great stuff for a grand total of $0? Host a swap party. Here's how it works.

Invite friends of all shapes, sizes, and tastes to bring items they don't want anymore — gently used clothes, jewelry, handbags, scarves, nail polish, perfume, watches, and more. Then let the swapping begin.

To make it easier, give your guests one clothespin with their name on it for each item they brought. As they browse, they pin their favorite items. When the shopping spree is over, everyone claims the items they pinned. If more than one person pinned an item, have a drawing. That way everyone goes home with as many items as they brought.

Get ready to show off your finds, share snacks, and crank up the music. Saving has never been this fun. Plus, when you're done, you can donate leftovers to a thrift store or charity.

**Trade in a party for a virtual switcheroo with more variety.** Want more options? Branch out with online swap stores. Each has its own set of rules, so you may have to explore a little to find one you like.

Some stores give you points when you sign up and when people choose your stuff. Then you use the points to place bids on the goods you want. On other sites, you browse through the options, and when you and another member agree on a swap, you just pay shipping and handling.

*Swapstyle.com* and *Listia.com* are two popular swap sites. When using these, always make sure the person you're swapping with has good reviews.

## Cash-back rewards serve up sizzling online incentives

Shopping is not what it used to be. More and more people are trading in rolling buggies for virtual shopping carts. That's great news for the thrifty buyer because online shopping has created new ways to save that you've probably never thought of. The most surprising are cash-back super sites. Here's what you need to know — and what retailers hope you never find out.

**Earn money back just for shopping online.** Cash-back or rebate sites work much like credit card cash-back programs. When you purchase an item from one of their affiliated retailers, the site earns a commission, and you get a percentage of the purchase price back, as little as 2 percent or as much as 40 percent. Here's how it works:

1. Sign up. Set up a free account, and browse thousands of retailers, such as Amazon, Target, and Walmart.

2. Shop. Find a deal you like and use the cash-back link to complete the purchase.

3. Get paid. Within several weeks or months, you'll receive a percentage of the purchase price by check or PayPal.

**Get cash back from the right site.** *Ebates.com*, one of the leaders in online cash-back shopping, has been around since 1998. But it's not the only site that has received an "A" rating from the Better Business Bureau. Others include *FatWallet.com*, *CouponCactus.com*, *BeFrugal.com*, and *CouponCabin.com*.

Before choosing a rebate site for shopping, compare deals and research each site's reputation. Never use one that requires a membership fee or asks for personal information.

**Sidestep surprises by being in the know.** Using a rebate site can mean more money in your pocket. Just follow these tips to make sure everything goes smoothly.

• Read the fine print. For instance, when you shop Amazon, you may only be allowed to get cash back on certain categories, like clothing.

• Most sites don't give you money back instantly. They have to check in with the retailer, make sure the purchase goes through, and then credit your account. Don't be upset if this process takes a few months.

- Cash-back sites track your purchases with cookies. If you visit a lot of websites to compare rates, this cookie trail can get lost, and the purchase may not get credited to your account. Make sure the rebate site you want to use was the last one you clicked before making a purchase. When in doubt, clear your cookies.

- The thought of never paying full price for clothing again is exciting. But don't hop on a deal just for the cash back if it's not something you would normally buy.

- These sites are best for people who do a lot of online shopping. For example, a one-time purchase of $50 at 3 percent cash back would get you only $1.50 credited to your account. But if you're a consistent online shopper, these savings could add up.

## Make leather shoes last on a shoestring budget

Leather shoes just don't seem to get comfy until you break them in. Unfortunately, that can mean worn heels, scuffed toes, and other unsightly rips and tears. Buying a new pair is expensive and means you'll just have to go through the whole breaking-in process again. But you can stay in step with your budget by repairing instead of re-buying.

**Refurbished footwear looks like new but fits like an old shoe.** You can often get high-end leather shoes refurbished where you bought them. For example, instead of getting a brand new pair of Allan Edmonds oxford leather shoes, which could cost you close to $400, you can get them restored to near-new condition. A standard toe-to-heel recrafting package goes for $125 and includes replacing soles, welting, laces, heels, and the cork layer under the insoles.

Don't worry if the store where you purchased your leather shoes doesn't offer refurbishing services. You can usually get them repaired and renewed for less than $100 from a shoe repair professional.

**If the shoe fits, repair it.** You may not want to go all out on a total shoe renewal. But don't toss the old loafers just because the bottoms are a little worse for wear. Instead, restore the worn-down heels or replace the old soles.

New heels and a shine will cost just over $20 if you take them to a cobbler. Or get them resoled, cleaned, and polished for about $40. You can resole quality men's shoes seven to 10 times, according to the Shoe Service Institute of America. How does buying one good pair of shoes that will last you 30 years sound?

## Cheaper sneakers put a spring in your step for $120 less

Run faster. Run longer. Those pricey shoes — the ones that cost three times the average brand — better lend wings to your feet. But most who shell out the big bucks actually end up less satisfied, says Jens Jakob Andersen, founder of RunRepeat.com, a website where runners and experts review, rank, and compare running shoes.

**Affordable sneakers run circles around high-end shoes.** Maybe you've heard rumors that low-cost shoes are just as good as the expensive varieties. Now a new study, led by Andersen, confirms what people have suspected for years. Big-ticket running shoes aren't all they're cracked up to be.

Researchers took reviews from over 130,000 users and analyzed nearly 400 pairs of running shoes from brands like Nike, Skechers, Adidas, Reebok, and New Balance. They found the top 10 most expensive, listed at an average price of $181, were rated about 8 percent worse than the 10 cheapest, which sold for an average of $61.

**Comfort is key in the long run.** This isn't the only study that claims people are choosing shoes for the wrong reasons. A new review published in *The British Journal of Sports Medicine* says athletes should ignore trendy shoe designs and pay attention to how shoes feel. Runners who simply picked the most comfortable footwear suffered fewer injuries.

## Diamond experts spill secrets — you save over $1,800

It's called buying shy — a term coined by Fred Cuellar, president of Diamond Cutters International. It means you buy diamonds that weigh just under half-carat or full-carat weights rather than the full weight. The look of the diamond isn't much different, but the savings are spectacular.

For example, buy a .90-carat diamond instead of a 1-carat diamond and you could hang on to $1,864 of your hard-earned money. To get a better idea of the kinds of savings you might find by buying shy, take a look at these midrange prices for round, colorless diamonds posted on *PriceScope.com*, an independent diamond and jewelry site that provides competitive prices from reputable vendors.

| Carats | Price | Savings |
|---|---|---|
| .49 | $1,094 | $506 |
| .50 | $1,600 | |
| .90 | $4,871 | $1,864 |
| 1.00 | $6,735 | |
| 1.49 | $11,068 | $1,903 |
| 1.50 | $12,971 | |
| 1.90 | $20,842 | $1,959 |
| 2.00 | $22,801 | |

# Celebrate the good times for less

# Vacation destinations

## Fill up your days with cheap (and unusual) adventures

Looking for neat things to do on your next vacation, or even in your free time? Consider these.

**Tour for treats.** Take factory tours such as Hershey's Chocolate World in Pennsylvania, or the Jelly Belly Center in Wisconsin. Many tours are cheap or free, and you may get yummy free samples. To find tours near your destination, visit *factorytoursusa.com*, where more than 500 tours are listed by state.

**Visit a seed library.** Who knew you could find seeds in a library? Visit *seedlibraries.net*, and you'll find plenty of places where you can borrow seeds to grow your own flowers and vegetables.

Just imagine the different types of seeds you'll find while traveling. It's a cheap and easy way to try something new in your garden.

If the plants grow well, let a few go to seed, and bring or send the seeds back to the library. You'll be continuing the cycle and helping other gardeners.

**Try a different kind of treasure hunt.** If you're traveling with kids and have a sense of adventure, try geocaching. (Try it even if you don't have kids!) Everyone sees the famous tourist attractions, but geocaching can help you step off the beaten path and explore new places. You may even learn secrets that only the locals know.

How does it work? When you go geocaching, you use a hand-held GPS or your smartphone to find caches hidden by other geocaching fans. Larger caches include "treasure" — small, fun items you can take with you if you replace them with similar items.

To start geocaching, create a free account at *geocaching.com*, or download the free Geocaching app on your phone. On the site or app, find out which caches are near you, and choose one to find.

You can also use Google Maps. It will serve as a GPS for your geocaching treasure hunt if you enter the cache's latitude and longitude.

Don't forget to pack a few trinkets to hide yourself. When you find the cache, you can trade yours for some of the hidden treasures. Record the trades in the logbook or in the Geocaching app, and re-hide the cache for the next treasure hunter.

As you search, don't be surprised if you tour parts of your vacation spot that most people never discover. The best part? You won't have to fight the crowds at the popular tourist attractions.

## Pay up to 50 percent less for your hotel room

Use an online booking site and you'll never pay full price for a hotel room again. Sounds great, but is it really the best place to get the deepest discount? Try one of these other clever ideas, and you may save $70 or more on a one-week stay.

**Visit travel websites, but don't book yet.** It doesn't hurt to check the big travel websites like *Expedia.com* and *Hotels.com*, but only to comparison shop. Once you learn their rates, you may get a better deal by calling the hotel directly.

Hotels have to pay a commission to these travel sites, so if you book through them, the hotel doesn't get as much money. That's why they may be willing to negotiate.

For example, say you find a room for $110 a night on one of the big travel sites. If you book it through the website, the hotel pays a $15 commission on the booking and only gets to keep $95.

But if you call the hotel's front desk, the clerk may offer you a $100 rate if you book through the hotel. They make an extra $5 a night, and you save $10 a night. That's $70 in savings for a one-week stay. A win-win situation.

**Ask for the discounts you deserve.** Let your senior status work for you. If you qualify for a discount, ask for it when you call the hotel, and you may get up to 50 percent off. Otherwise, try some of these strategies.

- If you don't think your plans will change, tell them you want the cheapest nonrefundable rate, rather than the best deal or best rate.

- Ask for the AAA discount if you're a member.

- Ask about any other discounts you're eligible for, such as military or AARP.

- Quote the best online rate you found for the hotel, and ask if the hotel clerk can match it.

Also, ask for a breakdown of the fees, so your discount won't be wiped out by unexpected charges.

Make sure you research your vacation destination thoroughly before you book your hotel. You may uncover hidden deals, dodge unexpected expenses or problems, and discover attractions and restaurants you'd hate to miss.

## 10 great vacations that give you more bang for your buck

Discover the 10 best vacation destinations for seniors. Enjoy lower prices along with good food and lots to do. In some cases, you'll also find smaller crowds at these great vacation spots — and you won't even need a passport to get there.

**Take your Florida beach vacation in Tampa-St. Petersburg.** Choose Tampa instead of Miami and you'll save $88 a night. That's the difference in average hotel rates between the two cities. A week-long vacation in Tampa may add up to more than $600 in hotel savings alone.

What's more, you can enjoy white-sand beaches like Clearwater or Ben T. Davis Beach for free. Clearwater Beach even adds restaurants and dolphin watching to your options.

When you've had enough sun, take the old-fashioned streetcar from downtown Tampa to Ybor City to experience the food and culture of Tampa's historic "Latin Quarter."

**Savor spectacular scenery on an Alaskan cruise.** Want to see the glaciers and mountains of the 49th state, but can't do a lot of hiking? Take an Alaskan cruise starting from Seattle, Washington.

Touring Alaska by cruise ship is the best way to see the state's majestic scenery. You just relax and enjoy the ride in comfort, while experts handle the planning, meals, and other work of traveling.

So many companies offer Alaska cruise tours that the deals for seniors are almost endless. You're bound to find a great bargain on a cruise that fits your schedule. Visit *cruisecritic.com* to get the lowdown about Alaskan cruises, and then shop around for the best deal.

**Enjoy historic Savannah at a relaxed Southern pace.** Imagine a pleasant summer night strolling under oak trees swagged in

Spanish moss, on your way to enjoy some of the South's most delicious foods. Not a bad way to spend an evening.

Savannah also features gorgeous architecture, picturesque scenery, historic sites, and free ways to get around downtown. You can even see quirky attractions like celebrity gravestones.

Hotels average $142 a night. To save at least $50 over downtown rates, book a hotel near the airport.

**Non-gamblers save big in Las Vegas.** Las Vegas offers inexpensive meals and buffets, discount coupons, and either deals or low prices on attractions and getting around.

Even hotel rates and air fares are budget friendly, but shop around to get the best bargain. You can also visit free attractions like:

- the wildly popular Fountains of Bellagio water show that wows spectators with performing fountains and lights.

- the Fall of Atlantis water show at Caesar's Palace featuring towering talking statues and fireworks.

- the Mirage's manmade volcano, which stands 50 feet high and puts on its own show every night with eruptions of lava and fire.

Just skip gambling to make sure you stay under budget!

**Experience the American Southwest in Santa Fe.** Nestled at the southern end of the Rocky Mountains, this New Mexico city is a literal Rocky Mountain high at an altitude of nearly 7,000 feet. Yet, with hotel rates averaging around $100 a night, it's more affordable than other Southwestern favorites like Sedona, Arizona.

Near the center of Santa Fe, you'll find plenty of art galleries, shopping, and restaurants, but hotel prices may be up to $60 lower outside downtown.

**Sample barbecue and jazz in Kansas City.** You can literally tour dozens of delicious barbecue places in Kansas City. But if you're not a barbecue fan, you'll find plenty of other food at reasonable prices.

If you love jazz, enjoy the free Jazz in the Woods Festival in June, or try the American Jazz museum for $10. Visiting New Orleans for your jazz fix would cost around $184 per night, so you'll save $65 daily by choosing Kansas City instead. The crowds and prices are better too.

Not in the mood for jazz? Kansas City offers free admission to several art museums and historical sites. Plus, free movies and live music are regularly available at the Crown Center. Surf to *visitkc.com* for more information.

**Try historic freebies in Philadelphia.** Boston is famous for its historical attractions, but hotel rates average over $200, so save more than $50 a night by visiting Philly and its Liberty Bell instead. Both the Liberty Bell and Independence Hall are free, and you can take a free self-guided tour of the U.S. Mint to see how money is made.

Philadelphia also has good restaurants, and you won't want to miss the historic Reading Terminal Market, where you can find everything from Amish cheese to an authentic Philly cheesesteak.

**Discover why so many people visit Branson.** This affordable Missouri favorite offers a variety of live shows and music, plus golf, museums, shopping, and plenty of food. While many shows focus on country music, other shows vary widely, offering everything from acrobats to comedians.

For a few exciting minutes of free entertainment, visit the Branson Landing at Lake Taneycomo to enjoy a spectacular water, light, and sound show.

**Choose Washington D.C. over the Big Apple.** A New York City hotel room can average around $250 while a room in the nation's capital may be $90 cheaper every night. Many popular attractions like the Lincoln Memorial, the Washington Monument, and the Pentagon, are free to tour.

**Pay next to nothing at scenic national parks.** A hotel room near the Grand Canyon or the Great Smoky Mountains National Park costs less than the national average of $120 a night. But some parks do charge admission. For example, the Grand Canyon National Park entrance fees start at $15.

Here's where your "mature" age is a plus. If you're 62 or older, you can buy a $10 senior pass that gives you free lifetime admission to more than 2,000 federal recreation sites, national parks, and national wildlife refuges.

The pass covers other people in the car with you in parks that charge by the vehicle. In some places, you'll even get 50 percent off on guided tours, camping, and other services.

Afraid you won't be able to get around because of your walker or wheelchair? Don't cross National Parks off your list quite yet. The Park Service wants everyone to enjoy the nation's magnificent parks, so all parks include features like accessible bathrooms, parking, and boardwalks or pathways to scenic sites.

Some parks provide more services and features than others, so find out what's available by checking the park's website before you visit. You can also call ahead to learn about wheelchair accessibility, especially for shuttles and trams.

Score extra discounts by visiting during your destination's off-season or the "shoulder" period immediately before or after the peak season. An added bonus — crowds are smaller then.

# Gifts and Gift cards

## Save 50 percent and give 'em what they want

Remember the old song lyrics, "Johnny wants a pair of skates; Suzy wants a dolly"? Well, not anymore. Nowadays, what young Johnny and Suzy really want are gift cards from the most popular stores. A National Retail Federation 2014 survey found 60 percent of holiday shoppers not only purchased gift cards for others, but asked to receive them, as well.

So bring on the gift cards. And the discounts.

**Never pay full price.** Purchase everybody's favorite cards at *Gift CardGranny.com* and you could save as much as 50 percent. Or snag a savings of up to 35 percent when you shop at a site like *Cardpool.com*. And don't forget to check the warehouse clubs. BJ's, Costco, and Sam's Club slash gift card prices by up to 20 percent. There are scammers out there, so avoid fraud and only purchase from reputable dealers.

**Your purchase is protected.** A Bankrate.com survey found that two out of three retailers will replace your gift card if it's lost or stolen. Just remember, you may have to register it first or provide the card number. And always hang on to that receipt. Helpful hint: snap a picture of the front and back of each card you purchase. Just in case.

Johnny doesn't want to use his gift card right away? That's fine. The 2009 Credit Card Accountability Responsibility and Disclosure (CARD) Act says gift cards cannot expire within five years from their activation date. The CARD Act also limits inactivity fees.

**Don't buy off the rack.** Thieves take gift cards from store display racks and then use portable scanners to read codes under the scratch-off strips. Once the card is activated, they use the stolen codes to make their own purchases. By the time Suzy gets her card to the store, her money's all gone. Avoid this swindle by purchasing your gift card at the store's customer service counter or pick one up online.

## They'll love the gift, you'll love the savings

Weddings. Graduations. Retirement parties. Baby showers. What do all these events have in common? Each one requires a thoughtful gift. But don't let gift buying leave you broke. Here are some easy ways to buy much more — and spend a lot less.

**Save the date and up to 7 percent.** How? It's easy. Just hit the stores on a state tax-free weekend. To find out if and when your state offers shoppers this helpful tax break, go to *freetaxweekend.com*.

**Ship it to me. For free.** When is a $5 hat not a $5 hat? When you have to pay an extra $6 for shipping. Nordstrom and L.L.Bean are just two of the many retailers that will ship orders right to your door — or your gift recipient's door — for free. Other retailers (think JCPenney and Macy's) offer free shipping if you spend over a certain dollar amount. Or, you can order online at Walmart, Kohl's, or Bed Bath & Beyond, select the in-store delivery option, and your merchandise will be ready for pickup lickety-split at your local store. And, yes, for free.

Of course, if free shipping is not available, there's always the good old post office. For $6.80, USPS will ship an 8-5/8" x 5-3/8" x 1-5/8"

> Hit the stores during your state's sales tax-free weekend and save up to 7 percent — right off the bat. To save the date for this helpful tax break, go to *freetaxweekend.com*.

package by priority mail anywhere in the U.S. Find more options at *postcalc.usps.com*.

**While you were sleeping.** Don't miss the bargains that pop up overnight. At sites like *clarkhoward.com*, you can scan for daily deals while you sip your morning coffee. Download shopping apps like *RetailMeNot.com* for coupon codes you can use in-store and online. Just check your phone while you shop to get up-to-the-minute details on the best buys in town.

**Customer loyalty adds up.** You regularly shop at stores that offer customer rewards, right? Bloomingdale's and Kohl's are among the many retailers that dole out discounts to their loyal shoppers. Put those extra savings toward some extra-special gifts. And if you're a card-carrying CVS or Walgreens customer, redeem your points and coupons to save big bucks on greeting cards and gift wrap.

**Cash in on senior specials.** Some retailers like Belk, Michaels, and Ross offer discounts for seniors, but only on certain days. Check your calendar and call your local store before you plan your shopping trip.

**Don't bite into your budget.** If you're headed out to the mall, why not carpool with a friend and split the gas money? But don't stop for lunch. Those food court costs can add up fast. Instead, treat yourself to a penny-pinching pick-me-up. Show your military ID at a Cinnabon for a 15 percent discount, or whip out your AARP card at any Dunkin' Donuts shop for a free doughnut with the purchase of a cup of coffee. Now those are sweet deals.

## Gifts from the heart — fun, festive, and free

Kahlil Gibran wrote, "It is when you give of yourself that you truly give." This is undeniably the best strategy behind lovely, personalized gifts that won't break the bank. Here are some chic — but cheap — customized gifts that take just a bit of your time, but say you care.

**Memories in a jar.** Give a meaningful gift to a forever friend. On pieces of card stock or heavy paper, have friends and family describe a special time they shared with that extraordinary person. Distribute the papers well in advance of the big day so everyone has time to get their stories just right. Collect the papers and place them in a decorative jar. Who wouldn't enjoy reliving a favorite memory with a friend?

Hint: Instead of a jar, place the papers in a photo album, one per page. Add pictures to create a memory album they'll cherish.

**Make it letter perfect.** How well do you know your best friend? Find out with a customized crossword puzzle. Come up with clues that are unique to the person you're celebrating. Where did she meet her husband? In what month did he propose? Or name the family's favorite vacation spot.

Making the puzzle is as easy as ABC. Just go to an online puzzle creator like *education.com* or *www.discoveryeducation.com/ free-puzzlemaker*. Enter your clues, and let the site do all the work. For free. Once completed, the framed puzzle makes a delightful keepsake.

**Get in on the act.** In what year was Grandma born? Celebrate her birthday with a personalized game of charades. On slips of paper, write important events or inventions that made their debut the year she was born. You'll find lots of ideas at sites like *writersdreamtools.com*. Place the papers in a box or bag. Choose your teams, and get the camera ready as your guests start acting out.

Grandma will love being the center of attention, and the grandkids will get a laugh-out-loud history lesson they'll never forget.

At the end of the game, arrange the papers in a small photo album for Grandma to enjoy time after time.

**Welcome home.** Here's a useful housewarming gift that's sure to melt the ice with new neighbors. Draw a map of your neighborhood and label the locations of supermarkets, schools, and stores. Attach coupons they can use when they shop. You can even include a gift certificate from your favorite local restaurant. They'll thank you warmly for a grand night out on their brand new town.

**Spell it out.** Is your sister expecting a new grandchild? A niece getting married? A co-worker retiring? Design a customized sign. Select a word that fits the celebration, and spell it out with items that fit your theme. For example, to celebrate a friend who loves to cook, spell the word "chef" with kitchen gadgets. To form the letters of a baby's name, choose rattles, teething rings, or diaper pins. Try chalk, crayons, and other school supplies for a favorite teacher. Clean out your junk drawer and let your imagination take over.

Once you've spelled the word, attach the items to a prepared board. And there you have it. A one-of-a-kind present they'll treasure forever.

**Photo shop.** If you can't find the right items for your sign, you can frame images that represent different letters, instead. Check out sites like *letter-photo.com* for photographs you can purchase online. Or, for an extra personal touch, take the pics yourself.

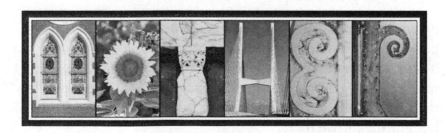

## Hit pay dirt with hassle-free gift returns

Did you receive a gift you're certain you'll never, ever use? You know the one. The fancy French press coffee maker from your uncle. (You're strictly a tea-drinker.) The book titled "Cats of the World." (Your co-worker doesn't know you're more of a dog person.) And don't forget the 5,000-piece jigsaw puzzle of the Gobi Desert. (Uh, thanks, cousin Myrtle.)

So what do you do with the gift that just isn't your style? If you know where it was purchased, returning it means that gift money isn't lost forever.

**The sooner the better.** Run, do not walk, to return your unwanted gift. Bookstore giant Barnes and Noble gives you only two weeks to make up your mind about that cat book. Sears and Kmart are among those that limit your returns on most items to just 30 days. Wait any longer and you'll be stuck with the Gobi Desert. But if you're lucky, your French press came from Nordstrom or Costco. Those two stores, along with several others, will accept most returns no matter when your uncle made his purchase.

**Don't open that box.** If you've already unwrapped, untied, and unsealed, especially in the case of electronics, the store may charge you a restocking fee of up to 15 percent of the purchase price. CDs and DVDs may not be returnable at all if they've been opened. Sellers on Amazon can charge a restocking fee of 20 percent for unopened media and up to 50 percent if the item is out of its plastic wrap.

**Keep those receipts.** Without one, you may only be able to get store credit or a gift card. Sears, Kmart, and Barnes and Noble all have strict no-receipt, no-return policies. Walmart is more forgiving. You never need a receipt for items that cost less than $25, and you can even get cash back. Let's hope Myrtle bought the puzzle there.

**Many happy returns.** Some stores boast super flexible return policies. Online retailer, Zappos, offers free shipping on every order and free returns if you're not satisfied with your purchase. Other stores with generous returns include Kohl's, Lands End, L.L.Bean, and Bloomingdale's. Check stores' websites for details.

**Cash a card in.** Your boss surprised you with a gift card to the new Japanese restaurant in town. Great, huh? Except you're more into sirloin than sushi. Turn that tofu into T-bone by selling your gift card at a site like *giftcards.com*. You may only get 70 percent of its face value, but that could be enough to buy a couple orders of chili cheese fries at your favorite steakhouse.

And you're not limited to selling just restaurant cards. Websites like *giftcards.com*, *raise.com*, and *cardcash.com* accept cards from Academy Sports to Zales, and everything in between.

## Regifting ABCs — spend less, give more

So you received the perfect gift — for someone else. The car care kit Uncle Joe sent for your birthday is right up your neighbor's alley. Giving it away will not only keep a perfectly useful item from the landfill, but will save you money, to boot. The question that has you dithering — when do you have the green light to regift?

First, heed this cautionary tale. At her shower, a bride tears open the pretty package. She sees the picture of an expensive food processor on the box and shrieks with delight. But her happiness turns to horror when she discovers dried food plastered to the processor's blades and bowl. A regift disaster. Don't let it happen to you.

Regifting can be as easy as ABC, and, well, D.

**Avoid giving an item you've already used.** The regifter in the story above forgot she'd made salsa with that processor six months ago. Learn from her mistake. Take the soon-to-be regift out of the box, and thoroughly check it for signs of use. Make sure that package of car wax is still sealed before you wrap it up for your neighbor.

**Be certain the friend who gave you the gift does not know, and will never know, the person getting the regift.** Sure the scarf your niece knitted for you looks great on Mom. But what happens when Mom wears your regift to the family reunion? Makes for awkward moments and hurt feelings.

**Check for hidden gift tags, monograms, and other person-alization.** Turn the sweater inside-out. Examine the book from cover to cover. Did Uncle Joe tape a gift card to the bottom of the box? Don't want to miss that. And while you're at it, inspect the item from every angle to make sure there's no damage.

**Dress it up.** Presentation is everything. You've already saved cold, hard cash on the gift, so you can afford to invest a little more in its wrapping. Spring for some nice paper, fancy ribbon, and a thoughtful note.

## Say it with flowers and still save bunches

A vase of pretty pink carnations says thanks to a kind friend. A bright bunch of sunny daffodils wishes Grandma a happy birth-day. Flowers make lovely gifts for all kinds of occasions. But the high cost of blossom-buying can quickly take the bloom off your rose.

**Dig deep when ordering online.** Sure, it's easy-peasy, but you'll pay in spades for the convenience. When you call or click to order those mums for Mom, the company you contact turns right around and phones a florist down the street, adding up to 25 percent to the cost of your flowers. Then that florist fills the order and tacks on his fees, leaving you with less bloom for your buck. So ask yourself, is the convenience really worth all the extra expense?

That depends. If you're having a floral emergency — a birthday was forgotten, a new baby was overlooked, your anniversary snuck up on you — then the online and over-the-phone florists will be happy to lead you down their garden paths. At *consumeraffairs.com*, search for "online flowers" and you'll find a list of cyber-florists to choose from. Be sure to use online coupon codes to help trim your costs.

But let the buyer beware. According to a 2014 J.D. Power survey, one in five online customers said they had a problem with their flower shipment, and one-fourth of those customers complained that the issue was not resolved to their satisfaction. So before you buy, take a look at the company's policy on replacements or refunds. You don't want Mom stuck with a bunch of limp lilies or droopy daisies.

**Come out smelling like a rose. And save.** Want to keep the quality of a traditional florist, but pare down the expense? Find out what day of the week fresh flowers arrive, and place your order then. For many floral shops, it's Monday. That way you'll be sure to get the freshest flowers available. Or call on Friday or Saturday to see what inventory they might be willing to discount before Monday's delivery. If you live nearby, you can even supply your own vase — a money-saving strategy that keeps more cash in your pocket.

Another smart way to buy buds on the cheap is to choose flowers that are in season. Visit sites like *theflowerexpert.com* to find out when your favorites will bloom. Still stumped about what to pick? Explain to your florist that you're on a budget, and ask what $25, for example, will get you. And don't forget to request that military, senior citizen, or special organization discount.

**Make other arrangements for bargain blooms.** Why not swing by the grocery store for milk, juice, bread — and roses. Wait a minute. Roses? At the grocery store? You bet. Your local grocer offers some of the best flower deals in town. And at superstores like Costco and Sam's Club you could gather up a budget bouquet. Try these other locations for cheap, even free, fresh-cut flowers:

- local farmers' market

- wholesale flower market

- downtown street vendors

- your own garden

---

## Keep your flowers fresher, longer

Whether your bouquet is cheering up a friend or brightening your own kitchen table, help it maintain that fresh-from-the-garden look. Just add one of these homemade flower preservatives to your vase.

To a quart of warm water, add one of the following combinations:

- 1 tablespoon sugar plus 1/4 teaspoon bleach

- 2 tablespoons sugar plus 2 tablespoons either lemon juice or vinegar

- 2 tablespoons sugar plus 2 tablespoons white vinegar plus 1/2 teaspoon bleach

Stir each until the sugar dissolves, then let cool. For best results, replace the solution every few days.

# Index

# E

# F